CONNECTICUT REAL ESTATE SALES EXAM

LEARNINGEXPRESS®

NEW YORK

Library of Congress Cataloging-in-Publication Data:
Connecticut real estate sales exam / by LearningExpress.
    p. cm.
  Includes bibliographical references and index.
  ISBN: 978-1-57685-579-9 (alk. paper)
  1. Real estate agents—Licenses—Connecticut—Examinations, questions, etc.
2. Real estate business—Licenses—Connecticut—Examinations, questions, etc.
I. LearningExpress (Organization)
HD278.C66 2006
333.33076—dc22

                                                        2006036804

Printed in the United States of America

9 8 7 6 5 4 3 2 1

ISBN 978-1-57685-579-9

For more information or to place an order, contact LearningExpress at:
   55 Broadway
   8th Floor
   New York, NY 10006

Or visit us at:
   www.learnatest.com

Contributors ▶

Christopher O'Brien Ashe, ABR, GRI, PSCS, Mediator, has been actively involved in Connecticut real estate since 1978 as a salesperson, broker, manager, trainer, and consultant. He teaches for his own school, Learning Unlimited, colleges and universities, state and local associations of REALTORS®, and real estate companies, and was voted Educator of the Year by the Connecticut Association of REALTORS® in 2001. Chris is currently devoting full time to teaching, training, consulting, and speaking throughout the United States.

Robert D. Mercer-Falkoff, J.D., has been a real estate attorney and educator in Connecticut since 1980. He teaches both Real Estate Principles and Practices and Continuing Education. He is an adjunct mathematics professor at the Housatonic Community College, a graduate of the U.S. Military Academy at West Point, a graduate of the University of Notre Dame Law School, and a retired U.S. Army Lieutenant Colonel.

Contents

CONNECTICUT REAL ESTATE SALES EXAM

1 ▶ Connecticut Real Estate Sales Exam

CHAPTER SUMMARY

A career in real estate sales can be challenging, rewarding, and profitable. Connecticut has a broad range of properties. You can sell anything from mansions in Westport to farms in Tolland. Licensed, knowledgeable, and qualified salespeople are in demand. This is great news for you, because you have already decided that you want to get your Connecticut Real Estate Salesperson License.

T REQUIRES MORE than simply passing an exam to become a licensed salesperson in Connecticut. There are other steps you must complete both before and after the exam in order to arrive at your ultimate goal—receiving your Connecticut Real Estate Salesperson License. This chapter will guide you through these steps, including the requirements, the exam application process, the exam content and format, and the salesperson license application process.

This chapter also serves as a guide for using this book effectively. LearningExpress wants you to succeed, so use this book to maximize your preparation for your upcoming exam.

The state of Connecticut has a reciprocal or an expedited license process with 14 other states. The rules vary by state. The state of Connecticut will also consider reciprocal applicants from any state on an individual basis, depending on how that applicant's licensing state treats a person with a Connecticut license who applies there. To receive a copy of the current rules, contact the Connecticut Real Estate Commission at 860-713-6050, or go online to www.ct.gov/dcp/cwp/view.asp?a=1622&Q=287752&PM=1.

► Who Needs to Take the Connecticut Real Estate Sales Exam?

Anyone wishing to make official, licensed real estate transactions in Connecticut must have a valid Connecticut Real Estate Salesperson License and be employed by a broker licensed by the state of Connecticut. In order to receive your license, you must first pass the licensing exam.

List of Reciprocal States

Arizona	Nebraska
Colorado	New York
Georgia	North Carolina
Illinois	Ohio
Indiana	Oklahoma
Massachusetts	Rhode Island
Mississippi	Tennessee

► Attorney Exemption

If you are a Connecticut attorney in good standing, you are not required to take a Real Estate Principles and Practices Course, but you will still be required to take the licensing exam. Consult the Real Estate Commission's website for more information.

Note: You may not legally provide real estate salesperson services before associating with a sponsoring licensed real estate broker.

► Eligibility Requirements

The Connecticut Real Estate Commission requires that all real estate salesperson applicants meet the following minimum requirements:

- **Age**—You must be at least 18 years old.
- **Moral Character**—Conviction of a criminal offense or failure to file all state tax returns and pay all state taxes required by law may be cause for denial of your application.

If you have Internet access, consult the Connecticut Department of Consumer Protection (the parent agency for the Connecticut Real Estate Commission) website for more information:

www.ct.gov/dcp/site/default.asp

If you do not have Internet access, or if you are unable to get your question(s) answered on the website, please contact the Connecticut Real Estate Commission for all examination and licensing questions:

The Connecticut Real Estate Commission
Department of Consumer Protection
165 Capitol Avenue
Hartford, CT 06106-1630
Voice: 860-713-6050
Fax: 860-713-7239
Website: www.ct.gov/dcp/site/default.asp

- **Education**—You must successfully complete a 60-hour classroom course in Real Estate Principles and Practices, which includes a passing score on a test of the material covered. The course and the school must be approved by the Real Estate Commission. Information about the schools approved to provide this course can be found on the Connecticut Real Estate Commission's website.
- **Examination**—You must pass a two-part exam, which is administered by Promissor Examination Services, a private company engaged by the state of Connecticut for this purpose.
- **Sponsoring Broker**—You must be sponsored by and associated with a real estate broker licensed in Connecticut. You don't need this to take the exam, but you must have a sponsoring broker before you will receive your license.
- **Fees**—You must submit separate fees to the state of Connecticut for the examination, the license application, and the Real Estate Guaranty Fund. You must also submit an additional fee to Promissor Examination Services for the test.

▶ Applying for the Exam

Once you complete your education requirements, you will have one year to pass the license exam. You will receive an official *Grade Report Form* from the school at which you completed the approved course. Your school will also provide you with a license application form. Fill it out completely and honestly; otherwise, you may experience long delays, or worse—rejection. Submit it to the Connecticut Department of Consumer Protection at the address shown on the application form.

You are not required to submit a separate application form for the exam itself.

Some license application instructions and portions of the Real Estate Commission's website may state that you are required to provide written character references and statements. However, this is no longer a requirement under Connecticut law, and these letters should not be submitted.

The exam has two parts: national (general topics) and state (Connecticut). You must pass each part. You have up to four attempts to pass both parts. You must make these attempts to pass within one year after you graduate from your pre-licensing course. Once you pass either part, you do not have to retake it within this one-year period. You simply retest on the part you did not pass. If you do not pass both parts within this year, you may not retake the exam unless you retake and pass a new and complete approved 60-hour pre-licensing course. You will also have to retake both parts of the exam in that case.

You must pay a $55 fee to Promissor each time to schedule a time to take the exam, whether you take one or both parts at the exam time.

Once the Real Estate Commission gives your license application preliminary approval, your information is automatically and electronically sent to Promissor. Promissor will send the approved candidates an *Examination Eligibility Mailer*. You will need to receive the eligibility mailer before contacting Promissor to make an exam reservation. You must allow two business days for your information to be received and processed by Promissor and allow an additional seven to ten business days for receipt of the eligibility mailer via U.S. mail. The mail notification will provide you with a testing identification number, instructions, and a toll-free telephone contact at Promissor. Call this contact and schedule a time to take the exam or visit the Promissor website (www.promissor.com). You should make a reservation by phone at least 24 hours in advance or on the website at least four business days in advance. All questions regarding exams should be directed to Promissor at 1-800-470-8759. You must pay Promissor $55 by credit card or another arrangement when you schedule the exam.

You must make a reservation. Walk-in exams are not available.

Exam Fees

Exam Fee	$40
Promissor Fee	$55

The exam fee must be paid by personal check, cashier's check, or money order, made payable to "Treasurer, State of Connecticut," and submitted with your initial license application before you take the exam.

The Promissor fee must be paid directly to Promissor by credit card or by other arrangements you make with Promissor, after you are notified that your application to take the exam has been accepted. The notice from Promissor will include instructions on how to do this.

Exams are given in the following cities:

Code	Location	Schedule
0705	Wallingford, CT	Tuesday through Saturday
0706	Wethersfield, CT	Tuesday through Saturday
0272	West Springfield, MA	Friday and Saturday
4011	East Providence, RI	Tuesday through Thursday and Saturday

Note: Locations and schedules are subject to change.

What to Bring to the Exam

- Two forms of signature identification, one of which must be a picture ID (you will not be admitted without proper identification).
- The confirmation number provided to you at the time of the reservation.
- A noiseless, tapeless, battery-operated, pocket-sized, handheld electronic calculator with no printing capability or alphabetic keyboard (no PDAs or cell phones will be permitted).
- It is a good idea to bring a calculator with which you are already familiar and make sure you have extra batteries.
- No personal items are to enter the testing center. Promissor will not be responsible for any personal items and suggests that you leave them locked in the trunk of your car.

▶ Exam Content

You will have 240 minutes to complete your Connecticut Real Estate Sales Exam. You must receive a score of at least 70% on each of the two portions of the exam to pass.

There are usually a few additional questions added to each test. These are future sample questions that are being tried out on test takers. You will also receive one minute for each of these questions. The sample questions will not be counted against your score, but unfortunately, you will not know which questions are real and which are samples.

The following are the major sections that will be tested on the exam. This list of items covered in the Connecticut Real Estate Sales Exam is from the Candidate Information Bulletin on the Promissor website and can be found online at www.asisvcs.com/publications/pdf/090700.pdf.

Real Estate Principles and Practices—80 questions (National Portion—General Topics)

I. **Real property, characteristics, definitions, ownership, restrictions, and transfer—16 questions**
   A. Definitions, descriptions, and ways to hold title
   B. Land use controls and restrictions
   C. Transfer/alienation of title to real property

II. **Property valuation and the appraisal process—6 questions**
   A. Principles, types, and estimates of property value
   B. Investment analysis

III. **Contracts and agency relationships with buyers and sellers—21 questions**
   A. Contract elements, types (e.g., valid, enforceable), and terminology
   B. Types of contracts used in real estate
   C. Agency relationships and fiduciary responsibilities

IV. **Property conditions and disclosures—6 questions**
   A. Environmental issues and hazards and hazardous materials
   B. Material and other disclosures
   C. Liability considerations

V. Federal laws governing real estate activities (e.g., Federal Fair Housing Act, Americans with Disabilities Act, antitrust, marketing controls)—6 questions

VI. **Financing the transaction and settlement—17 questions**
   A. Financing components
   B. Lender requiems and obligations
   C. Settlement (including calculations)

VII. **Leases, rents, and property management—6 questions**
   A. Types and elements of leasehold estates, leases, lease clauses, and rental agreements
   B. Lessor and lessee rights, responsibilities, and recourse
   C. Property management contracts and obligations of parties

VIII. **Brokerage operations—2 questions**
   A. Broker management of funds
   B. Broker-salesperson relationship
   C. Advertising
   D. Ethical and legal business practices

Connecticut License Law—30 questions
   I. **Duties and powers of the Real Estate Commission**
      A. Fines
      B. License suspension and revocation
      C. General powers

   II. **Licensing requirements**
      A. Activities requiring a license
      B. Types of licenses
      C. License transfer
      D. License renewal/continuing education
      E. License qualification

   III. **Statutory requirements governing activities of licensees**
      A. Advertisement
      B. Broker-salesperson relationship
      C. Commissions
      D. Handling of documents
      E. Handling of money
      F. Listings
      G. Material misrepresentation
      H. Agency/disclosure/conflict of interest

   IV. **State requirements**
      A. Guaranty funds
      B. Discrimination practices

Real Estate Math

If you are worried about the math that will be covered on the exam—relax. The math problems on the exam will not be very complex, and they will all relate to real estate. You may have already tackled problems like these in your real estate courses. Because LearningExpress understands that math can intimidate many people, especially on exams, there is an entire chapter in this book dedicated to reviewing real estate math to help you brush up on those skills.

Remember to take the problem step by step, reading it carefully and using the scratch paper provided at the test site to set up the problem before you start punching in numbers. Always round off calculations when applicable.

Exam Day

Try to get a good night's sleep the night before the exam and allow plenty of time in the morning to get to your exam location, especially if you are unfamiliar with the area. You should report to the exam center 30 minutes or more before your exam in order to sign in, present your identification, and get yourself settled.

The exam is given by computer and is composed entirely of multiple-choice responses. You may take a short tutorial and ask for any assistance you need if you do not understand how to operate the keyboard or mouse for the exam. Do this before you start to take the test, or the time to help you will count against your allowed time.

Receiving Your Connecticut Salesperson License

You will not receive your license at the testing site. After you pass the exam, you must find a sponsoring real estate broker who will sign a sponsoring broker form. Forward this form to the Real Estate Commission with your license application fee and a $20 fee for the Real Estate Guaranty Fund. The instructions on how to do this are contained in the Candidate Information Bulletin on the Promissor website. If you wait more than one year after you pass the exam to begin working for a broker, contact the Real Estate Commission for its current policy regarding such delays.

License Application Fees

Your license application fee is between $56.25 and $225. (The fee is prorated from month to month.) You also must pay $20 to the Real Estate Guaranty Fund. The Real Estate Commission will send you a written notice after you pass the exam, and the notice will inform you of the exact amount you need to pay.

How to Prepare for the Exam

You have made it this far—you have completed the required real estate course and have made the decision to read this book—so you have already shown that you have the commitment it will take to prepare for the exam. This book is designed to be a valuable tool in preparing you for the big day.

Test-Taking Techniques

Chapter 2, The LearningExpress Test Preparation System, does exactly as the title suggests—it teaches you how to prepare for the test effectively. In this chapter, you will learn to:

- set up a realistic study plan
- use your study time and exam time efficiently
- overcome test anxiety

The best approach for effective studying is to be disciplined, stay on your study schedule, and do not procrastinate.

Study Materials

Utilize all of your study materials. By reviewing information from a variety of sources, you are more likely to cover all of the material that might be included on the exam. This book is a great source of information and can be used as a foundation for your study plan. In addition, use your study materials, notes, exams, and texts from your real estate course.

Using This Book

In addition to this chapter and the LearningExpress Test Preparation System, this book contains three content and review chapters and four practice exams. We suggest that you take the first practice exam (Chapter 3) before moving on to the content and review material. This way, you will be able to better assess your personal strengths and weaknesses, allowing you to direct your time where you need it the most.

Chapter 4, the Connecticut Real Estate Refresher Course, is an overview of real estate concepts and criteria that will be covered on the exam.

Chapter 5 is dedicated to Real Estate Math Review. This chapter reviews the types of problems and computations you will face on the exam, allowing you to practice and polish your math skills.

Chapter 6 is a Real Estate Glossary, providing an excellent list of real estate terminology needed for the exam and your career.

Although you should focus most of your efforts on the areas in which you need the most improvement, you should read all of the chapters in this book to ensure that you do not miss out on valuable information. You will find that some of the information and terminology in Chapters 4 through 6 is repeated, but this will only help reinforce your knowledge.

Use the other three practice tests in the book (Chapters 7, 8, and 9) to gauge your progress as you go along, so you can continue to focus your concentration where needed. Based on the exam content and time allotted for the actual 110-question multiple-choice exam, the practice tests in this book each have 110 questions.

Do not forget about the bonus CD-ROM included with this book. It includes practice questions, so you can practice on a computer if you wish. The CD-ROM is designed to be user friendly; however, please consult the "How to Use the CD-ROM" section located in the back of the book should you have any questions.

Important Note

This book covers the most commonly used key terms and concepts that are likely to be covered on the exam. However, it would be impossible to include everything; thus, we suggest that you utilize a variety of study materials. Please note that real estate laws and regulations change from time to time, so it is important that you be aware of the most up-to-date information (consult the Connecticut Real Estate Commission). Our book is intended to be just one of the many study tools you will use, and is designed to reinforce and round out your knowledge of real estate sales. In addition, information about application processes, fees, and practices may change. For the most accurate information, visit the Connecticut Department of Consumer Protection website for more information: www.ct.gov/dcp/site/default.asp.

The Path to Success

Each person has his or her own personal goals and individual path to take to achieve those goals. Desire, dedication, and know-how are essential, no matter what path you take. You have already shown that you have the desire and dedication, just by reading this chapter. You are well on your way to a new career in real estate! You have shown that you are serious; now let this book help give you the know-how you need to pass your exam.

2 ▶ The LearningExpress Test Preparation System

CHAPTER SUMMARY

Taking the Connecticut Real Estate Sales Exam can be tough. It demands a lot of preparation if you want to achieve a top score. Your career depends on your passing the exam. The LearningExpress Test Preparation System, developed exclusively for LearningExpress by leading test experts, gives you the discipline and attitude you need to be a winner.

FACT: TAKING THE real estate licensing exam is not easy, and neither is getting ready for it. Your future career as a real estate salesperson depends on your getting a passing score, but there are all sorts of pitfalls that can keep you from doing your best on this exam. Here are some of the obstacles that can stand in the way of your success:

- being unfamiliar with the format of the exam
- being paralyzed by test anxiety
- leaving your preparation to the last minute
- not preparing at all!
- not knowing vital test-taking skills: how to pace yourself through the exam, how to use the process of elimination, and when to guess
- not being in tip-top mental and physical shape
- arriving late at the test site, having to work on an empty stomach, or shivering through the exam because the room is cold

What's the common denominator in all these test-taking pitfalls? One word: control. Who's in control, you or the exam?

Here's some good news: The LearningExpress Test Preparation System puts you in control. In nine easy-to-follow steps, you will learn everything you need to know to make sure that you are in charge of your preparation and your performance on the exam. Other test takers may let the test get the better of them; other test takers may be unprepared or out of shape, but not you. You will have taken all the steps you need to take to get a high score on the real estate licensing exam.

Here's how the LearningExpress Test Preparation System works: Nine easy steps lead you through everything you need to know and do to get ready to master your exam. Each step discussed in this chapter includes both reading about the step and one or more activities. It's important that you do the activities along with the reading, or you won't be getting the full benefit of the system. Each step tells you approximately how much time that step will take you to complete.

Step 1. Get Information	50 minutes
Step 2. Conquer Test Anxiety	20 minutes
Step 3. Make a Plan	30 minutes
Step 4. Learn to Manage Your Time	10 minutes
Step 5. Learn to Use the Process of Elimination	20 minutes
Step 6. Know When to Guess	20 minutes
Step 7. Reach Your Peak Performance Zone	10 minutes
Step 8. Get Your Act Together	10 minutes
Step 9. Do It!	10 minutes
Total	3 hours

We estimate that working through the entire system will take you approximately three hours, although it's perfectly okay if you work faster or slower. If you take an afternoon or evening, you can work through the whole LearningExpress Test Preparation System in one sitting. Otherwise, you can break it up, and do just one or two steps a day for the next several days. It's up to you—remember, you are in control.

▶ Step 1: Get Information

Time to complete: 50 minutes
Activity: Read Chapter 1, The Connecticut Real Estate Sales Exam

Knowledge is power. The first step in the LearningExpress Test Preparation System is finding out everything you can about the Connecticut Real Estate Sales Exam. Once you have your information, the other steps in the LearningExpress Test Preparation System will show you what to do about it.

Part A: Straight Talk about the Connecticut Real Estate Sales Exam

Why do you have to take this exam, anyway? You have already been through your pre-license course; why should you have to go through a rigorous exam? It's simply an attempt on the part of your state to be sure you have the knowledge and skills necessary for a licensed real estate agent. Every profession that requires practitioners to exercise financial and fiduciary responsibility to clients also requires practitioners to be licensed—and licensure requires an exam. Real estate is no exception.

It's important for you to remember that your score on the Connecticut Real Estate Sales Exam does not determine how smart you are, or even whether you will make a good real estate agent. There are all kinds of things an exam like this can't test: whether you have the drive and determination to be a top salesperson, whether you will faithfully exercise your responsibilities to your clients, or whether you can be trusted with confidential information about people's finances. Those kinds of things are hard to evaluate, while a computer-based test is easy to evaluate.

This is not to say that the exam is not important! The knowledge tested on the exam is knowledge you will need to do your job. And your ability to enter the profession you've trained for depends on your passing this exam. And that's why you are here—using the LearningExpress Test Preparation System to achieve control over the exam.

Part B: What's on the Test

If you haven't already done so, stop here and read Chapter 1 of this book, which gives you an overview of the Connecticut Real Estate Sales Exam.

▶ Step 2: Conquer Test Anxiety

Time to complete: 20 minutes
Activity: Take the Test Stress Quiz

Having complete information about the exam is the first step in getting control of the exam. Next, you have to overcome one of the biggest obstacles to test success: test anxiety. Test anxiety not only impairs your performance on the exam itself, but also keeps you from preparing! In Step 2, you will learn stress management techniques that will help you succeed on your exam. Learn these strategies now, and practice them as you work through the exams in this book, so they will be second nature to you by exam day.

Test Stress Quiz

You need to worry about test anxiety only if it is extreme enough to impair your performance. The following questionnaire will provide a diagnosis of your level of test anxiety. In the blank before each statement, write the number that most accurately describes your experience.

0 = Never   1 = Once or twice   2 = Sometimes   3 = Often

___ I have gotten so nervous before an exam that I simply put down the books and didn't study for it.

___ I have experienced disabling physical symptoms such as vomiting and severe headaches because I was nervous about an exam.

___ I did not show up for an exam because I was scared to take it.

___ I have experienced dizziness and disorientation while taking an exam.

___ I have had trouble filling in the little circles because my hands were shaking too hard.

___ I have failed an exam because I was too nervous to complete it.

___ **Total: Add up the numbers in the blanks above.**

Your Test Stress Score

Here are the steps you should take, depending on your score. If you scored:

0–2: Your level of test anxiety is nothing to worry about; it's probably just enough to give you that little extra edge.

3–6: Your test anxiety may be enough to impair your performance, and you should practice the stress management techniques listed in this section to try to bring your test anxiety down to manageable levels.

7+: Your level of test anxiety is a serious concern. In addition to practicing the stress management techniques listed in this section, you may want to seek additional help.

Combating Test Anxiety

The first thing you need to know is that a little test anxiety is a good thing. Everyone gets nervous before a big exam—and if that nervousness motivates you to prepare thoroughly, so much the better. It's said that Sir Laurence Olivier, one of the foremost British actors of the twentieth century, felt ill before every performance. His stage fright didn't impair his performance; in fact, it probably gave him a little extra edge—just the kind of edge you need to do well, whether on a stage or in an examination room.

Above is the Test Stress Quiz. Stop and answer the questions to find out whether your level of test anxiety is something you should worry about.

Stress Management before the Test

If you feel your level of anxiety getting the best of you in the weeks before the test, here is what you need to do to bring the level down again:

- **Get prepared.** There's nothing like knowing what to expect and being prepared for it to put you in control of test anxiety. That's why you are reading this book. Use it faithfully, and remind yourself that you are better prepared than most of the people taking the test.
- **Practice self-confidence.** A positive attitude is a great way to combat test anxiety. This is no time to be humble or shy. Stand in front of the mirror and say to your reflection, "I am prepared. I am full of self-confidence. I am going to ace this test. I know I can do it." Say it into a tape recorder and play it back once a day. If you hear it often enough, you will believe it.
- **Fight negative messages.** Every time someone starts telling you how hard the exam is or how it's almost impossible to get a high score, start saying your self-confidence messages. Don't listen to the negative messages. Turn on your tape recorder and listen to your self-confidence messages.
- **Visualize.** Imagine yourself reporting for duty on your first day as a real estate salesperson. Think of yourself talking with clients, showing homes, and best of all, making your first sale. Visualizing success can help make it happen—and it reminds you of why you are going through all this work in preparing for the exam.
- **Exercise.** Physical activity helps calm your body down and focus your mind. Besides, being in good physical shape can actually help you do well on the exam. Go for a run, lift weights, go swimming—and do it regularly.

Stress Management on Test Day

There are several ways you can bring down your level of test anxiety on test day. They will work best if you practice them in the weeks before the test, so you know which ones work best for you.

- **Deep breathing.** Take a deep breath while you count to five. Hold it for a count of one, then let it out on a count of five. Repeat several times.
- **Move your body.** Try rolling your head in a circle. Rotate your shoulders. Shake your hands from the wrist. Many people find these movements very relaxing.
- **Visualize again.** Think of the place where you are most relaxed: lying on the beach in the sun, walking through the park, or whatever. Now close your eyes and imagine you are actually there. If you practice in advance, you will find that you need only a few seconds of this exercise to experience a significant increase in your sense of well-being.

When anxiety threatens to overwhelm you right there during the exam, there are still things you can do to manage the stress level:

- **Repeat your self-confidence messages.** You should have them memorized by now. Say them silently to yourself, and believe them!
- **Visualize one more time.** This time, visualize yourself moving smoothly and quickly through the test answering every question right and finishing just before time is up. Like most visualization techniques, this one works best if you have practiced it ahead of time.

- **Find an easy question.** Find an easy question, and answer it. Getting even one question finished gets you into the test-taking groove.
- **Take a mental break.** Everyone loses concentration once in a while during a long test. It's normal, so you shouldn't worry about it. Instead, accept what has happened. Say to yourself, "Hey, I lost it there for a minute. My brain is taking a break." Put down your pencil, close your eyes, and do some deep breathing for a few seconds. Then you will be ready to go back to work.

Try these techniques ahead of time, and see if they work for you!

▶ Step 3: Make a Plan

Time to complete: 30 minutes
Activity: Construct a study plan

Maybe the most important thing you can do to get control of yourself and your exam is to make a study plan. Too many people fail to prepare simply because they fail to plan. Spending hours on the day before the exam poring over sample test questions not only raises your level of test anxiety, but is simply no substitute for careful preparation and practice over time.

Don't fall into the cram trap. Take control of your preparation time by mapping out a study schedule. On the following pages are two sample schedules, based on the amount of time you have before you take the Connecticut Real Estate Sales Exam. If you are the kind of person who needs deadlines and assignments to motivate you for a project, here they are. If you are the kind of person who doesn't like to follow other people's plans, you can use the suggested schedules here to construct your own.

Even more important than making a plan is making a commitment. You can't review everything you learned in your real estate courses in one night. You have to set aside some time every day for study and practice. Try for at least 20 minutes a day. Twenty minutes daily will do you much more good than two hours on Saturday.

Don't put off your study until the day before the exam. Start now. A few minutes a day, with half an hour or more on weekends, can make a big difference in your score.

Schedule A: The 30-Day Plan

If you have at least a month before you take the Connecticut Real Estate Sales Exam, you have plenty of time to prepare—as long as you don't waste it! If you have less than a month, turn to Schedule B.

TIME	PREPARATION
Days 1–4	Skim over the written materials from your training program, particularly noting areas you expect to be emphasized on the exam and areas you don't remember well. On Day 4, concentrate on those areas.
Day 5	Take the first practice exam in Chapter 3.
Day 6	Score the first practice exam. Use "Exam I for Review" to see which topics you need to review most. Identify two areas that you will concentrate on before you take the second practice exam.
Days 7–10	Study the two areas you identified as your weak points. Don't forget, there is the Connecticut Real Estate Refresher Course in Chapter 4, the Real Estate Math Review in Chapter 5, and the Real Estate Glossary in Chapter 6. Use these chapters to improve your score on the next practice test.
Day 11	Take the second practice exam in Chapter 7.
Day 12	Score the second practice exam. Identify one area to concentrate on before you take the third practice exam.
Days 13–18	Study the one area you identified for review. Again, use the Refresher Course, Math Review, and Glossary for help.
Day 19	Take the third practice exam in Chapter 8.
Day 20	Once again, identify one area to review, based on your score on the third practice exam.
Days 20–21	Study the one area you identified for review. Use the Refresher Course, Math Review, and Glossary for help.
Days 22–25	Take an overview of all your training materials, consolidating your strengths and improving on your weaknesses.
Days 26–27	Review all the areas that have given you the most trouble in the three practice exams you have taken so far.
Day 28	Take the fourth practice exam in Chapter 9. Note how much you have improved!
Day 29	Review one or two weak areas by studying the Refresher Course, Math Review, and Glossary.
Day before the exam	Relax. Do something unrelated to the exam and go to bed at a reasonable hour.

Schedule B: The Ten-Day Plan

If you have two weeks or less before you take the exam, use this ten-day schedule to help you make the most of your time.

TIME	PREPARATION
Day 1	Take the first practice exam in Chapter 3 and score it using the answer key at the end. Use "Exam 1 for Review" to see which topics you need to review most.
Day 2	Review one area that gave you trouble on the first practice exam. Use the Connecticut Real Estate Refresher Course in Chapter 4, the Real Estate Math Review in Chapter 5, and the Real Estate Glossary in Chapter 6 for extra practice in these areas.
Day 3	Review another area that gave you trouble on the first practice exam. Again, use the Refresher Course, Math Review, and Glossary for extra practice.
Day 4	Take the second practice exam in Chapter 7 and score it.
Day 5	If your score on the second practice exam doesn't show improvement on the two areas you studied, review them. If you did improve in those areas, choose a new weak area to study today.
Day 6	Take the third practice exam in Chapter 8 and score it.
Day 7	Choose your weakest area from the third practice exam to review. Use the Refresher Course, Math Review, and Glossary for extra practice.
Day 8	Review any areas that you have not yet reviewed in this schedule.
Day 9	Take the fourth practice exam in Chapter 9 and score it.
Day 10	Use your last study day to brush up on any areas that are still giving you trouble. Use the Refresher Course, Math Review, and Glossary.
Day before the exam	Relax. Do something unrelated to the exam and go to bed at a reasonable hour.

▶ Step 4: Learn to Manage Your Time

Time to complete: 10 minutes to read, many hours of practice!
Activity: Practice these strategies as you take the sample tests in this book

Steps 4, 5, and 6 of the LearningExpress Test Preparation System put you in charge of your exam by showing you test-taking strategies that work. Practice these strategies as you take the sample tests in this book, and then you will be ready to use them on test day.

First, you will take control of your time on the exam. It's a terrible feeling to know there are only five minutes left when you are only three-quarters of the way through the test. Here are some tips to keep that from happening to *you*.

- **Follow directions.** Because the Connecticut Real Estate Sales Exam is given on the computer, you should take your time reviewing the tutorial before the exam. Read the directions carefully and ask questions before the exam begins if there's anything you don't understand.
- **Pace yourself.** There is a timer on the screen as you take the exam. This will help you pace yourself. For example, when one-quarter of the time has elapsed, you should be a quarter of the way through the test, and so on. If you are falling behind, pick up the pace a bit.
- **Keep moving.** Don't waste time on one question. If you don't know the answer, skip the question and move on. You can always go back to it later.
- **Don't rush.** Although you should keep moving, rushing won't help. Try to keep calm and work methodically and quickly.

▶ Step 5: Learn to Use the Process of Elimination

Time to complete: 20 minutes
Activity: Complete worksheet on Using the Process of Elimination

After time management, your next most important tool for taking control of your exam is using the process of elimination wisely. It's standard test-taking wisdom that you should always read all the answer choices before choosing your answer. This helps you find the right answer by eliminating wrong answer choices. And, sure enough, that standard wisdom applies to your exam, too.

Let's say you are facing a question that goes like this:

Alicia died, leaving her residence in town and a separate parcel of undeveloped rural land to her brother Brian and her sister Carrie, with Brian owning one-quarter interest and Carrie owning three-quarters interest. How do Brian and Carrie hold title?

a. as tenants in survivorship

b. as tenants in common

c. as joint tenants

d. as tenants by the entirety

You should always use the process of elimination on a question like this, even if the right answer jumps out at you. Sometimes, the answer that jumps out isn't right after all. Let's assume, for the purpose of this exercise, that you are a little rusty on property ownership terminology, so you need to use a little intuition to make up for what you don't remember. Proceed through the answer choices in order.

So you start with choice **a**. This one is pretty easy to eliminate; this tenancy doesn't have to do with survivorship. Because the Connecticut Real Estate Sales Exam is given on a computer, you won't be able to cross out answer choices; instead, make a mental note that choice **a** is incorrect.

Choice **b** seems reasonable; it's a kind of ownership that two people can share. Even if you don't remember much about tenancy in common, you could tell it's about having something "in common." Make a mental note, "Good answer, I might use this one."

Choice **c** is also a possibility. Joint tenants also share something in common. If you happen to remember that joint tenancy always involves equal ownership rights, you mentally eliminate this choice. If you don't, make a mental note, "Good answer" or "Well, maybe," depending on how attractive this answer looks to you.

Choice **d** strikes you as a little less likely. Tenancy by the entirety doesn't necessarily have to do with two people sharing ownership. This doesn't sound right, and you have already got a better answer picked out in choice **b**. If you are feeling sure of yourself, you can mentally eliminate this choice.

If you're pressed for time, you should choose choice **b**. If you have got the time to be extra careful, you could compare your answer choices again. Then, choose one and move on.

If you are taking a test on paper, like the practice exams in this book, it's good to have a system for marking good, bad, and maybe answers. We recommend this one:

X = bad

✓ = good

? = maybe

If you don't like these marks, devise your own system. Just make sure you do it long before test day—while you're working through the practice exams in this book—so you won't have to worry about it just before the exam.

Even when you think you are absolutely clueless about a question, you can often use process of elimination to get rid of one answer choice. If so, you are better prepared to make an educated guess, as you will see in Step 6. More often, the process of elimination allows you to get down to only two possibly right answers. Then you are in a strong position to guess. And sometimes, even though you don't know the right answer, you find it simply by getting rid of the wrong ones, as you did in the previous example.

Try using your powers of elimination on the questions in the worksheet Using the Process of Elimination. The questions aren't about real estate work; they're just designed to show you how the process of elimination works. The answer explanations for this worksheet show one possible way you might use the process to arrive at the right answer.

The process of elimination is your tool for the next step, which is knowing when to guess.

Using the Process of Elimination

Use the process of elimination to answer the following questions.

1. Ilsa is as old as Meghan will be in five years. The difference between Ed's age and Meghan's age is twice the difference between Ilsa's age and Meghan's age. Ed is 29. How old is Ilsa?
   a. 4
   b. 10
   c. 19
   d. 24

2. "All drivers of commercial vehicles must carry a valid commercial driver's license whenever operating a commercial vehicle." According to this sentence, which of the following people need NOT carry a commercial driver's license?
   a. a truck driver idling his engine while waiting to be directed to a loading dock
   b. a bus operator backing her bus out of the way of another bus in the bus lot
   c. a taxi driver driving his personal car to the grocery store
   d. a limousine driver taking the limousine to her home after dropping off her last passenger of the evening

3. Smoking tobacco has been linked to
   a. increased risk of stroke and heart attack.
   b. all forms of respiratory disease.
   c. increasing mortality rates over the past ten years.
   d. juvenile delinquency.

4. Which of the following words is spelled correctly?
   a. incorrigible
   b. outragous
   c. domestickated
   d. understandible

Answers

Here are the answers, as well as some suggestions as to how you might have used the process of elimination to find them.

1. d. You should have eliminated choice **a** right away. Ilsa can't be four years old if Meghan is going to be Ilsa's age in five years. The best way to eliminate other answer choices is to try plugging them in to the information given in the problem. For instance, for choice **b**, if Ilsa is 10, then Meghan must be 5. The difference in their ages is 5. The difference between Ed's age, 29, and Meghan's age, 5, is 24. Does 24 equal 2 times 5? No. Then choice **b** is wrong. You could eliminate answer **c** in the same way and be left with choice **d**.

2. c. Note the word *not* in the question, and go through the answers one by one. Is the truck driver in choice **a** "operating a commericial vehicle"? Yes, idling counts as "operating," so he needs to have a commercial driver's license. Likewise, the bus operator in choice **b** is operating a commercial vehicle; the question doesn't say the operator has to be on the street. The limo driver in choice **d** is operating a commercial vehicle, even if it doesn't have passenger in it. However, the cabbie in choice **c** is not operating a commercial vehicle, but his own private car.

3. a. You could eliminate choice **b** simply because of the presence of the word *all*. Such absolutes hardly ever appear in correct answer choices. Choice **c** looks attractive until you think a little about what you know—aren't fewer people smoking these days, rather than more? So how could smoking be responsible for a higher mortality rate? (If you didn't know that *mortality rate* means the rate at which people die, you might keep this choice as a possibility, but you would still be able to eliminate two answers and have only two to choose from.) And choice **d** is not logical, so you could eliminate that one, too. And you are left with the correct choice, **a**.

4. a. How you used the process of elimination here depends on which words you recognized as being spelled incorrectly. If you knew that the correct spellings were *outrageous*, *domesticated*, and *understandable*, then you were home free. You probably knew that at least one of those words was wrong!

▶ Step 6: Know When to Guess

Time to complete: 20 minutes
Activity: Complete worksheet on Your Guessing Ability

Armed with the process of elimination, you are ready to take control of one of the big questions in test taking: Should I guess? The first and main answer is *yes*. Some exams have what's called a "guessing penalty," in which a fraction of your wrong answers is subtracted from your right answers—but the Connecticut Real Estate Sales Exam doesn't work like that. The number of questions you answer correctly yields your raw score. So you have nothing to lose and everything to gain by guessing.

The more complicated answer to the question "Should I guess?" depends on you—your personality and your "guessing intuition." There are two things you need to know about yourself before you go into the exam:

- Are you a risk taker?
- Are you a good guesser?

You will have to decide about your risk-taking quotient on your own. To find out if you are a good guesser, complete the worksheet Your Guessing Ability. Frankly, even if you are a play-it-safe person with lousy intuition, you're still safe in guessing every time. The best thing would be if you could overcome your anxieties and go ahead and mark an answer. But you may want to have a sense of how good your intuition is before you go into the exam.

Your Guessing Ability

The following are ten really hard questions. You are not supposed to know the answers. Rather, this is an assessment of your ability to guess when you don't have a clue. Read each question carefully, just as if you did expect to answer it. If you have any knowledge at all of the subject of the question, use that knowledge to help you eliminate wrong answer choices.

1. September 7 is Independence Day in
   a. India.
   b. Costa Rica.
   c. Brazil.
   d. Australia.

2. Which of the following is the formula for determining the momentum of an object?
   a. $p = mv$
   b. $F = ma$
   c. $P = IV$
   d. $E = mc^2$

3. Because of the expansion of the universe, the stars and other celestial bodies are all moving away from each other. This phenomenon is known as
   a. Newton's first law.
   b. the big bang.
   c. gravitational collapse.
   d. Hubble flow.

4. American author Gertrude Stein was born in
   a. 1713.
   b. 1830.
   c. 1874.
   d. 1901.

5. Which of the following is NOT one of the Five Classics attributed to Confucius?
   a. the *I Ching*
   b. the *Book of Holiness*
   c. the *Spring and Autumn Annals*
   d. the *Book of History*

6. The religious and philosophical doctrine that holds that the universe is constantly in a struggle between good and evil is known as
   a. Pelagianism.
   b. Manichaeanism.
   c. neo-Hegelianism.
   d. Epicureanism.

7. The third chief justice of the U.S. Supreme Court was
   a. John Blair.
   b. William Cushing.
   c. James Wilson.
   d. John Jay.

8. Which of the following is the poisonous portion of a daffodil?
   a. the bulb
   b. the leaves
   c. the stem
   d. the flowers

9. The winner of the Masters golf tournament in 1953 was
   a. Sam Snead.
   b. Cary Middlecoff.
   c. Arnold Palmer.
   d. Ben Hogan.

10. The state with the highest per capita personal income in 1980 was
   a. Alaska.
   b. Connecticut.
   c. New York.
   d. Massachusetts.

Answers

Check your answers against the correct answers below.

1. c.
2. a.
3. d.
4. c.
5. b.
6. b.
7. b.
8. a.
9. d.
10. a.

▶ How Did You Do?

You may have simply gotten lucky and actually known the answer to one or two questions. In addition, your guessing was more successful if you were able to use the process of elimination on any of the questions. Maybe you didn't know who the third chief justice was (question 7), but you knew that John Jay was the first. In that case, you would have eliminated choice **d** and, therefore, improved your odds of guessing right from one in four to one in three.

According to probability, you should get $2\frac{1}{2}$ answers correct, so getting either two or three right would be average. If you got four or more right, you may be a really terrific guesser. If you got one or none right, you may be a really bad guesser.

Keep in mind, though, that this is only a small sample. You should continue to keep track of your guessing ability as you work through the sample questions in this book. Circle the numbers of questions you guess on as you make your guesses; or, if you don't have time while you take the practice exams, go back afterward and try to remember which questions you guessed on. Remember, on an exam with four answer choices, your chances of getting a right answer is one in four. So keep a separate "guessing" score for each exam. How many questions did you guess on? How many did you get right? If the number you got right is at least one-fourth of the number of questions you guessed on, you are at least an average guesser, maybe better—and you should always go ahead and guess on the real exam. If the number you got right is significantly lower than one-fourth of the number you guessed on, you would, frankly, be safe in guessing anyway, but maybe you would feel more comfortable if you guessed only selectively, when you can eliminate a wrong answer or at least have a good feeling about one of the answer choices.

▶ Step 7: Reach Your Peak Performance Zone

Time to complete: 10 minutes to read, weeks to complete!
Activity: Complete the Physical Preparation Checklist

To get ready for a challenge like a big exam, you have to take control of your physical, as well as your mental, state. Exercise, proper diet, and rest will ensure that your body works with, rather than against, your mind on test day, as well as during your preparation.

Exercise

If you don't already have a regular exercise program going, the time during which you are preparing for an exam is actually an excellent time to start one. And if you are already keeping fit—or trying to get that way—don't let the pressure of preparing for an exam fool you into quitting now. Exercise helps reduce stress by pumping wonderful good-feeling hormones called endorphins into your system. It also increases the oxygen supply throughout your body, including your brain, so you will be at peak performance on test day.

A half hour of vigorous activity—enough to raise a sweat—every day should be your aim. If you are really pressed for time, every other day is okay. Choose an activity you like, and get out there and do it. Jogging with a friend always makes the time go faster, or take a radio.

But don't overdo it. You don't want to exhaust yourself. Moderation is the key.

Diet

First of all, cut out the junk. Go easy on caffeine and nicotine, and eliminate alcohol and any other drugs from your system at least two weeks before the exam. Promise yourself a binge the night after the exam, if need be.

What your body needs for peak performance is simply a balanced diet. Eat plenty of fruits and vegetables, along with protein and carbohydrates. Foods high in lecithin (an amino acid), such as fish and beans, are especially good "brain foods."

The night before the exam, you might "carbo-load" the way athletes do before a contest. Eat a big plate of spaghetti, rice and beans, or your favorite carbohydrate.

Rest

You probably know how much sleep you need every night to be at your best, even if you don't always get it. Make sure you do get that much sleep, though, for at least a week before the exam. Moderation is important here, too. Extra sleep will just make you groggy.

If you are not a morning person and your exam will be given in the morning, you should reset your internal clock so that your body doesn't think you are taking an exam at 3:00 A.M. You have to start this process well before the exam. The way it works is to get up half an hour earlier each morning, and then go to bed half an hour earlier that night. Don't try it the other way around; you will just toss and turn if you go to bed early without having gotten up early. The next morning, get up another half an hour earlier, and so on. How long you will have to do this depends on how late you are used to getting up. Use the Physical Preparation Checklist on the next page to make sure you are in tip-top form.

▶ Step 8: Get Your Act Together

Time to complete: 10 minutes to read, time to complete will vary
Activity: Complete Final Preparations worksheet

You are in control of your mind and body; you are in charge of test anxiety, your preparation, and your test-taking strategies. Now it's time to take charge of external factors, like the testing site and the materials you need to take the exam.

Find Out Where the Exam Is and Make a Trial Run

Do you know how to get to the testing site? Do you know how long it will take to get there? If not, make a trial run, preferably on the same day of the week at the same time of day. Make note on the Final Preparations worksheet of the amount of time it will take you to get to the exam site. Plan on arriving 30–45 minutes early so you can get the lay of the land, use the bathroom, and calm down. Then figure out how early you will have to get up that morning and make sure you get up that early every day for a week before the exam.

Gather Your Materials

The night before the exam, lay out the clothes you will wear and the materials you have to bring with you to the exam. Plan on dressing in layers; you won't have any control over the temperature of the examination room. Have a sweater or jacket you can take off if it's warm. Use the checklist on the Final Preparations worksheet to help you pull together what you will need.

Don't Skip Breakfast

Even if you don't usually eat breakfast, do so on exam morning. A cup of coffee doesn't count. Don't eat doughnuts or other sweet foods, either. A sugar high will leave you with a sugar low in the middle of the exam. A mix of protein and carbohydrates is best: Cereal with milk or eggs with toast will do your body a world of good.

▶ Step 9: Do It!

Time to complete: 10 minutes, plus test-taking time
Activity: Ace the Connecticut Real Estate Sales Exam!

Physical Preparation Checklist

For the week before the exam, write down what physical exercise you engaged in and for how long and what you ate for each meal. Remember, you are trying for at least half an hour of exercise every other day (preferably every day) and a balanced diet that's light on junk food.

Exam minus 7 days

Exercise: _____ for _____ minutes
Breakfast: _____
Lunch: _____
Dinner: _____
Snacks: _____

Exam minus 6 days

Exercise: _____ for _____ minutes
Breakfast: _____
Lunch: _____
Dinner: _____
Snacks: _____

Exam minus 5 days

Exercise: _____ for _____ minutes
Breakfast: _____
Lunch: _____
Dinner: _____
Snacks: _____

Exam minus 4 days

Exercise: _____ for _____ minutes
Breakfast: _____
Lunch: _____
Dinner: _____
Snacks: _____

Exam minus 3 days

Exercise: _____ for _____ minutes
Breakfast: _____
Lunch: _____
Dinner: _____
Snacks: _____

Exam minus 2 days

Exercise: _____ for _____ minutes
Breakfast: _____
Lunch: _____
Dinner: _____
Snacks: _____

Exam minus 1 day

Exercise: _____ for _____ minutes
Breakfast: _____
Lunch: _____
Dinner: _____
Snacks: _____

Fast-forward to exam day. You are ready. You made a study plan and followed through. You practiced your test-taking strategies while working through this book. You are in control of your physical, mental, and emotional state. You know when and where to show up and what to bring with you. In other words, you are better prepared than most of the other people taking the Connecticut Real Estate Sales Exam with you. You are psyched.

Just one more thing. When you are done with the exam, you will have earned a reward. Plan a celebration. Call up your friends and plan a party, or have a nice dinner for two—whatever your heart desires. Give yourself something to look forward to.

Final Preparations

Getting to the Exam Site

Location of exam: _____

Date: _____

Departure time: _____

Do I know how to get to the exam site? Yes _____ No _____
If no, make a trial run.

Time it will take to get to exam site: _____

Things to Lay out the Night Before

Clothes I will wear	_____
Sweater/jacket	_____
Watch	_____
Photo ID	_____
No. 2 pencils	_____
Calculator	_____
_____	_____
_____	_____

And then do it. Go into the exam, full of confidence, armed with the test-taking strategies you have practiced until they're second nature. You are in control of yourself, your environment, and your performance on the exam. You are ready to succeed. So do it. Go in there and ace the exam. And look forward to your future career as a real estate salesperson!

3 ▶ Connecticut Real Estate Sales Exam 1

CHAPTER SUMMARY

This is the first of the four practice tests in this book based on the Connecticut Real Estate Sales Exam. Take this test to see how you would do if you took the exam today, and to get a handle on your strengths and weaknesses.

L IKE THE OTHER practice tests in this book, this test is based on the actual Connecticut Real Estate Sales Exam. See Chapter 1 for a complete description of this exam. Take this exam in as relaxed a manner as you can, without worrying about timing. You can time yourself on the other three exams. You should, however, make sure that you have enough time to take the entire exam in one sitting. Find a quiet place where you can work without interruptions.

The answer sheet you should use is on the following page, and is followed by the exam. After you have finished, use the answer key and explanations to learn your strengths and your weaknesses. Then use the scoring section at the end of this chapter to see how you did overall.

► Connecticut Real Estate Sales Exam 1 Answer Sheet

1.	ⓐ	ⓑ	ⓒ	ⓓ	38.	ⓐ	ⓑ	ⓒ	ⓓ	75.	ⓐ	ⓑ	ⓒ ⓓ
2.	ⓐ	ⓑ	ⓒ	ⓓ	39.	ⓐ	ⓑ	ⓒ	ⓓ	76.	ⓐ	ⓑ	ⓒ ⓓ
3.	ⓐ	ⓑ	ⓒ	ⓓ	40.	ⓐ	ⓑ	ⓒ	ⓓ	77.	ⓐ	ⓑ	ⓒ ⓓ
4.	ⓐ	ⓑ	ⓒ	ⓓ	41.	ⓐ	ⓑ	ⓒ	ⓓ	78.	ⓐ	ⓑ	ⓒ ⓓ
5.	ⓐ	ⓑ	ⓒ	ⓓ	42.	ⓐ	ⓑ	ⓒ	ⓓ	79.	ⓐ	ⓑ	ⓒ ⓓ
6.	ⓐ	ⓑ	ⓒ	ⓓ	43.	ⓐ	ⓑ	ⓒ	ⓓ	80.	ⓐ	ⓑ	ⓒ ⓓ
7.	ⓐ	ⓑ	ⓒ	ⓓ	44.	ⓐ	ⓑ	ⓒ	ⓓ	81.	ⓐ	ⓑ	ⓒ ⓓ
8.	ⓐ	ⓑ	ⓒ	ⓓ	45.	ⓐ	ⓑ	ⓒ	ⓓ	82.	ⓐ	ⓑ	ⓒ ⓓ
9.	ⓐ	ⓑ	ⓒ	ⓓ	46.	ⓐ	ⓑ	ⓒ	ⓓ	83.	ⓐ	ⓑ	ⓒ ⓓ
10.	ⓐ	ⓑ	ⓒ	ⓓ	47.	ⓐ	ⓑ	ⓒ	ⓓ	84.	ⓐ	ⓑ	ⓒ ⓓ
11.	ⓐ	ⓑ	ⓒ	ⓓ	48.	ⓐ	ⓑ	ⓒ	ⓓ	85.	ⓐ	ⓑ	ⓒ ⓓ
12.	ⓐ	ⓑ	ⓒ	ⓓ	49.	ⓐ	ⓑ	ⓒ	ⓓ	86.	ⓐ	ⓑ	ⓒ ⓓ
13.	ⓐ	ⓑ	ⓒ	ⓓ	50.	ⓐ	ⓑ	ⓒ	ⓓ	87.	ⓐ	ⓑ	ⓒ ⓓ
14.	ⓐ	ⓑ	ⓒ	ⓓ	51.	ⓐ	ⓑ	ⓒ	ⓓ	88.	ⓐ	ⓑ	ⓒ ⓓ
15.	ⓐ	ⓑ	ⓒ	ⓓ	52.	ⓐ	ⓑ	ⓒ	ⓓ	89.	ⓐ	ⓑ	ⓒ ⓓ
16.	ⓐ	ⓑ	ⓒ	ⓓ	53.	ⓐ	ⓑ	ⓒ	ⓓ	90.	ⓐ	ⓑ	ⓒ ⓓ
17.	ⓐ	ⓑ	ⓒ	ⓓ	54.	ⓐ	ⓑ	ⓒ	ⓓ	91.	ⓐ	ⓑ	ⓒ ⓓ
18.	ⓐ	ⓑ	ⓒ	ⓓ	55.	ⓐ	ⓑ	ⓒ	ⓓ	92.	ⓐ	ⓑ	ⓒ ⓓ
19.	ⓐ	ⓑ	ⓒ	ⓓ	56.	ⓐ	ⓑ	ⓒ	ⓓ	93.	ⓐ	ⓑ	ⓒ ⓓ
20.	ⓐ	ⓑ	ⓒ	ⓓ	57.	ⓐ	ⓑ	ⓒ	ⓓ	94.	ⓐ	ⓑ	ⓒ ⓓ
21.	ⓐ	ⓑ	ⓒ	ⓓ	58.	ⓐ	ⓑ	ⓒ	ⓓ	95.	ⓐ	ⓑ	ⓒ ⓓ
22.	ⓐ	ⓑ	ⓒ	ⓓ	59.	ⓐ	ⓑ	ⓒ	ⓓ	96.	ⓐ	ⓑ	ⓒ ⓓ
23.	ⓐ	ⓑ	ⓒ	ⓓ	60.	ⓐ	ⓑ	ⓒ	ⓓ	97.	ⓐ	ⓑ	ⓒ ⓓ
24.	ⓐ	ⓑ	ⓒ	ⓓ	61.	ⓐ	ⓑ	ⓒ	ⓓ	98.	ⓐ	ⓑ	ⓒ ⓓ
25.	ⓐ	ⓑ	ⓒ	ⓓ	62.	ⓐ	ⓑ	ⓒ	ⓓ	99.	ⓐ	ⓑ	ⓒ ⓓ
26.	ⓐ	ⓑ	ⓒ	ⓓ	63.	ⓐ	ⓑ	ⓒ	ⓓ	100.	ⓐ	ⓑ	ⓒ ⓓ
27.	ⓐ	ⓑ	ⓒ	ⓓ	64.	ⓐ	ⓑ	ⓒ	ⓓ	101.	ⓐ	ⓑ	ⓒ ⓓ
28.	ⓐ	ⓑ	ⓒ	ⓓ	65.	ⓐ	ⓑ	ⓒ	ⓓ	102.	ⓐ	ⓑ	ⓒ ⓓ
29.	ⓐ	ⓑ	ⓒ	ⓓ	66.	ⓐ	ⓑ	ⓒ	ⓓ	103.	ⓐ	ⓑ	ⓒ ⓓ
30.	ⓐ	ⓑ	ⓒ	ⓓ	67.	ⓐ	ⓑ	ⓒ	ⓓ	104.	ⓐ	ⓑ	ⓒ ⓓ
31.	ⓐ	ⓑ	ⓒ	ⓓ	68.	ⓐ	ⓑ	ⓒ	ⓓ	105.	ⓐ	ⓑ	ⓒ ⓓ
32.	ⓐ	ⓑ	ⓒ	ⓓ	69.	ⓐ	ⓑ	ⓒ	ⓓ	106.	ⓐ	ⓑ	ⓒ ⓓ
33.	ⓐ	ⓑ	ⓒ	ⓓ	70.	ⓐ	ⓑ	ⓒ	ⓓ	107.	ⓐ	ⓑ	ⓒ ⓓ
34.	ⓐ	ⓑ	ⓒ	ⓓ	71.	ⓐ	ⓑ	ⓒ	ⓓ	108.	ⓐ	ⓑ	ⓒ ⓓ
35.	ⓐ	ⓑ	ⓒ	ⓓ	72.	ⓐ	ⓑ	ⓒ	ⓓ	109.	ⓐ	ⓑ	ⓒ ⓓ
36.	ⓐ	ⓑ	ⓒ	ⓓ	73.	ⓐ	ⓑ	ⓒ	ⓓ	110.	ⓐ	ⓑ	ⓒ ⓓ
37.	ⓐ	ⓑ	ⓒ	ⓓ	74.	ⓐ	ⓑ	ⓒ	ⓓ				

► Connecticut Real Estate Sales Exam 1

1. In Connecticut, an agent can work with a buyer as a
 a. subagent of the seller.
 b. client.
 c. customer.
 d. all of the above

2. Net listings are
 a. illegal in Connecticut.
 b. allowed with the proper disclosure notice.
 c. can be used only for condominiums.
 d. permitted only at the request of the seller.

3. In Connecticut, unsolicited telephone canvassing
 a. is illegal.
 b. cannot be done between the hours of 9:00 P.M and 9:00 A.M.
 c. requires the written permission of the person being called.
 d. could result in the loss of your real estate license.

4. Connecticut law requires an assessment ratio of
 a. 90% of market value.
 b. 80% of market value.
 c. 70% of market value.
 d. 60% of market value.

5. The maximum security deposit a landlord can collect is
 a. one month's rent.
 b. two months' rent.
 c. There is no maximum amount.
 d. two months' rent for people under 62 years of age, one month's rent for people 62 years of age or older.

6. Connecticut's version of the Interstate Land Sales Full Disclosure Act covers any subdivision with
 a. more than five lots.
 b. more than ten lots.
 c. more than 15 lots.
 d. all subdivisions.

7. Using the gross rent multiplier method of evaluation, what would be the value of a three-family house that had an annual gross income of $40,000 if the average selling price of a three-family house in the community is $300,000 and the average annual gross income of the properties is $30,000?
 a. $400,000
 b. $40,000
 c. $600,000
 d. $300,000

8. The residential property condition disclosure is NOT required for
 a. a For Sale by Owner.
 b. two-family houses.
 c. condominiums.
 d. new construction.

9. Real estate agents in Connecticut have buyers and sellers sign
 a. a full contract of sale.
 b. a nonbinding binder.
 c. nothing. The attorney does the paperwork.
 d. all of the above

10. The Connecticut Real Estate Commission has
   a. up to six members.
   b. up to eight members.
   c. up to ten members.
   d. up to 12 members.

11. Which of the following is NOT permitted with a Connecticut Real Estate License?
   a. selling commercial or industrial real estate
   b. working with real estate investors
   c. representing developers
   d. doing appraisals

12. On the sale of a single-family primary residence, an individual has a capital gain exclusion of
   a. $250,000
   b. $500,000
   c. $750,000
   d. no exclusion

13. Unlicensed personal assistants can
   a. show a property to a prospective buyer.
   b. do clerical work only.
   c. write up an offer.
   d. consult with a seller about marketing options.

14. A real estate agent can do all of the following for a buyer without entering into a written agreement EXCEPT
   a. give the buyer property information.
   b. give the buyer information about the licensee's firm.
   c. discuss the buyer's finances and motivation.
   d. give the buyer information on mortgage rates and lending institutions.

15. Agents cannot put a For Sale sign on a property without
   a. written permission of the owner.
   b. a listing agreement with the owner.
   c. both **a** and **b**
   d. none of the above

16. Common interest properties are
   a. condominiums.
   b. cooperatives.
   c. planned unit developments.
   d. all of the above

17. A property is three-quarters of a mile in length, half a mile in width, and sells for $25,000 per acre. What is the selling price?
   a. $60,000
   b. $550,175
   c. $6,000,000
   d. $3,750,000

18. The most common form of legal description in Connecticut is the
   a. government survey system.
   b. monument reference system.
   c. metes and bounds system.
   d. none of the above

19. Property taxes are
   a. collected by both the state and local governments.
   b. an *ad valorem* tax.
   c. based on rates set by the state of Connecticut each January.
   d. a minor source of revenue for towns.

20. An owner who sells his or her land and remains as a tenant of the new owner is an example of
   a. freehold.
   b. sale and leasehold.
   c. secondary financing.
   d. installment contract.

21. Connecticut towns are required to physically reassess real estate
   a. at least every ten years.
   b. at least every 12 years.
   c. at least every 15 years.
   d. It is up to the town to decide.

22. A condition in the lease in which the tenant is entitled to peaceful possession is called
   a. prevention of waste.
   b. quiet enjoyment.
   c. escheat.
   d. tenancy at sufferance.

23. Mary, an associate with ABC Realty, is looking at the property of John and Susie Seller in preparation for doing a listing presentation to the Sellers later in the week. While Mary is looking at the property, she and Susie discuss why the Sellers are moving and how much money the Sellers need to get for the property. Which of the following is true?
   a. This discussion was completely proper.
   b. Mary can discuss how much money the Sellers need to get, but not their motivation.
   c. When Mary first met the Sellers, she should have disclosed to the Sellers that she is not yet their agent and nothing they tell her is confidential.
   d. Mary can discuss motivation, but not finances.

24. Most purchase and sales agreements will have a clause stating the title shall be free from all
   a. appurtenances.
   b. encumbrances.
   c. riparian.
   d. torrens.

25. A mortgage in which the seller will deliver a deed upon receipt of the final mortgage payment is
   a. a purchase money mortgage.
   b. a secondary mortgage.
   c. a land sales contract.
   d. an equity mortgage.

26. A landlord's rules and regulations must do all of the following EXCEPT
   a. promote the convenience, safety, or welfare of the tenants.
   b. apply to all tenants equally and fairly.
   c. hold the landlord harmless in the event of an accident.
   d. be made known to the tenant when he or she enters into the rental agreement.

27. Bob Broker negotiated a lease for Mr. Smith, a landlord. Mr. Smith refused to pay Bob the agreed upon commission. Which of the following is true?
   a. Bob can take Mr. Smith to court to force him to pay.
   b. Bob can keep part of the security deposit to cover the fee he is owed.
   c. Bob is out of luck.
   d. When dealing with leases, an agent should always get paid up front.

28. In Connecticut, planning commissions are created by the towns
   a. based on the local town constitution.
   b. using powers conferred on them through the federal planning acts.
   c. under the powers given to them by state enabling acts.
   d. based on traditional power of the towns.

29. In Connecticut, the first step a landlord takes to evict a tenant is to
   a. file a Suit for Eviction.
   b. turn off the utilities.
   c. serve a Notice to Quit.
   d. call the police.

30. Applicants for a Connecticut real estate license will automatically be rejected if
   a. they have a criminal record.
   b. they are under 18 years of age.
   c. they can't get three letters of reference.
   d. they had their real estate license revoked two years ago.

31. In Connecticut, all contracts pertaining to real estate must
   a. be in writing.
   b. have the broker's name on them.
   c. be in the state-mandated format.
   d. be signed by the broker of record.

32. At a meeting, a group of brokers agrees that they will not charge less than a 5% commission on their listings. This would be an example of
   a. price fixing.
   b. adverse negotiation.
   c. a commission split.
   d. a bilateral contract.

33. Connecticut taxes are based on the mil rate. What is one mil?
   a. $.0001
   b. $.001
   c. $.01
   d. $.10

34. A seller who fails to fill out the Connecticut property condition disclosure
   a. has a void contract.
   b. has a voidable contract.
   c. has done nothing wrong.
   d. can be required to pay the buyers $300 at the closing.

35. Tenant Ford is leasing a store in the Burlington Mall and she has to pay a fixed amount of rent for the space plus a certain amount of the gross receipts. This would be called a
   a. gross lease.
   b. net lease.
   c. triple net lease.
   d. percentage lease.

36. Which of the following is NOT considered negotiating in Connecticut?
   a. telling a buyer about financing options
   b. showing a buyer another firm's listings
   c. discussing a possible offer with a buyer
   d. discussing the buyer's motivation

37. In Connecticut, most married couples take title to real estate as
   a. tenants in common.
   b. tenants by the entirety.
   c. tenants in trust.
   d. joint tenants.

38. To have a right to an easement by prescription in Connecticut, a person must have been using the property for
  a. 15 years.
  b. 20 years.
  c. 25 years.
  d. There is no time period as long as the usage was open and notorious.

39. An income property has a gross income of $36,638 and operating expenses of $23,910. If you want to achieve a 9% capitalization rate, what is the maximum price you should pay for the property?
  a. $142,500
  b. $142,000
  c. $141,800
  d. $140,000

40. ABC Realty has taken a listing and has the seller's permission to advertise it on the agency's website. Under Connecticut law, ABC Realty is obligated to
  a. put the listing on the first page of the website.
  b. include the address of the property and the seller's e-mail.
  c. update the information on the website at least every 72 hours.
  d. show a photograph of the listing.

41. In Connecticut, deeds are recorded
  a. in the town hall where the owner lives.
  b. in the town hall where the property is located.
  c. at the county courthouse.
  d. none of the above

42. To be considered marketable record title in Connecticut, the chain of title must be unbroken for at least
  a. 20 years.
  b. 30 years.
  c. 40 years.
  d. 50 years.

43. What is the most compensation a person can receive from the Real Estate Guaranty Fund for a single transaction?
  a. $10,000
  b. $15,000
  c. $20,000
  d. $25,000

44. Applications for a real estate license in Connecticut
  a. must be made on or before May 31.
  b. must be in writing.
  c. can be completed after taking the state exam.
  d. have to be notarized.

45. Landlord Mary executed a residential lease for 24 months with a new tenant. This lease
  a. must be recorded at the town hall.
  b. has to be countersigned by a notary.
  c. is illegal in Connecticut.
  d. requires a three-month security deposit.

46. Bob and Mary hired Ralph's Homebuilding Contractors to construct their new home. They signed a contract and gave Ralph a deposit of $15,000. According to the contract, work was to begin on May 1. It is now June 22 and work still has not begun. Bob and Mary

    a. just have to wait until Ralph gets around to starting construction.

    b. will have to sue Ralph to get their deposit back.

    c. can attach Ralph's business in order to force the construction to begin.

    d. are entitled to get their deposit back because no substantial work has been done since the promised start date.

47. In Connecticut, the role of the broker at the closing

    a. is to prepare the deed.

    b. is to prepare the mortgage.

    c. is to prepare the closing statement.

    d. The broker has no official role.

48. Tom is sitting an open house for his company. The Smiths walk in. The first thing Tom should do after greeting them is

    a. describe his company's policies on agency.

    b. have them sign the guest book.

    c. take them on a tour of the home.

    d. ask them if they are working with an agent.

49. Fred wants to send an e-mail to all of his past customers telling them about his new listings. Fred's e-mail must contain

    a. the prices of the listings.

    b. a disclaimer about the information being deemed accurate, but not guaranteed.

    c. the broker's name and address.

    d. the date when the listings expire.

50. All of the following persons must give a Connecticut Property Condition to a buyer EXCEPT

    a. a For Sale by Owner.

    b. properties valued in excess of $500,000.

    c. property owned by an attorney.

    d. the builder of a new home.

51. John has just taken an offer and deposit from a buyer. John must be sure that the deposit is in the company's escrow account within three banking days of

    a. the day the deposit was taken.

    b. the day when the last signature goes on the accepted offer.

    c. the day the counteroffer was made.

    d. There is no required time limit.

52. Sally, the listing agent, told the buyers that the roof didn't leak and was "as good as new" when, in fact, it was 14 years old. Sally

    a. made a material misrepresentation and could be fined or lose her license.

    b. did nothing wrong because the roof didn't leak.

    c. was correct in looking out for the best interests of her client, the sellers.

    d. was just "puffing," which is allowed by law.

53. Putting a client's funds in the operating bank account of the brokerage is a crime called

    a. commingling.

    b. confiscation.

    c. conversion.

    d. contamination.

54. Advising a consumer on how to break his or her contract with another agency would be
   a. allowed if the client asked for the information.
   b. interfering with an agency relationship and punishable by fine and/or loss of license.
   c. not a good idea, but not really illegal.
   d. a good business practice.

55. The principal duty of a planning commission is to
   a. look out for the best interests of property owners.
   b. stabilize the community so things stay the way they are.
   c. prepare, adopt, and amend a plan of development for the town.
   d. divide the town into various land use zones.

56. Stigmatized property in Connecticut is called
   a. property with a nonmaterial defect.
   b. psychologically impacted property.
   c. stigmatized property.
   d. a problem property.

57. In Connecticut, the person who is responsible for preparing the closing documents is the
   a. transaction closer.
   b. real estate broker.
   c. escrow agent.
   d. closing attorney.

58. In Connecticut, an inspection for lead-based paint is required
   a. if a child under six years of age living in the house has been diagnosed with elevated levels of lead.
   b. for all of the units in a multifamily dwelling if a child under six years of age from one of the units has elevated levels of lead.
   c. if the building will be used as a day care center.
   d. all of the above

59. Residential underground storage tanks are gradually being removed because
   a. the state requires that they all be removed prior to January 15, 2010.
   b. lenders and insurance companies are insisting on the removal.
   c. of Connecticut's in-ground tank amnesty program.
   d. local ordinances require the seller to remove the tank prior to transfer of title.

60. Mary is the listing agent for Crumbling Manor, which has just had a home inspection paid for by prospective purchasers. The inspection revealed a failed septic system, serious problems with the foundation, and a roof that needs to be replaced. The buyers have backed out and Mary has put the property back on the market. Which of the following is true?
   a. Mary must tell any future buyers about the problems discovered by the inspection.
   b. Mary does not have to tell the buyers because of the doctrine of *caveat emptor*.
   c. Mary has a duty to protect her clients, the sellers, so she should not divulge the inspection results.
   d. The purchasers paid for the inspection and Mary cannot disclose its contents without their written permission.

61. The consequences of a seller allowing a buyer to inspect the home for lead paint could be that
   a. the seller would have to pay for the inspection if evidence of lead was found.
   b. if lead is found, and the buyers have children under the age of six, they are prohibited from purchasing the home.
   c. if lead is discovered, the seller would have to pay for removal or abatement.
   d. There are no consequences for the seller.

62. Connecticut real estate license laws are administered by the
a. Connecticut Association of REALTORS®.
b. Connecticut Housing Council.
c. Connecticut Real Estate Commission.
d. Connecticut Housing Authority.

63. The Real Estate Guaranty Fund is designed to compensate
a. a broker when the client refuses to pay him or her.
b. a consumer who has been damaged by a broker.
c. a cooperating broker who doesn't receive proper payment.
d. all of the above

64. A real estate agent can act as a mortgage broker and real estate broker in the same transaction if
a. there is a written agreement between the broker and the client for both services.
b. the client is not prohibited from using other mortgage brokers also.
c. the broker gets a fee for mortgage services only if he or she is successful in obtaining the financing that the client uses.
d. all of the above

65. In order for the Connecticut Real Estate Commission to audit a broker's escrow account, it must
a. give 48 hours' notice.
b. give five days' notice.
c. give ten days' notice.
d. It is not required to give any notice.

66. Tenancy by the entirety is a special form of ownership
a. for corporations.
b. for individuals.
c. that is not recognized in Connecticut.
d. for limited partnerships.

67. The holder of a life estate may do all of the following EXCEPT
a. pay property taxes.
b. maintain the property.
c. mortgage the life interest.
d. leave the property to his or her children.

68. What is the formula for determining the value of an income property?
a. net operating income ÷ capitalization rate = value
b. potential gross income ÷ capitalization rate = value
c. effective gross income ÷ capitalization rate = value
d. replacement cost × capitalization rate = value

69. Riparian rights say that the owner of land adjacent to a river owns
a. to the edge of the water.
b. to the middle of the river.
c. to the high-water mark.
d. to the edge of the 50-year flood plain.

70. Before a septic system can be installed, there must be successful
a. percolation and deep hole tests.
b. field tests.
c. soil sample certifications.
d. No tests are required.

71. A salesperson may be hired by the broker as
   a. an independent contractor.
   b. a salaried full-time employee.
   c. an hourly part-time employee.
   d. all of the above

72. A subagency relationship can be created only
   a. in writing.
   b. with the specific permission of the seller.
   c. if the seller and seller's agent agree to be liable for the actions of the subagent.
   d. all of the above

73. Which of the following is NOT a freehold estate?
   a. fee simple estate
   b. life estate
   c. estate for years
   d. defeasible fee estate

74. The owner of real property has
   a. air rights.
   b. surface rights.
   c. subsurface rights.
   d. all of the above

75. If a house had no closets in the bedrooms, this would be an example of what kind of depreciation?
   a. physical
   b. functional
   c. economic
   d. environmental

76. What would most affect the value of a parcel of real estate?
   a. the appraisal
   b. the book value
   c. the location
   d. the age of the building

77. If you owned a unit in a condominium, what would you own exclusively?
   a. the tennis courts
   b. the hallways in the building
   c. an undivided share of each unit
   d. the air space in your unit

78. A husband and wife jointly own a multifamily building that they don't live in. When they sell the property, they will have an exclusion from capital gains of
   a. $0
   b. $250,000
   c. $500,000
   d. $100,000

79. In the settlement statement, the earnest money deposit is
   a. not shown.
   b. a debit to the seller.
   c. a debit to the buyer.
   d. a credit to the buyer.

80. A store was leased for three years. The first year's rent was $1,000 per month and was to increase 10% each year thereafter. The broker received a 7% commission for the first year, 5% for the second year, and 3% for the balance of the lease. The total commission for the broker was
   a. $840
   b. $1,161
   c. $1,935.60
   d. $2,748

81. The type of deed in which the grantee receives the property with a promise that the property will be free of any encumbrances is a
- **a.** quitclaim deed.
- **b.** warranty deed.
- **c.** certificate of title.
- **d.** trust deed.

82. In a transaction involving a subagency, what is the legal theory that says the principal may be held responsible for the acts of the subagent?
- **a.** *caveat emptor*
- **b.** escheat
- **c.** vicarious liability
- **d.** *fructas naturales*

83. Before a new building can be occupied, the municipality must issue a
- **a.** building permit.
- **b.** conditional use permit.
- **c.** variance.
- **d.** certificate of occupancy.

84. The exculpatory clause in a lease is intended to relieve the landlord from liability for
- **a.** back rent.
- **b.** the security deposit.
- **c.** a tenant's personal injury in a common area.
- **d.** repairs to the unit.

85. In Connecticut, a lease must be in writing if
- **a.** there is no security deposit.
- **b.** it is for longer than one year.
- **c.** it is with a minor.
- **d.** the rent exceeds $1,500 per month.

86. Continuing education classes in Connecticut
- **a.** can be taken in a classroom.
- **b.** can be taken on the Internet.
- **c.** must be taken every two years.
- **d.** all of the above

87. A seller wants to net $330,000 from the sale of a property and the broker's commission is 5%. What should the sale price be to accomplish this?
- **a.** $347,638
- **b.** $346,500
- **c.** $345,313
- **d.** $330,000

88. In a cooperative, the buyer of a unit becomes
- **a.** a unit owner.
- **b.** a stockholder in the cooperative.
- **c.** an adverse tenant.
- **d.** an estoppel tenant.

89. A cap rate is used in what kind of appraisal?
- **a.** cost approach
- **b.** income approach
- **c.** market comparison approach
- **d.** competitive market analysis

90. An income property has a gross income of $51,408 and operating expenses of $36,680. If you want to achieve a cap rate of 8%, what is the maximum price you should pay for the property?
- **a.** $117,824
- **b.** $148,100
- **c.** $180,400
- **d.** $184,100

91. Which of the following would be considered part of the real estate?
   a. a ceiling fan permanently installed by a tenant
   b. a picture hanging in the den
   c. a bird bath standing in the back yard
   d. a bookcase standing in the living room

92. Under Connecticut law, all contracts between a real estate broker and a client
   a. must be for at least 60 days' duration.
   b. must be in writing.
   c. must be notarized.
   d. must be on the state-mandated forms.

93. In Connecticut, a minor is
   a. a person under the age of 16.
   b. a person under the age of 18.
   c. a person under the age of 21.
   d. We don't have minors in Connecticut.

94. An agent who has been hired by a seller and allows another agent to be a subagent
   a. is liable for the statements and actions of the subagent.
   b. has no liability for the actions or statements of the subagent.
   c. is considered a facilitator in the transaction.
   d. becomes a buyer's agent.

95. An agent who has two buyers for the same property is a
   a. dual agent.
   b. single agent in two transactions.
   c. facilitator.
   d. designated agent.

96. In some towns in Connecticut, contracts entered into on Sunday are
   a. void.
   b. unenforceable.
   c. voidable.
   d. valid.

97. The alloidal system gives an individual
   a. the right to own personal property.
   b. the right to own real property.
   c. the right of personality.
   d. the right to a mortgage.

98. A ticket to attend a concert is considered a(n)
   a. license.
   b. easement.
   c. freehold.
   d. encroachment.

99. In Connecticut, a property manager is required to have a
   a. broker's license.
   b. salesperson's license.
   c. college degree.
   d. none of the above

100. The two most common forms of deeds of conveyance in Connecticut are
   a. warranty and quitclaim deeds.
   b. warranty and special warranty deeds.
   c. grant and sheriff's deeds.
   d. warranty and trust deeds.

101. If the selling price of a property is $300,000 and the bank requires a $60,000 down payment, then the loan-to-value ratio would be
   a. 80%.
   b. 70%.
   c. 40%.
   d. 10%.

102. A Connecticut community has an annual budget of $1,206,000 and a total assessed property value of $24,500,000. What is the mil rate?
 a. 42
 b. 49.22
 c. 20.31
 d. 203

103. Connecticut is
 a. a title theory state.
 b. a lien theory state.
 c. a modified lien theory state.
 d. a full encumbrance state.

104. At the closing, who usually has the obligation to provide a "good and marketable title"?
 a. the buyer
 b. the buyer's attorney
 c. the home inspector
 d. the seller

105. In Connecticut, a will may be prepared by anyone who is of sound mind and at least
 a. 16 years of age.
 b. 18 years of age.
 c. 20 years of age.
 d. 21 years of age.

106. John bought a rectangular parcel of land that measures 1,250 feet by 3,760 feet. How many acres did John purchase?
 a. 10.79 acres
 b. 107.90 acres
 c. 227.560 acres
 d. 280 acres

107. Connecticut law prohibits discrimination based on
 a. creed.
 b. sexual orientation.
 c. emotional disability.
 d. all of the above

108. With regard to zoning laws, the real estate agent
 a. should join the zoning board of appeals.
 b. does not need to worry about them.
 c. needs a thorough knowledge of the zoning laws in the communities he or she serves.
 d. should give gifts to the inspectors and stay on friendly terms.

109. Which of the following applies to rental security deposits in Connecticut?
 a. They cannot exceed two months' rent.
 b. They must be deposited in a special escrow account.
 c. The landlord must pay interest on them.
 d. all of the above

110. Fred has received a Notice to Quit from the landlord. How long does he have to vacate the apartment?
 a. ten days
 b. 30 days
 c. 45 days
 d. It depends on the type of leasehold estate Fred has.

► Answers

1. **d.** Connecticut allows all of these forms of representation with proper disclosures.
2. **a.** Net listings are always illegal.
3. **b.** Calls can be made only during the daytime hours and only to people who are not on the "Do not call" list.
4. **c.** Connecticut requires an assessment ratio of 70%.
5. **d.** One month for tenants 62 and older and two months for tenants under 62 years of age.
6. **a.** Anything five lots or more is covered by Connecticut law; federal law covers 25 or more lots.
7. **a.** The gross multiplier is determined by dividing the average selling price by the annual income.
   $300,000 ÷ $30,000 = gross multiplier of 10
   Gross multiplier of 10 × $40,000 = $400,000
8. **d.** New construction does not require a property condition disclosure.
9. **d.** Practices vary throughout Connecticut with regard to the drawing up of sales agreements. Local custom dictates what form, if any, will be used.
10. **b.** The Real Estate Commission can have up to eight members.
11. **d.** In order to do appraisals, a person must have an appraiser's license.
12. **a.** An individual has an exclusion of $250,000 if he or she has lived in the property two out the past five years and it is his or her primary residence.
13. **b.** Unlicensed assistants cannot work directly with buyers and sellers. They can do only clerical tasks.
14. **c.** The buyer's financial information and motivation are confidential information and should be discussed only with people who have employed the licensee as their agent.

15. **c.** An agent must have a listing agreement and written permission from the owner to put a sign on a property.
16. **d.** Common interest properties include condominiums, cooperatives, and planned developments.
17. **c.** $\frac{3}{4}$ of a mile = 3,960 feet
    $\frac{1}{2}$ of a mile = 2,640 feet
    3,960 feet × 2,640 feet = 10,454,400 square feet
    10,454,400 square feet ÷ 43,560 square feet in an acre = 240 acres
    240 acres × 25,000 = $6,000,000
18. **c.** The metes and bounds description is the most common in Connecticut, although the lot and block system is also used.
19. **b.** Property taxes are levied *ad valorem* (according to value).
20. **b.** This is a sale and leasehold or sale and leaseback.
21. **b.** Connecticut towns are required to reassess at least every 12 years.
22. **b.** This gives the tenant the right to peaceful possession.
23. **c.** Mary should discuss agency at the first substantive meeting where the Sellers real estate needs are discussed and advise them not to tell her confidential information about their finances or motivation.
24. **b.** Most purchase and sales agreements expressly state that title should be free of all encumbrances.
25. **c.** The deed is not executed until the final loan payment is made.
26. **c.** "Hold harmless" clauses are generally unenforceable in Connecticut.
27. **a.** Bob can take the landlord to court.
28. **c.** The state of Connecticut delegates powers to the local communities through enabling acts.

29. **c.** Serving a Notice to Quit is the first step in the eviction process.

30. **b.** An applicant must be 18 years of age.

31. **a.** All real estate contracts must be in writing.

32. **a.** Price fixing is illegal.

33. **b.** A mil is one-tenth of a cent ($.001).

34. **d.** Failure to complete the property condition disclosure can result in a $300 credit to the purchasers at the closing.

35. **d.** This is a lease in which the tenant pays a fixed amount plus a percentage of the gross sales.

36. **a.** Discussing financing options is not "negotiating" as long as you don't discuss the buyer's personal finances.

37. **d.** Most married couple own real estate as joint tenants with right of survivorship.

38. **a.** You must use the property for 15 years to claim a prescriptive easement.

39. **d.** The maximum price should not exceed $141,422.

Gross income	$36,638
Operating expenses	−23,910
Net income	$12,728

$12,728 ÷ .09 = 141,422$

40. **c.** In Connecticut, a broker is required to update the information on the website at least every 72 hours.

41. **b.** Deeds are recorded in the town where the property is located.

42. **c.** Title must be unbroken for at least 40 years.

43. **d.** The most that can be paid for a single transaction is $25,000.

44. **b.** Applications must be written.

45. **a.** Leases for longer than one year must be in writing and recorded at the town hall.

46. **d.** If requested by a consumer, a contractor must return the deposit if 30 days have passed since the promised start date and no substantial work has been completed.

47. **d.** The broker plays no official role in the closing.

48. **d.** When meeting a potential client/customer for the first time, you should always begin by asking if he or she is working with another agent.

49. **c.** Any electronic advertising must contain the name and address of the broker as it is registered with the real estate commission.

50. **d.** New homes don't require a property condition disclosure.

51. **b.** It must be deposited within three banking days of the last signature on the accepted offer.

52. **a.** A material misrepresentation in Connecticut can be grounds for a fine and/or loss of license.

53. **a.** Putting a client's funds in the firm's regular bank account is the crime of commingling.

54. **b.** Interfering with an agency relationship can result in fines and/or loss of license.

55. **c.** The primary duty of the planning commission is to prepare, adopt, and amend a plan of development for the town.

56. **a.** We used to call them psychologically impacted property. Now we refer to them as properties with a nonmaterial defect.

57. **d.** The closing attorneys prepare the paperwork.

58. **d.** If a child under six years of age has elevated levels of lead, the building he or she lives in (single or multifamily) must be inspected and all day care centers must pass inspection prior to licensure.

59. **b.** Many lenders and insurance companies are insisting on the removal of tanks or they won't work with the property.

60. **a.** The results of the inspection are material facts and must be disclosed.

61. **b.** If lead was discovered, the buyers could decide not to purchase, but there are no consequences for the seller.

62. **c.** The Connecticut Real Estate Commission administers real estate license law.

63. **b.** The Guaranty Fund is meant to compensate members of the public who have won a judgment against a broker and are unable to collect.

64. **d.** All of these disclosures are required for a real estate broker to also be a mortgage broker.

65. **d.** The Real Estate Commission can audit a broker's escrow account at any time with no advance notice.

66. **c.** Tenancy by the entirety is a special form of joint tenancy for married couples that is not recognized in Connecticut.

67. **d.** When the life tenant dies, the property goes to the remainder person and can't be willed to the life tenant's heirs.

68. **a.** Net operating income divided by the capitalization rate determines the market value.

69. **b.** You own the land to the middle of the river and the right to use the water so long as your use doesn't interfere with other owners whose property borders the river.

70. **a.** Deep hole and percolation tests must be done to determine the soil type and rate of drainage.

71. **d.** The state does not regulate the type of relationship between brokers and salespersons.

72. **d.** Subagency requires a specific written agreement between the subagent, the seller, and the seller's agent in which the seller and the seller's agent acknowledge their liability for the acts of the subagent.

73. **c.** An estate for years is a leasehold estate and not a freehold estate.

74. **d.** Real property ownership includes air, surface, and subsurface rights. These are separate rights and can be individually sold or transferred.

75. **b.** No closets in the bedrooms would be functional depreciation.

76. **c.** The location would have the most effect on the value.

77. **d.** When you own a condominium, you own air space, not land.

78. **a.** You get a capital gains exclusion only for owner-occupied property.

79. **d.** The earnest money is a credit to the purchaser.

80. **c.** The first year's rent is $12 \times \$1,000 = \$12,000 \times 7\% = \$840$ commission in year one. The rent increased 10% in year two to $\$1,100$ per month $\times 12 = \$13,200$ annual rent $\times 5\% = \$660$ commission in year two. The rent increased 10% again in year three ($\$1,100 + 110$) to $\$1,210$ per month $\times 12 = \$14,520$ annual rent $\times 3\% = \$435.60$ commission. $840 + 660 + 435.60 = \$1,935.60$.

81. **b.** The warranty deed promises that the property will be free of encumbrances.

82. **c.** The legal concept of vicarious liability says that a principal is responsible for the acts of his or her agents and subagents.

83. **d.** The building department must issue a certificate of occupancy before new construction can be occupied.

84. **c.** The exculpatory or hold harmless clause is intended to protect the landlord from liability for personal injuries in common areas. In Connecticut, the landlord would have to prove that it was the tenant's fault that the injury occurred in order to have protection.

85. **b.** Leases for longer than one year must be in writing.

86. **d.** All of the answers are correct.

87. **a.** $100\% - 5\% = 95\%$; $\$330,000 \div .95 = \$347,368$

88. b. The owner in a cooperative owns shares of stock in the corporation and has a proprietary lease on his or her unit.

89. b. A cap rate is used in the income approach to appraisal.

90. d. The maximum price should not exceed $184,100.

Gross income	$51,408
Minus operating expenses	−36,680
Net operating income	$14,728

$14,728 \div .08 = \$184,100$

91. a. Once an item becomes permanently attached to the property, it is part of the real estate.

92. b. All real estate contracts, with the exception of leases for less than one year, must be in writing.

93. b. A minor is a person under the age of 18.

94. a. An agent is fully liable for the statements and actions of a subagent.

95. b. A single agent in two separate transactions. A dual agent represents both sides in the *same* transaction.

96. d. Sunday contracts are valid and enforceable everywhere in Connecticut.

97. b. The alloidal system gives the right to own real property.

98. a. A concert ticket is a license.

99. d. No particular license or education is required to be a property manager in Connecticut.

100. a. Warranty and quitclaim deeds are by far the most common types of deeds recorded in Connecticut.

101. a. $300,000 − $60,000 = $240,000 (amount of the loan)

$240,000 \div 300,000 = .80 = 80\%$

102. b. $1,206,000 \div \$24,500,000 = .4922$ or 49.22 mils

103. c. We act as a lien theory state, but because of the way our statutes are drafted, we are considered a modified lien theory state.

104. d. The seller is usually obligated to provide "good and marketable title."

105. b. Eighteen years of age is considered the age of consent in Connecticut and this applies to making out a will.

106. b. $1,250 \times 3,760 = 4,700,000$ square feet. $4,700,000 \div 43,560$ (the number of square feet in one acre) $= 107.90$ acres

107. d. Connecticut prohibits discrimination for any of these reasons.

108. c. An agent should be knowledgeable about the zoning regulations in all of the towns he or she serves.

109. d. All of these things are true about security deposits in Connecticut.

110. d. Different types of leasehold estates have different time lines.

▶ Scoring

Evaluate how you did on this practice exam by first finding the number of questions you answered correctly. Only the number of correct answers is important—questions you skipped or got wrong don't count against your score. At the time this book was printed, a passing score for the exam was 70%. On this practice exam, a passing score would be 77 correct.

Use your scores in conjunction with the Learning-Express Test Preparation System in Chapter 2 of this book to help you devise a study plan using the Connecticut Real Estate Refresher Course in Chapter 4, the Real Estate Math Review in Chapter 5, and the Real Estate Glossary in Chapter 6. You should plan to spend more time on the sections that correspond to the questions you found hardest and less time on the lessons that correspond to areas in which you did well.

For now, what is much more important than your overall score is how you performed on each of the areas tested by the exam. You need to diagnose your strengths and weaknesses so that you can concentrate your efforts as you prepare. The different question types are mixed in the practice exam, so in order to diagnose where your strengths and weaknesses lie, you will need to compare your answer sheet with the following table, which shows which of the categories each question falls into.

Once you have spent some time reviewing, take the second practice exam in Chapter 7 to see how much you have improved.

EXAM 1 FOR REVIEW

Connecticut Real Estate Sales Exam 1 Subject Areas	Question Numbers (Questions 1–110)
Property Ownership and Land Use Controls and Registrations	6, 16, 18, 20, 22, 26, 28, 29, 33, 35, 38, 45, 55, 59, 66, 67, 69, 70, 73, 74, 77, 81, 83, 84, 88, 91, 98, 110
Valuation and Market Analysis	68, 75, 76, 89
Financing	12, 25
Laws of Agency	1, 2, 27, 36, 72, 82, 94, 95
Mandated Disclosures	23, 34, 48, 50, 58, 60, 61
Contracts	31, 85, 92, 96
Transfer of Property	24, 41, 42, 47, 57, 78, 79, 100, 103, 104, 105
Practice of Real Estate	4, 9, 19, 21, 32, 37, 46, 52, 54, 71, 97, 108
License Law/Rules and Regulations	3, 5, 8, 10, 11, 13, 14, 15, 30, 40, 43, 44, 49, 51, 53, 56, 62, 63, 64, 65, 86, 93, 99, 109
Real Estate Math	7, 17, 39, 80, 87, 90, 101, 102, 106
Fair Housing	107

4 ▶ Real Estate Refresher Course

CHAPTER SUMMARY

If you want to review real estate concepts for your exam, this is the chapter you need. Using this chapter, you can review just what you need to know for the test.

H OW YOU USE this chapter is up to you. You may want to proceed through the entire course in order, or perhaps, after taking the first practice exam, you know that you need to brush up on just one or two areas. In that case, you can concentrate only on those areas. Following are the major sections of the real estate refresher course and the page on which you can begin your review of each one. (This list of items covered in the Connecticut Real Estate Sales Exam is from the Real Estate Candidate Handbook on the Promissor website and can be found online at www.asisvcs.com/publications/pdf/090700.pdf.)

▶ Real Estate Principles and Practices (General Portion)

Property Ownership

Land Use Controls and Regulations

Valuation and Market Analysis

Financing

Laws of Agency

Mandated Disclosures

Contracts

Transfer of Property

Practice of Real Estate

Real Estate Calculations

Specialty Areas

- Property Management
- Landlord/Tenant
- Subdivisions
- Commercial Property/Income Property

▶ Connecticut Real Estate Law (State Portion)

Duties and Powers of the Real Estate Commission

Licensing Requirements

Requirements Governing the Activities of Licensees

State Requirements

Property Ownership

Real versus Personal Property

Property can be divided into two classes: **real property** and **personal property**.

Land includes the Earth's surface, the ground, the minerals and water below the surface, the air space above the surface, and things naturally attached to the land (trees, rocks, etc.). **Real estate** is **land** plus improvements (artificial objects permanently attached to the land, i.e., buildings, pavement). **Real property** is **land** plus **real estate** and also all of the legal interests, rights, and rights included in owning the **land** and **real estate**.

Personal property (also known as **personalty**) is any property that cannot properly be defined as **real property**. Easily movable **personal property** is often called a **chattel**. Ownership of personal property is usually transferred by a **bill of sale**.

There are two types of personal property: **tangibles**, such as a car, refrigerator, or chandelier; and **intangibles**, such as a patent, which is considered intellectual property.

Items Affixed to the Property

Fixtures are permanent man-made additions to real property, such as fences, lights, and other improvements. When an item of personal property is permanently attached to real estate, it becomes real property and is identified as a fixture. Fixtures become appurtenances and remain with the property when ownership transfers to a new owner. An exception occurs when a commercial tenant installs a business fixture to be used in the business for which the space has been leased. In the absence of a contract between the landlord and tenant stating otherwise, **trade fixtures**

remain the property of the tenant and may be removed by the tenant at the end of the lease. The tenant is obligated to repair any damage caused by the removal of a trade fixture.

The determination of a fixture is made by asking and answering the following questions.

1. How is the item attached?
2. Have the improvements been modified to accommodate the item?
3. What was the intent of the parties?
4. Is there a contractual agreement that defines the item as a fixture or as a chattel?

Growing things can be real property or personal property, depending on how they are grown. Plants and trees that occur naturally or as part of the landscaping are part of the real estate. **Emblements** are annually cultivated crops and are personal property. Corn would be considered personal property, but orange trees would be considered real property, as trees are perennial. The oranges may be considered personal property if commercially grown.

Property Rights

The **bundle of rights of ownership** interest in real property includes the **rights of possession**, **control**, **enjoyment**, **exclusion**, and **disposition** (transfer title to someone else by **sale**, **gift**, **will**, or **exchange**). **Corporeal** rights affect the physical land themselves (i.e., the right to use the land and build on it). **Incorporeal** rights are not tangible (i.e., the right to grant others an easement).

Limits to Property Rights

Government Rights

Eminent domain is the right of the government to take ownership of privately held real property. Typically, real property is taken for schools, freeways, parks, public housing, urban renewal, economic development, and other social and public purposes. When direct negotiations with the property owner are unsuccessful, the legal proceeding involved in exercising the right of eminent domain is called **condemnation**. The property owner must be provided a reasonable opportunity to a fair hearing on the taking and also be paid the fair market value of the property taken.

An **inverse condemnation** is a proceeding brought about by a property owner demanding that a government entity purchase his or her land. A property owner might choose this proceeding if his or her land has been adversely affected by the taking of neighboring land. For instance, homeowners at the ends of airport runways may try to force airport authorities to buy their homes because of the noise of aircraft during takeoffs.

A state government may enact laws and enforce them to protect the safety, health, morals, and general welfare of the public and property within the state. This government authority is called **police power**. Examples of police power are **zoning laws** and **building codes**.

Zoning ordinances designate which land parcels in a city can be used for specific property uses (i.e., single-family homes, multifamily homes, commercial uses). A **nonconforming use** is a use that was in existence before the current zoning regulation went into effect. Such property improvements typically will be allowed to remain, though are subject to strict rules regarding future modifications. A **conditional use permit** or **special permit** allows a property use that is not specified for the zoned area, but is nevertheless considered for the public good.

All new construction or modification of existing structures must comply with the **setback** requirements (the minimum distance from property boundaries or other buildings).

A **variance** may be granted for a deviation from a zoning requirement. Normally, variances need approval by the local **zoning board of appeals**.

Building codes are minimum construction standards for building, framing, plumbing, electrical wiring, and other components.

These laws restrict the property owner's use of their land but do not constitute a taking (see **eminent domain**). Consequently, there is no payment to the property owner who suffers a loss of value through the exercise of police power.

Taxation

The government has the right to collect property taxes from property owners to provide funds for services such as schools, fire and police protection, parks, and libraries. The federal government does not tax property, relying on income taxes for operating revenues, but cities levy taxes on real property. These taxes are levied according to the value of the property and are called *ad valorem* taxes.

Estates

Estates in real property are **freehold** (an ownership interest in the property) or **non-freehold** (a rental interest in the property).

Types of Freehold Estates

Fee simple is the highest and best form of ownership. Also known as **fee simple absolute**, the owner has the right to:

- occupy, rent, or mortgage the property
- sell, dispose of, or transfer ownership of the property
- build on the property (or destroy buildings already part of the property)
- mine or extract oil, gas, and minerals
- restrict or allow the use of the property to others

A **fee simple determinable estate** ends whenever a specific event happens (or does not happen) and the real property automatically reverts back to the grantor or his or her heirs. **Fee upon condition** gives the grantor the right to take back the property upon a particular event, but the property does not automatically revert to the grantor.

A **life estate** lasts only for the lifetime of the holder of the estate (or another identified living person, when a life estate *pur autre vie* is created).

The holder of a **life estate** has all the responsibilities of ownership while the estate is in effect and may not destroy the premises unless the vested holder of the life estate grants permission. The vested holder is the party that will own the property after the life estate holder is deceased.

A life estate is not inheritable unless it is a life estate *pur autre vie* and the person against whose life the estate is measured survives the original holder of the life estate. At the completion of the life estate, the property normally passes to a third party called a **remainderman**. If no remainder interest was created, the property returns by reversion (**life estate in reversion**) to the creator of the life estate or his or her heirs.

Forms of Ownership

There are many different entities that can acquire ownership in real property: an individual, a group of individuals, a large corporation, a government entity (at any level of government), and more. In addition, there are many different forms of ownership. **Estate in severalty** (sole ownership) occurs when property is held by one person or a single legal entity. The individual's interest is severed from everyone else's.

Concurrent ownership is ownership by more than one party.

Tenancy in common involves two or more individuals who own an undivided interest in real property without rights to survivorship. Undivided means that each tenant has an interest in the entire property.

The interest in the estate can vary among the tenants in common. One party can have 40%, another 25%, and another 35%. If a deed conveying property is made out to two people but does not stipulate their relationship, they are presumed to be tenants in common with equal interest. A party can freely dispose of his or her interest by sale, gift, devise, or descent without affecting the rights of the other owners. The new owner will be a **tenant in common** with the other owners.

Joint tenancy also involves two or more people, but includes a right of survivorship. Four unities must exist to create a valid joint tenancy:

1. **Unity of time**—All tenants must acquire their interest at the same moment. This means that no new tenants can be added at a later time.
2. **Unity of title**—All tenants must acquire their interest from the same source—the same deed, will, or other conveyance.
3. **Unity of interest**—Each tenant has an equal percentage ownership.
4. **Unity of possession**—Each tenant enjoys the same undivided interest in the whole property and right to occupy the property.

Joint tenancy also includes the **right of survivorship**. This means that a joint tenant cannot will his or her ownership interest; when a co-owner dies, the surviving co-owners share equally in the deceased owner's interest. The last survivor becomes the sole owner.

Tenancy by the entirety is a form of joint tenancy specifically for married couples. Neither spouse can sell the property independently; both must sign the deed in order to transfer the property. **Tenancy by the entirety**, like a **joint tenancy**, provides the right of survivorship for the remaining spouse.

Transfer of Rights

Deeds

A **deed** is a written document that conveys property from the **grantor** (owner) to the **grantee** (buyer). The requirements for a valid deed are as follows:

- It must be **in writing**.
- The grantor(s) must be of sound mind (legally capable).
- It must contain an **identification of all parties** (sometimes deeds will include the terms *et al.* meaning "and others" and *et ux.* meaning "and wife").
- It must identify the property adequately; preferably with a full **legal description** (metes and bounds, lot and block, government survey, etc., will be discussed in detail later in this chapter).
- It must contain a **granting clause**—also called words of conveyance—that contains the appropriate words ("I hereby grant, transfer, and convey," etc.).
- It must state the **consideration** (something of value, like money or love) given.
- It must have a **proper execution**—the deed must be signed by the grantor.
- It must be **delivered** to and **accepted** by the grantee.

A deed must also be dated, witnessed, and **acknowledged**, signed before a notary public, and sometimes signed by the grantee in order to be **recorded** at the place where the public records of real property transfers are stored. A deed does not need to be recorded in order to be valid. However, recording a deed provides **constructive notice** (assumed or publicly available notice) of the conveyance to parties who would otherwise not know about the recording (i.e., those who did not have **actual knowledge** of the deed). Recorded deeds are organized according to the **book/volume** and **page** reference number where recorded. A recorded deed provides **constructive notice** (assumed or publicly available notice) of the conveyance.

In Connecticut, deeds are recorded in the **land records** located in the **town clerk's office** of the town in which the property is located.

There are many different types of deeds:

- A **general warranty deed** carries the grantor's **express** or **implied assurances** (called **warranties** or **covenants**) regarding the validity of the title.
- A **special** (or **"limited"**) **warranty deed** carries the grantor's assurances only as to the state of the title after the grantor acquired ownership.
- A **bargain and sale deed** contains no warranties against encumbrances, but implies that the grantor has the right to sell the property (e.g., tax collector deed or foreclosure sale deed).
- A **quitclaim deed** transfers whatever interest the grantor may own, but does not warrant that the grantor actually has any interest in the described property.
- The types of deeds involving a trust are:
  - A **deed of trust** (sometimes called **deed in trust**) conveys the property to a trust from the grantor (often called the **settlor** or **trustor**).

- A **trustee deed** conveys the property from a trust to anyone but the original creator of the trust (the trustor).
- A **reconveyance deed** conveys the property from the trust back to the original trustor.

Will or Inheritance

A person who dies with a will, **testate**, will have his or her property distributed as specified in the will. An owner who has died without a will has died **intestate**. When someone dies **intestate**, his or her possessions will be distributed based on the **laws of descent**.

A transfer of personal property by will is called a **bequest** or **legacy** (money). A transfer of real estate by will is called a **devise**.

Escheat is the state's right to claim ownership of property when a person dies and leaves no heirs and no will. Ownership of the property reverts to the state. This reversion to the state is called **escheat**, from the Anglo-French word meaning "to fall back."

Adverse possession may be used to acquire title to property against the owner's will. The occupancy must be **open, notorious** (not secretive), **continuous**, and **without permission**. Most states also require the person claiming ownership to be acting in good faith. Adverse possession can be used only against private property, not public property.

Eminent domain is the right of the government (federal or state) to take private property for a public purpose.

Foreclosure is the legal act of selling property because the terms of a note were not met (normally for nonpayment).

Encumbrances and Liens

An **encumbrance** is a right or interest in a property that does not belong to an owner or tenant. An encumbrance is **voluntary** if it is imposed with the consent of the owner. It is **involuntary** if it can be imposed without the consent of the owner. Encumbrances consist of **liens** (a claim to property to ensure payment of a debt to another) and items that affect the use and physical condition of the property, such as **encroachments** or **easements**.

An **encroachment** occurs when a property improvement extends onto an adjoining parcel of land. An encroachment may be so slight as to be unnoticeable or unobjectionable, as with a fence line that deviates by only one or a few inches from the defined property boundary. The remedy may be removal of the encroachment or money damages. If no legal action is taken (or permission granted) by the owner of the burdened land, such action may become a **claim of adverse possession**.

Easements grant a right to use a portion of a property owner's land for a specific purpose. The **dominant tenement** is a parcel of land that benefits from an easement over an adjoining or adjacent parcel. An **easement appurtenant** is one that runs with the land because it is transferred when title to the dominant tenement is transferred. The **servient tenement** is the parcel of land that is burdened with the easement; that is, the parcel over which the owner of the dominant tenement is allowed to travel.

An **easement in gross** does not benefit any one parcel of real estate but rather benefits a number of parcels to bring such things as utilities.

An easement may be acquired by:

- **express grant** in a deed
- **easement by necessity** when a parcel is landlocked and there is no method of ingress or egress other than over someone else's land
- **easement by prescription**, which is obtained in a manner similar to that of adverse possession. The right to be obtained is a right of use rather than ownership, but the use must be without the permission of the property owner, open and notorious, and must continue for a statutory number of years.

Unlike an easement, which is permanent, a **license** is the temporary permission to come onto someone's land. The holder of a ticket for a baseball game has a license to enter the stadium for the game. A license can be revoked by the licensor.

If a married person owns property in his or her name only, upon death, the surviving spouse is entitled to a one-third life interest in the property. If the surviving spouse is the wife, the right is called **dower**. If the surviving spouse is the husband, the right is called **curtesy**. Most states have adopted modern probate statutes to replace these concepts. Connecticut has adopted the Uniform Probate Code and its definition of **widow's (widower's) election**. Under this law, a surviving spouse may elect either to accept what the spouse receives under the deceased spouse's will, or elect to receive a life estate interest in one-third of the estate's assets.

Liens are claims against property that secure payment of a financial obligation owed by the property or the property owner. They come in many varieties. Liens may be created voluntarily or by operation of law. A **specific lien** is a lien on one specific property, such as a mortgage or city tax lien. A **general lien** is a lien on all of a person's property, such as a judgment or IRS tax lien. A **mechanic's lien** is an example of an involuntary lien. In general, a mechanic's lien is available to anyone who provides material or labor for an improvement to real estate if he or she has not been paid for services or materials.

Water Rights

Water rights are defined by state law and depend on the water source and use.

Even though real property may border a body of water, the legal doctrine of **prior appropriation** determines that the state government controls access to the water. This rule is particularly important in areas where water is a scarce resource.

- **Riparian rights**—on a navigable body of water, the property owner's boundary will extend to the water's edge or the accretion line of the water. On a non-navigable body of water, the property owner's boundary will extend to the center of the body of water.
- **Littoral rights**—the rights of a landowner whose property borders on a non-flowing body of water, such as a lake, ocean, or other body of still water.

- **Accretion**—the gradual additional of land resulting from the natural deposit of soil by streams, lakes, or rivers.
- **Avulsion**—the sudden loss of land when a stream or other body of water suddenly changes its course.
- **Erosion**—the gradual loss of land by wind, water, and other natural processes.
- **Reliction**—the gradual adding of land due to the withdrawal of water.
- **Alluvion**—the soil carried by a moving body of water that is deposited on someone's land.
- **Accession**—acquiring ownership of land due to the deposit of soil by natural forces (wind or water).

Condominiums/Cooperatives/Time-Sharing Leases and Options

Condominiums

A condominium is created by a recorded **declaration of condominium** (sometimes called the **master deed**), which identifies the property, each unit, and the percentage ownership that the individual owns in the land and the **common areas** of the structures. The **declaration** or **master deed** is recorded at the appropriate office to record all other types of deeds. A **unit deed** is recorded for each sale of an individual unit. Each unit owner agrees to be bound by the **bylaws** and rules and regulations of the condominium. The **bylaws** (or **Declaration of Trust**) are recorded to establish the condominium association, define its legal authority, and also define the roles of the **trustees** and their authority.

Condominium fees are determined by the annual operating **budget** of the condominium. Normally, fees are due monthly and are based on the unit's percentage of ownership.

Some of the **common areas** are for the use of all of the unit owners (e.g., the foundation, elevator, pool), while some of the common areas will be defined as limited common elements and will be designated for the exclusive use of a specific unit, such as a balcony.

An advantage of condominium ownership over cooperative ownership is that a default in payment of taxes, mortgage payment, or monthly assessment affects only the specific unit. Each unit is defined as a separate parcel of real estate and is owned fee simple.

In order to transfer a condominium unit to another owner in Connecticut, the current owner must procure a **resale certificate** from the association, which discloses the status of all of the condominium fees and common charges. The current owner also needs to procure an **insurance certificate** showing that the new owner (and his or her mortgage holder) will be covered under the condominium master insurance policy.

Some condominium associations have a **right of first refusal** to purchase a unit before it is sold to someone else. This right will be explained in the resale certificate and the declaration.

Cooperatives

Cooperatives are apartments owned by a corporation that holds titles to the entire cooperative property, holds a blanket mortgage on the entire property, and is responsible for the *ad valorem* taxes for the entire property. The cooperative is taxed as one entity.

Each purchaser of an apartment unit is a stockholder in the corporation and receives a **stock certificate in the corporation**. The purchaser obtains the right to occupy through a **proprietary unit lease for the life of the corporation**. Each block of stock is tied to a specific right to occupy and carries a lease payment financial obligation that represents a *pro rata* share of the total cost of the operations expense and mortgage payments on the building.

A disadvantage of cooperative ownership over condominium ownership is that default of the monthly payment by a shareholder affects the entire cooperative and the other shareholders must make up the deficiency.

Time-Sharing

Time-shares are when multiple owners own a proportional interest in a single condominium unit with the exclusive right to use and occupy the unit for a specified period of time each year. The individual owners pay common expense, maintenance costs, and management fees based on the ratio between the ownership period and the total number of ownership periods available in the property. This type of ownership can be either a **fee simple** ("estate" time-share) or **leasehold** ("use" time-share) interest. Time-share owners can participate in an **exchange program** (either in-house for affiliated resorts or external) and exchange their time-share for another location.

Leases

Freehold versus Non-freehold

Estates in real property are **freehold** (an ownership interest in the property) or **non-freehold** (a rental interest in the property).

A **non-freehold** estate gives the holder of the estate a right to occupy the property until the end of the lease when the right will revert to the fee simple holder. The **lessor** permits the **lessee** to use the property for the period and under the **terms** specified in the **lease**. **Demise** is another legal term meaning to lease.

Types of Tenancy

TYPE	CHARACTERISTIC	EXAMPLE
Estate/Tenancy for Years	A lease with a definite termination date	one-year residential apartment lease
Tenancy for Period to Period	A lease with an automatic renewal option	90-day house lease that will renew for another 90 days unless proper notice is given by either party
Tenancy at Will	A lease without a termination date. It terminates when proper notice is given by either party.	
Tenancy at Sufferance	Also called **holdover tenant**. The tenant remains in possession of the property after the termination of a lease. If the lessor accepts rent from the holdover tenant, a tenancy at will is created; otherwise, the tenant at sufferance may be evicted.	

Common Leases

Leases must be signed by the landlord and the tenant, but need not be recorded to be enforceable. An individual who wishes to notify the public of a leasehold interest may record a memorandum of lease.

A lease must include a sufficient property description. A legal description as used in a deed is appropriate, although in certain residential leases, a street address and apartment number are sufficient.

There are several kinds of leases:

- A **gross lease** specifies that the landlord pay all expenses: property taxes, insurance, maintenance. This kind of lease is often used for apartments and other residential properties.
- A **net lease** specifies that the tenant pay certain expenses. The most common arrangement requires the tenant to pay property taxes, insurance, and maintenance. This is called a net, net, net or triple net lease.
- A **percentage lease** requires the tenant to pay a percentage of gross sales as rent in addition to a base rental amount specified in the lease. Percentage leases are often used in shopping centers.
- A **graduated lease** calls for periodic, stated changes in rent during the term of the lease.
- A **99-year lease** is a long-term land lease typically used for commercial development when the lessee prefers to spend his or her money on capital improvements or the owner does not want to sell (often used by fast-food restaurants).

When a lease is **assigned**, the original lessee transfers the remaining interest in a lease to a new party. With a **sublet**, only a portion of the lease is transferred. In both instances, the original lessee remains responsible. With **novation**, a new lease is substituted for the original lease, removing responsibility from the original lessee. Some leases expressly prohibit the lessee's interest to be transferred.

When a property sells and there are existing leases, the **leases are binding** on the new owner.

Obligation of Parties

The lessor (property owner or landlord) is obligated to provide:

- **utility services** (although the lessee may be required to pay for these services under the terms of the lease)
- a property that is **fit for habitation**
- a property **free of sanitary and building code violations**

The lessor of residential property will not be allowed to interfere with the tenant's **quiet enjoyment** of the leased property. This means that the lessor must recognize the tenant's right of possession of the property.

If the unit becomes unfit for habitation or the lessor interferes with the tenant's quiet enjoyment of the property, the lessee may vacate the apartment by **constructive eviction**.

The lessee is obligated to **avoid waste**, which means that he or she will use the property in the proper manner. The lessee is also obligated to:

- keep the leased property clean and dispose of trash in a sanitary manner
- use fixtures and appliances in a safe and sanitary manner, and in the rooms designated for their use
- not damage, deface, or otherwise destroy the property, or permit anyone else to do so

If a lessor takes a **security deposit**, he or she must hold the money in a separate, interest-bearing account. The lessee is entitled to interest on the security deposit.

Options

An **option** is a unilateral contract. An option to purchase enables a purchaser to purchase a property at a set price within a given time frame. An option may also be used with a lease. To create a valid option, the property owner must be paid some cash (valuable consideration), the option must be in writing, and time is of the essence. Options may be **assigned** without the consent of the optionor.

A **right of first refusal** gives the optionee the right to match another offer or rescind his or her option.

Property Management

The range of services that the property manager can perform for the landlord (property owner) includes marketing, leasing, maintenance, bill payment, preparing reports on monthly income and operating expenses, and rent collection.

Contracts/Deeds

Real Estate Contracts

A **listing** is a hiring contract between a real estate brokerage and the owner of a property for the sale of a specific property, spelling out the terms and consideration due.

A **binder** is a short, temporary agreement to sell property for a specified price, and this binder is usually quickly replaced by a more comprehensive **purchase agreement**.

An **offer to purchase** is normally a fill-in-the-blank form where the buyers specify the price and terms they are willing to pay for the property. It is not a contract, but a statement of the intentions of the buyers.

Normally, neither binders nor offers to purchase are used. The most common practice is for the buyers to complete, sign, and present to the sellers a **purchase agreement**. This agreement includes all of the terms and contingencies (such as home inspection and mortgage financing). After the sellers sign this agreement, it becomes the binding contract document upon which the sale will be based. Sometimes, a second contract (a **purchase and sale agreement**) with even more details is signed after the buyers have completed their home inspection.

A **lease** is a contract for the rental (possession) of property. The lessor permits the lessee to use the property for the period and under the terms specified in the lease.

A **deed** conveys title to real property. It must be in writing, executed, and delivered to transfer ownership of property.

The **mortgage note** is a primary financing instrument. The borrower agrees to pay the loan off according to a schedule of payments at a certain interest rate over a specified period of time (an IOU).

The **mortgage deed** is a pledge of property to secure the repayment of a debt (collateral). If the debt is not repaid as agreed between the lender and borrower, the lender can force the sale of the pledged property and apply the proceeds to repayment of the debt.

A **bilateral contract** is one in which both parties exchange promises to do or refrain from doing something. A real estate sales contract is bilateral because both sides have an obligation to perform—the turning over of title to the property in exchange for money or other considerations.

A **unilateral contract** is one in which one party makes a promise and the other party does not promise, but can make the contract a binding agreement by taking some action.

An **option** is a unilateral contract. An option to purchase enables a purchaser to purchase a property at a set price within a given time frame. To create a valid option, the property owner must be paid some cash (valuable consideration), the option must be in writing, and time is of the essence.

A contract is **executory** when it has not yet been fully performed.

A contract is **executed** when all contract terms have been met and the transaction is completed.

Essential Elements of Contracts

A contract is a legally enforceable agreement between two parties to do something (performance) or to refrain from certain acts (forbearance). A contract must:

- have **offer** and **acceptance** (mutual assent)
- include **consideration** (does not need to be money)
- have a **lawful objective**
- involve **legally competent parties**
- be in writing as required by the **Statute of Frauds** (one notable exception is a lease for one year or less)
- be signed by the parties to the agreement signifying their **consent** to the contract

If a notary witnesses the parties' signatures, the notary certifies that neither party is acting under duress and signing the contract of its own free act.

Termination of an Offer

The offer to purchase can be terminated by one of the following:

- death of either party
- expiration of the time frame listed in the offer
- revocation by the offeror before receiving notice of acceptance by offeree
- bankruptcy of either party
- condemnation or destruction of the property
- outright rejection or a counteroffer by the offeree (a counteroffer constitutes a rejection of the previous offer)

Valid/Void/Voidable Contracts

A contract can be construed by the courts to be valid, void, or voidable.

A **valid** contract meets all the requirements of law. It is binding upon its parties and legally enforceable in a court of law.

A **void** contract has no legal effect and, in fact, is not a contract at all. Even though the parties may have intended to enter into a contract, no legal rights are created and no party is bound. The word *void* means the absence of something. An example of a void contract is a contract to commit a crime.

A **voidable** contract binds one party but not the other. For example, when one party is guilty of fraud, the other party may void the contract. But, if the offended party wishes to fulfill the contract, then the party who committed fraud is still bound to the terms of the contract. A contract with a minor is voidable at the option of the minor party.

Real Property Purchase Agreement

The Real Property Purchase Agreement includes the following:

- **names** of all parties to the transaction (seller is **vendor**; buyer is **vendee**)
- **description of the land**
- **sales price** (consideration)
- amount of buyer's earnest money **deposit**, which will be held in an escrow account
- **date** of the contract
- **signatures** of the buyer(s) and seller(s)

The Connecticut **Statute of Frauds** requires that a contract to sell real property must be in writing. (Most contracts dealing with real estate must be in writing. An exception is a lease that will terminate one year or less from the date of the agreement. Even then, it is in the best interests of both landlord and tenant to have a written agreement.)

Once a contract to purchase has been signed by both parties, the buyer has **equitable title** in the property (interest in real property, but the transaction is not yet complete). **Legal title** is title that is fully vested in the owner as evidenced by a deed, will, or court document. Legal title to land and its appurtenances encompasses the entire bundle of rights that an owner possesses.

Most real property purchase agreements allow the buyer the **right to assign** the contract to another party. If the contract is assigned, the original buyer is not relieved of his or her obligations if the assignee does not fulfill the responsibilities under the contract.

Legal Descriptions of Property

In order to convey real property, the deed must include an unmistakable description of the property. To satisfy the requirement for legal description in the deed, one of the following methods may be used.

- **Metes and bounds** system is one of the oldest methods of land measurement and description used in this country. The **bounds** (boundary lines) of property are measured from a specified point of beginning along measurements called **metes**, with each change of direction marked by a compass angle. **Markers** denote each turning point; in modern description, **natural monuments** (the old oak tree) have been replaced by **benchmarks** (metal pins). The description ends with the return to the **point of beginning** (POB).
- **Lot and block system** uses parcel numbers noted on a subdivision map (**plat map**). The plat is divided into blocks by streets. The blocks are then separated into lots.
- Government survey system (rectangular survey system) was developed to have a more uniform method of delineating property boundaries. Property is identified by reference to the intersection of a meridian (**principal meridian**) running north-south and a baseline running east-west. Land is separated into rectangles called **townships** of six miles squared (six miles to a side, or 36 square miles). Townships are counted in **tiers** north or south of a baseline and ranges east or west of a meridian. A township is divided into 36 sections. A **section** is one mile squared (one square mile) and contains 640 acres. An **acre** contains 43,560 square feet.

Breach of Contract

When one party fails to perform as required by the contract, a breach of contract or default has occurred. The wronged or innocent party has the following possible remedies:

- Sue for money **damages**. For example, if a seller cannot perform, but the buyer has already spent a large amount of money on inspections, appraisals, and so on, the buyer could sue to recover the money spent.
- Sue for **specific performance**. Specific performance means fulfilling the terms of the contract.
- Accept liquidated money damages. This remedy, available only to the seller, means **retaining the earnest money deposit**.
- Mutually **rescind** the contract. Sometimes, both parties are better off just walking away from the contract and canceling the agreement.

Recorded or Registered Title?

Twenty states have experimented with the Torrens system. Today, Torrens exists in nine states: Minnesota, Massachusetts, Colorado, Georgia, Hawaii, New York, North Carolina, Ohio, and Washington.

There are two primary systems of determining the status of real property ownership and encumbrances: the **abstract** (or **recording**) **system** and the **Torrens** (or **registration**) **system**.

Forty-one states have an abstract real property recording system in which the primary function of the public real property transfer records is to provide the opportunity for private parties to record their property documents (deeds, etc.) and to allow private parties to search the land records themselves in order to come to their own conclusions and opinions as to ownership and title. Proof of ownership is determined by private title searchers who search the land records for transactions that occurred over a number of years and often provide an abstract of title (title abstract) or summary of all of the recorded documents that concern a particular property during this period. Private companies then are paid to issue **title insurance policies** to ensure that a person actually owns his or her property.

An alternative recording system (now used in only nine states) is the **Torrens system**. This is a system of registering real property ownership. In this system, each parcel of real property is identified by the Register of Deeds by a numbered **Torrens Certificate** (or Registration Certificate), which identifies the title history of the property, its current owners, its legal description, and any outstanding encumbrances. Parties to a closing present their documents to the Register of Deeds and apply to register them. The status of this recording and the ownership of the property is confirmed by a government official who searches the title records and the existing Torrens Certificate. After a brief procedure before a special court, the government confirms the ownership in the new grantee and issues a new numbered **Torrens Certificate** to the private recording party (sometimes the Register of Deeds does not return the recorded deed of conveyance). With Torrens registered real property, the title has been searched by a government and approved by a court. The insurer of title and ownership is the government, not private searchers and companies. Some states have newer records by a recording system and older records by a Torrens-type registration system.

Connecticut has an abstract recording system of recording documents with the town clerk of the town where the property is located. Connecticut has never utilized a Torrens-type registration system.

Transfer Taxes

Most states charge a **transfer tax** (or **tax stamps**) whenever real property changes hands. The amount of the tax is based on the sales price of the property, and normally is an expense paid by the seller at closing. Currently, Connecticut has a complex system of transfer taxes called the **Connecticut conveyance tax**. The amount of the tax varies not only with the sales price, but also with the type of property and, in some cases, the town in which the property is located.

Title Search

A **title search** will reveal the chain of title, the history of conveyances, and encumbrances that can be found in the public records. The title search begins with the name of the present owner and the instrument that establishes title in that owner as the grantee. Working back through what is called the **grantee index**, the name of the grantor to the present owner is found on the deed in which that owner is the grantee. In this way, the person examining the title can go back to the first recorded document of the property. The **chain of title** is an account of the successive owners of the property. An **abstract of title** is a certified summary of the history of the recorded documents affecting the title.

Financing/Mortgages

Real Estate Cycle

Although there are many steps to the real estate cycle, typically they include:

1. Listing the real property
2. Qualifying the buyer
3. Showing the buyer properties
4. Offer/real property purchase agreement—the contract between the buyer and seller
5. Financing—most offer/purchase agreements have a financing contingency
6. Pass papers (also called a **closing** when title changes hands)

Financing Procedure

The first step to obtaining financing is submitting a **mortgage application**.

    Bank approval steps: The lender wants to make sure that the borrower is a good credit risk. To ensure this, the lender looks at several items:

- the property—the bank will send an appraiser to evaluate the property and ensure that the sales price is in line with other comparable properties that have recently sold nearby
- the borrower's ability to pay
- a check of the borrower's credit

    The standard real property purchase agreement includes a **financing contingency clause**. Standard contracts include this contingency, allowing the buyers a specific period of time to receive a mortgage commitment. If the buyers do not receive their commitment by the deadline, they can withdraw from the transaction and receive their earnest money deposit back.

Types of Lending Institutions

There are many sources of financing available to the buyer of real property. The borrower can apply to a **savings and loan association**, a **commercial bank**, a **mutual savings bank** (owned by their depositors), a **cooperative bank**, a **credit union**, a **mortgage company** (which is different from a mortgage broker, who does not actually loan money, but brings borrowers and lenders together), a **life insurance company**, or a **private lender**.

Money as a Commodity

The **discount rate** is the interest rate the Federal Reserve Bank charges when it makes a loan to another financial institution. The **prime rate** is the interest rate charged by banks to their preferred borrowers. Many home equity loans are based on the prime rate published by the Federal Reserve Bank. **Mortgage rates** are market-driven for long-term loans and do not necessarily rise or fall with changes in either the short-term discount rate or prime rate.

Some loans include **origination points** or **discount points**. Each point is 1% of the amount borrowed, so one point on a $100,000 loan would be $1,000. **Origination points** are costs of the loan and are the usual way for mortgage brokers to be paid. When a borrower pays **discount points**, he or she is prepaying the lending institution money at the beginning of the loan to receive a lower interest rate over the life of the loan. This can also be called a **buydown** because the borrower is "buying down" the interest rate of the loan.

Types of Mortgages

With a **direct reduction** mortgage, a portion of the principal is paid off with each mortgage payment.

A **construction loan** is short-term financing used by a developer or builder. The funds are released based on a predetermined schedule as phases of the construction are completed. Upon completion, the developer must pay off the construction loan and secure long-term financing.

A **blanket mortgage** is used by a developer or contractor to purchase more than one lot of land. A defining feature of the blanket mortgage is a **release clause**, which lets the developer sell off a parcel of the land while retaining the blanket mortgage on the rest of the property.

A **package mortgage** uses not only real estate for collateral, but also personal property.

A **demand mortgage** gives the lender the right to demand payment at any time.

With a **purchase money mortgage**, the seller holds the financing for the borrower (**seller financing**).

A **junior** or **second mortgage** is an additional loan on top of the borrower's primary financing. It is a **junior lien** and, in the case of a default by the borrower, will not be paid unless the primary loan is covered in full.

An **open-end mortgage** allows the mortgagor to borrow additional funds from the lender, up to a specified amount, without rewriting the mortgage.

A **wraparound mortgage** combines a new loan wrapped around an existing mortgage. The borrower makes payment on both mortgages to the wraparound mortgagee who then forwards the payments on the first mortgage to the first mortgagee.

With a **variable rate mortgage** (**adjustable rate**), the interest rate will vary over the life of the loan. The rate is adjusted at specified intervals throughout the loan based on some predetermined indicator, such as Treasury Bill rates (known as the **index**). The **margin** is a predetermined amount added to the index rate to determine the interest rate. For the borrower's protection, there is a **cap**, or limit, on the amount the rate can be increased for each specified rate change period and a **cap** for how high the rate can go to over the life of the loan.

A **balloon loan** usually charges a lower interest rate than a regular fixed rate loan. The loan will be structured as an amortized loan with a term of 30 years, but the loan will balloon after a certain period. That is, the loan becomes due and payable before the end of the amortization term. The loan may balloon in five, seven, or ten years, or however long the lender stipulates. At the end of the balloon period, the borrower must repay the loan and secure other financing.

In a **shared equity** loan, the lender gives the borrower a lower interest rate in exchange for a percentage of the equity of the property.

Negative amortization occurs when an adjustable rate goes up, but the monthly payment stays the same. The monthly payment is no longer large enough to cover both the interest and the amount of principal due. The amount of the shortfall is added to the remaining principal balance.

An **equity loan** is a second mortgage used to access the equity (the difference between the market value of the property and what is owed) in a property.

Conventional loans are those made without any form of government-backed insurance or guarantee. The lender looks to the borrower and the **security** (the property) for assurance that the loan will be repaid by the borrower (or by forced sale of the property).

VA-guaranteed loans carry the assurance of the **Department of Veteran Affairs (VA)** (established in 1944) that the lender will be protected in the event of default by the borrower. (Note that the VA is not lending the money itself, but guaranteeing it.)

- The **certificate of eligibility** is the VA's statement that the veteran is eligible for the loan guarantee program.
- The property must be appraised by a VA-approved appraiser and the VA will issue a **certificate of reasonable value** (**CRV**) based on that estimate.
- VA loans are for one- to four-family owner-occupied homes.
- The **funding fee** depends on the veteran's category and the amount of the down payment, which can range from zero (**100% financing**) to 10% or more.
- No prepayment penalty is allowed.
- The property may be sold and the **VA loan assumed** (even by a nonveteran), but the veteran must receive a written release of liability from the VA to be relieved of personal obligation in the event of a future foreclosure and deficiency.
- The veteran's entitlement can be reused on a subsequent home purchase, although the amount of entitlement will be reduced if there has been an assumption of a prior loan guarantee.

The **Federal Housing Administration** (**FHA**), established in 1934, insures loans for any qualified buyer. These loans are administered through the department of Housing and Urban Development (**HUD**). FHA-insured loans protect the lender in the event the borrower defaults on the mortgage. (Note that the FHA does not lend money itself, it insures the lender.)

- FHA sets maximum loan amounts that it will lend depending on the state and county in which the property is located.
- The borrower makes a one-time insurance payment at the time of the closing of the sale.
- The borrower and the property must meet FHA guidelines.
- No prepayment penalty is allowed.
- FHA loans are for one- to four-family owner-occupied homes.
- An FHA loan may be assumed.
- Because of the FHA insurance, a lower-than-usual down payment may be possible.

Borrowers who make a down payment of less than 20% of the sales price may be required to purchase **private mortgage insurance** (**PMI**). The insurance **premium** is usually a monthly charge added to the loan payment. It can be eliminated (with the lender's approval) when the borrower's equity in the home is at least 20% of the home's value. **MGIC** is one the nation's largest private mortgage insurance companies.

Depending on the loan, a buyer may be able to take over the seller's existing mortgage. If the buyer **assumes** the loan, then both the new owner and the seller are responsible in the event of a deficiency after a foreclosure. If the buyer takes the loan **"subject to,"** then only the seller is responsible if there is a deficiency after a foreclosure.

Secondary Mortgage Market

The **primary market** sells loans directly to borrowers, while the **secondary market** sells the loans made in the primary market to investors.

The major purchasers of home loans are:

- **Federal National Mortgage Association** (**Fannie Mae** or **FNMA**) is the largest purchaser of all types of home loans. The FNMA was originally a government agency, and then was converted to entirely private ownership and control, with some oversight by the federal government.
- **Federal Home Loan Mortgage Corporation** (**FHLMC** or **Freddie Mac**) is a federally chartered private corporation that primarily purchases conventional loans.
- **Government National Mortgage Association** (**GNMA** or **Ginnie Mae**) is a government corporation, which is a division of HUD and is a major purchaser of government-backed (FHA and VA) mortgage loans.

These entities buy so many loans that they virtually control how the loan origination or primary market operates. A loan that meets Fannie Mae's guidelines is called a **conforming loan.** Most conventional loans will use uniform instruments for loan applications, appraisal reporting forms, and closing statements.

Truth-in-Lending (Regulation Z)

The **Truth-in-Lending Act** (**TILA**), enacted by Congress in 1968, is part of the Consumer Protection Act. **Regulation Z** was created by the Federal Trade Commission under the direction and authority of the TILA. Regulation Z applies to creditors (lenders) involved in at least one of the following:

- more than 25 consumer credit transactions per year
- more than five transactions per year with a dwelling used as security
- the credit is offered to consumers
- credit is offered on a regular basis
- the credit is subject to a finance charge
- the arrangement requires more than four installments
- the credit is primarily for personal, family, or household purposes

If credit is extended to a business, or for a commercial or agricultural purpose, Regulation Z does not apply. The required Truth-in-Lending disclosures must be made in a **disclosure statement** that highlights certain information by using a box, boldface type, a different type style, or a different background color. The disclosure statement must be presented to the borrower within **three business days** of making the loan application; the day the application is completed by the borrower is not counted. Information to be disclosed includes (in addition to other items):

- amount financed
- finance charge
- annual percentage rate (**APR**)
- total amount that will be paid over the life of the loan
- prepayment penalties
- late-payment charges

When a consumer is refinancing a loan that qualifies under the Truth-in-Lending Act, which is enforced through Regulation Z as a consumer credit transaction, the borrower has three business days to **rescind** (or cancel) the mortgage (**right of rescission**).

Advertisements for consumer loans covered under Regulation Z must give the APR and provide other payment terms and conditions if specific credit terms are used. Remember, this is a disclosure law so consumers have a summary of the financial offer and can compare products available from other providers in the marketplace.

Mortgage Note and Mortgage Deed

A **mortgage deed** is a pledge of property made by a mortgagor (the borrower) to pledge collateral (the property) that may be sold at auction (foreclosure) when the borrower defaults and fails to fulfill the promises made in the mortgage instrument. The mortgage (pledge of the collateral) is given for the benefit of the mortgagee (the lender). Caution! Remember that in real estate terminology, words ending in *or* refer to the person giving something (The borrower gives the pledge.) and words ending in *ee* refer to the person receiving something (The lender receives the benefit of the pledge of the collateral.). Forget about the fact that the lender gives the money, it is the pledge of collateral that is important in this discussion.

When a lender makes a loan, the borrower signs a **mortgage note** that promises to repay the loan and defines the terms of the repayment.

The **mortgage deed** pledges the property as collateral. When the loan has been paid in full, the **defeasance clause** in the mortgage deed requires the lender (mortgagee) to issue a **discharge** (showing the release of the debt) that should be recorded to remove the encumbrance affecting the title to the property.

A **due-on-sale** clause (also known as **alienation** or **assumption clause**) means that the loan must be paid off in full when the property is sold and the loan cannot be assumed by another party.

A **subordination clause** states that the loan will be junior (subordinated) to another lien in the future.

A defaulting borrower faces penalties of varying severity. Late charges will be incurred if the borrower is late in making a payment. If the borrower remains in default, the lender may invoke an acceleration clause. An **acceleration clause** gives the lender the right to collect the balance of the loan immediately. Finally, if the debt remains unpaid, the **power of sale** clause in the mortgage deed allows the process of foreclosure to begin.

The mortgage deed is different from the **grantor/grantee deed**, which is the deed that transfers actual ownership (bundle of rights) from the grantor (seller) to the grantee (buyer).

Real Estate Settlement and Procedures Act (RESPA)

The **Real Estate Settlement and Procedures Act** (**RESPA**), enacted by Congress in 1974, is the federal law that requires disclosures by lenders, mortgage brokers, and closing agents in federally related transactions involving the sale or transfer of a dwelling of one to four units. (Second mortgages, seller financing, also known as purchase money mortgages and construction loans, are not subject to RESPA requirements.) The law requires:

- The lender or mortgage broker must provide the borrower with a copy of the special information booklet prepared by HUD within three business days of the loan application.
- The lender or mortgage broker must provide the borrower with a **good-faith estimate of closing costs.**
- A **Uniform Settlement Statement** (form **HUD-1**) must be made available to the borrower and seller at least one day prior to closing. The borrower and the seller will receive a copy of the form after the closing is completed.
- Fees, kickbacks, or other such payments to persons who do not actually provide loan services are strictly prohibited.
- Any affiliated business arrangement with an individual or entity offering settlement services must be disclosed.

Brokerage

Brokerage Definition

A **real estate broker** is any person who for another person and for a fee, commission, or other valuable consideration, or with the intention or in the expectation or upon the promise of receiving or collecting a fee, commission, or other valuable consideration, does any of the following: sells, exchanges, purchases, rents, or leases; or negotiates; or offers, attempts, or agrees to negotiate the sale, exchange, purchase, rental, or leasing of any real estate, or lists or offers, attempts, or agrees to list any real estate, or buys or offers to buy, sells or offers to sell, or otherwise deals in options on real estate, or advertises or holds himself or herself out as engaged in the business of selling, exchanging, purchasing, renting, or leasing real estate, or assists or directs in the procuring of prospects or the negotiation or completion of any agreement or transaction that results or is intended to result in the sale, exchange, purchase, leasing, or renting of any real estate.

Law of Agency

An **agent** is a person who represents the interest of another person or party (called the **principal**) in dealings with third persons. An agent acts as the fiduciary to his or her client.

A Mnemonic Trick

An agent's fiduciary duties to his or her client or principal can be remembered as OLD CAR:

- **O**bedience
- **L**oyalty
- **D**isclosure (of material facts concerning the transaction)
- **C**onfidentially
- **A**ccountability (of funds)
- **R**easonable care

In **single agency**, an agent is representing either the buyer or the seller. In **dual agency**, an agent is representing both the buyer and the seller. In Connecticut, a dual agent is always required to have informed, written consent of both parties before acting as a dual agent. A dual agent cannot give both parties all of the fiduciary duties.

There are two agency models for real estate companies:

1. All agents in the firm have the same relationship with the consumer (**seller** or **buyer agency**, not **designated agency**).
2. **Designated agency**—only the real estate agent listed on the disclosure form (**designated seller** or **buyer agent**) represents the client and other agents affiliated with the real estate company do not represent that client and may represent another party in the real estate transaction.

Connecticut licensees must disclose their relationship with the prospective buyer or seller. The relationship options are:

- **Seller's agent**—an agent who works for the best interest of the seller (**client**) and owes the seller fiduciary duties. The majority of agents who list property work with the seller as the seller's agent. A seller's agent can work with a buyer, but as a **customer**, not a client. The buyer must understand that the agent owes his or her fiduciary duties to the seller.
- **Buyer's agent**—an agent who works for the best interest of the buyer and owes the buyer fiduciary duties.
- **Facilitator** (**non-agent**)—no agency relationship exits with either party in the transaction. The facilitator's job is to bring both parties together. A facilitator has a duty to present all real property honestly and accurately, disclosing known material defects and accounting for funds. The facilitator does not have fiduciary duties. Connecticut does not allow facilitators.
- **Designated seller's and buyer's agent**—a designated agent represents his or her client (either buyer or seller) and owes fiduciary duties to his or her client. With the client's permission, the agent can be **designated** by another agent (the appointing agent, normally the broker or office manager) to be the office's sole representative for that particular client. All other agents affiliated with the real estate company do not represent that client. If the appointing agent designates another agent in the office to represent the other

party to the transaction, the appointing agent becomes a **dual agent** and must remain impartial, while the two designated agents (the **designated seller's** and **designated buyer's** agent) each represent his or her respective clients fully and owe his or her respective clients fiduciary duties. In Connecticut, in order to practice designated agency, an agent must have the informed, written consent of his or her client.

- **Dual agent**—an agent who represents both the buyer and the seller. In Connecticut, a dual agent is always required to have informed, written consent of both parties before acting as a dual agent. A dual agent cannot give both parties all of the fiduciary duties. **Undisclosed dual agency** is prohibited.

Creation of Agency

The listing agreement is the contract that establishes the **agency** relationship between an agent and his or her principal. These contracts can either be a listing agreement for the right to sell a property, or a buyer agency agreement for the right to help a buyer find a property. A written or oral listing agreement will establish an **express agency** (a hiring). **Implied agency** can be inferred by the conduct of the principal and agent (the parties act as if there had been an actual hiring). **Apparent authority** may establish an agency relationship. This occurs when a principal gives a third party reason to believe that another person is the principal's agent even though that person is unaware of the appointment. If the third party accepts the principal's representation as true, the principal may have established ostensible authority and therefore may be bound by the acts of his or her agent. This may happen, for example, when a seller gives the keys for a property to an agent. Other agents may reasonably rely upon the first agent's statement that authority exists for the first agent to show the property.

Listing agreements in Connecticut must be in writing.

Types of Listings

- An **open listing** is an agreement that a commission will be paid to the listing broker only if he or she is the procuring cause of the sale. A seller may enter into an open listing with an unlimited number of brokers. If the property is sold by another broker or by the sellers themselves, the listing broker is not entitled to a commission.
- An **exclusive agency listing** means that only one listing broker represents the seller. If the property sells through the efforts of the broker or through cooperation with MLS, the listing broker receives a commission. However, the seller retains the right to sell the property on his or her own without paying a commission.
- An **exclusive right to sell listing** provides the greatest protection to the listing broker, who will be paid a commission no matter who sells the property.
- A **net listing** offers the property owner a guaranteed sales price, with the listing broker taking any part of the purchase price over that amount. Net listings are illegal in Connecticut.

Multiple Listing System (MLS) is a system in which all members can share information regarding the properties they have for sale.

Duties of an Agent

The real estate listing agent owes the property owner (**principal**) the duties of a **fiduciary** if he or she is acting as a seller's agent. The agent must act in the owner's best interest. The buyer's agent owes the same responsibilities to the buyer.

When agents have a **personal interest in a property** and are selling or buying property for themselves, they must disclose that they are licensed real estate agents to the other party.

A broker must have a separate escrow bank account where all deposits for pending sales are kept in safekeeping. These funds must be kept separate from the broker's personal or business account. Any **commingling** of funds is prohibited.

Many properties sell through the cooperation offered in MLS. The agent working with the buyer is called a **cooperating broker**, or **co-broker** or **buyer's broker**.

Subagency is normally found when a potential buyer customer is interested in a parcel of property listed by broker firm "A," seeks assistance with the property from broker firm "B," but is not represented by either firm "A" or firm "B." This could be the desire of the potential buyer or by custom and practice in the state. Broker "B" becomes the **subagent** but does not represent the customer buyer. Broker "A" owes fiduciary duties to the seller and can only offer the buyer customer level services (fairness and honesty). In Connecticut, in order to practice subagency, the listing broker must obtain written permission from the seller. The written permission must include the following disclosure regarding **vicarious liability**: "Vicarious liability is the potential for a seller to be held liable for a misrepresentation or an act or omission of the subagent and that the seller authorizes the broker or salesperson to offer subagency in the signing of the notice."

While this type of subagency was widely used before the advent of real estate buyer agency, current buyer agency agreements and relationships have terminated much of the need for this type of subagency. Many states prohibit its use.

Termination of Agency

An agency contract can be terminated by:

- **completion of the objective**—either the property is sold or the buyer client has bought a house
- **expiration of the time limit** specified in the contract
- **mutual consent** (**rescission**)
- **revocation**—by either principal or agent. The breaching party may have to pay damages.
- **death of the principal or broker** (because the agency contract is between the broker owner of the real estate company and the principal, the agency relationship is not affected by the death of the agent)
- **destruction of the property**
- **bankruptcy of either party**

Commissions

The best way to ensure that an agent will be paid for the work he or she performs is to make sure that he or she is always working under a contract, a listing agreement, or a buyer agency representation agreement.

Commissions are negotiable and are set through an agreement of the parties. The Sherman Anti-Trust Law prohibits price fixing among real estate offices.

Sometimes, there is a dispute over a commission if a buyer has worked with more than one agent. The commission will be paid to the broker who is found to be the **procuring cause** in producing a ready, willing, and able buyer. (Determining procuring cause can be a difficult task because it is not necessarily the agent who was the first to show the property or the agent who wrote the offer.)

A broker is normally considered to have earned the commission when it has procured a ready, willing, and able buyer if the sale is not completed due to the wrongful act or interference of the seller.

Broker versus Salesperson

Two kinds of agency relationships are common in real estate practice:

- **General agency**—Real estate brokers typically have agents who act as their agents in working with their principals.
- **Special** (or **"limited"**) **agency**—A principal to a transaction (the seller or buyer) secures the advice and assistance of a real estate broker and the broker's agents. Although the agent normally signs the agency contract with the buyer or seller, the contract is between the broker owner of the real estate company and the principal.

Only the broker owner can sue a principal, not an agent. The agent's only recourse is through the broker owner.

A **REALTOR**® is a member of the National Association of REALTORS®. These are the only real estate agents authorized to use the REALTOR® registered trademark. REALTORS® agree to abide by the Association's Code of Ethics.

Commission Splits

Commissions are split into many pieces when a property is sold. When a listing office submits a listing to MLS, it includes the amount of commission it will offer to a cooperating broker (the buyer's broker), which procures a buyer who successfully completes the transaction. The amount of the **commission split** is determined by the listing office's office policy.

The remaining commission is now split between the broker owner and the agent. The way a broker owner shares a commission with an agent varies among different offices. Some offices take a percentage of the commission to cover operating expenses, advertising, and administrative help. Other offices charge agents a set monthly desk fee to cover overhead and the agent retains most of the commission.

Appraisal

Appraisal and Value

An **appraisal** is performed by a licensed, certified appraiser who gives an unbiased estimate of a property's **value** as of a certain time, based on supporting data. The **Uniform Standards of Professional Appraisal Practice** (**USPAP**) sets the minimum requirement for appraisals.

Market value is the most probable price that an informed buyer will be likely to pay and that an informed seller will be likely to accept in an arm's-length transaction, where neither party is acting under duress.

Establish Appraisal Purpose

Although real estate agents focus their attention on when a property owner wishes to sell, there are many other times when an owner wants to know the value of his or her property:

- **condemnation**—when the government takes private property by eminent domain, the owner must be paid fair market value for the property
- **assessed value**—determination for property tax purposes (the basis for taxation)
- **insurance purposes**—the maximum amount that an insurer would be willing to pay for an insured loss
- **estate settlement**—the value of the sum of a person's estate (real property and person property) when he or she dies
- **sales value for owner**—the price the property should bring in the open market
- **loan value**—the maximum loan that can be secured by the property
- **exchanges**—a transaction in which a property is traded for another property, rather than sold for money or other consideration

Elements of Value

An appraisal will specify the type of value sought. The elements that establish value can be remembered by the acronym **DUST**:

Demand for the type of property
Utility (desirable use) the property offers
Scarcity of properties available
Transferability of property to a new owner (lack of impediments to a sale)

Forces Affecting Value

- **social**—demographic and other trends that affect the demand for property
- **economic adjustments**—employment level, business start-ups, availability of credit, and other factors that influence the level of prosperity of a region
- **political/government regulations**—regulations that affect property use like zoning regulations, building codes, and environmental laws
- **physical**—changes caused by the elements, which can occur gradually or over a brief period of time

Economic Principles

Many principles of value underlie the appraisal process, including the following:

- **Supply and demand:** as the number of properties available for sale goes up relative to the number of potential buyers, prices will fall. As the number of properties declines while the number of potential buyers remains the same or increases, prices will rise.
- **Change:** forces to which all property is subject, which can either increase or decrease property values (these forces can be physical, political, economic, or social).

- **Substitution:** the principle that the typical buyer will want to pay no more for a property than would be required to buy another, equivalent property.
- **Highest and best use:** the legally allowed property use that makes maximum physical use of a site and generates the highest income.
- **Conformity:** individual properties in a neighborhood tend to have a higher value when they are of similar architecture, design, age, and size.
- **Progression:** the benefit to a property of being located in an area of more desirable properties; a small, plain house on a street of mansions will benefit from proximity to them.
- **Regression:** the detriment to a property of being located in a neighborhood of less desirable properties; a large, over-improved house on a street of small, plain houses will have a lower value than it would in a neighborhood of comparable houses.
- **Anticipation (of future betterments):** value is the present worth of the expected future benefits to be derived from owning the property, operating it (if the property has a commercial aspect), and potential gains when it is sold.
- **Assemblage:** bringing a group of adjoining parcels under the same ownership, which may make them more valuable for a particular purpose, such as construction of a residential or commercial development. If this common ownership does result in a greater value, the increase in value is called **plottage** or **plottage value**.
- **Law of decreasing returns:** in effect when property improvements no longer bring a corresponding increase in property value.
- **Law of increasing returns:** in effect as long as property improvements bring a corresponding increase in property value.
- **Contribution:** the value of any component is measured by what it adds to the property as a whole. If an improvement is excessively expensive or excessively large for the surrounding area and land, it is called an **over-improvement**.
- **Competition:** a potential for profit attracts competition to the market. When competition brings more sellers to the market, there is the potential for an oversupply of properties resulting in lower prices. When competition brings more buyers to the market, there is the potential for a shortage of properties resulting in higher prices.

The Appraisal Process

Following are the steps in the appraisal process:

1. State the problem—the nature of the appraisal assignment must be clearly understood. The assignment may be to find a market value of the subject property. If so, that should be stated.
2. Determine the kinds and sources of data necessary.
   - What are the characteristics of the subject property?
   - What economic or other factors will play a role in determining property value?
   - What approach(es) will be most appropriate in this appraisal, and what kind of data will be necessary?

3. Determine the highest and best use of the site.

4. Estimate the value of the site.

5. Estimate the property's value by each of the appropriate approaches (market data, cost, and/or income).

6. Reconcile the different values reached by the different approaches to estimate the property's most probable market value. This process is called **reconciliation** or **correlation**.

7. Report the estimate of value to the client in writing. There are several types of documents that may be prepared.

   ■ The **narrative appraisal report** provides a lengthy discussion of the factors considered in the appraisal and the reasons for the conclusion of value.

   ■ The **form report** is used most often for single-family residential appraisals. A **Uniform Residential Appraisal Report (URAR)** is required by various agencies and organizations.

Market Data Approach (Sales Comparison Approach)

If the property being appraised is a residential property, the most important determinant of value is the price that other similar properties have commanded in the open market. In using the market data approach, the appraiser will select **comparable properties** (**comps**) to compare to the property being appraised (subject property). An appraiser would prefer to have at least three comps for a market data appraisal and typically will use sales only within the last six months. The sales price of a comparable is adjusted down to compensate for the market value of a desirable feature that is present in the comp but not the subject property. The sales price of a comp is adjusted up to allow for desirable features that are present in the subject property and not the comp.

Example: The house at 29 Milo Avenue is being appraised. Comparable A sold last month for $350,000. The comp has a detached garage and the subject property does not. The estimated value of the garage is $9,600, which is subtracted from the sales price of $350,000 to derive an adjusted sales price for the comp of $340,400. After analyzing the sales prices of three comps this way and comparing the resulting adjusted figures, the appraiser estimates the value of the subject property at $340,000.

Land, whether or not it has any improvements (buildings), is often valued separately by using the market data approach.

Income Approach

If a property produces income in the form of rent and other **revenues**, its value is estimated by analyzing the amount and stability of the income it can produce. The income approach is used to value income producing properties.

Here is the formula for determining value by the income approach:

$$\text{value} = \text{net operating income} \div \text{capitalization rate}$$

Effective gross income is found by totaling income from all sources and subtracting an allowance for vacancy and collection losses.

Net operating income is found by subtracting **maintenance and operating expenses** from effective gross income. For appraisal purposes, operating expenses include variable expenses (such as salaries and utilities), fixed expenses (such as real estate taxes and insurance), and reserves for replacement (such as set-asides for a new roof and furnace), but not the costs of financing, income tax payments, depreciation deductions, and capital improvements.

The **capitalization rate** (**cap rate**) is a ratio used to estimate the value of a property that produces income. The cap rate is determined by dividing the annual net income by the current value of the property. However, its use is primarily by experienced appraisers or other real estate professionals or investors who, from experience, know roughly how much income a property of a certain value should produce. Therefore, they can quickly estimate the current value of the property by knowing how much income it produces. It is only a rough, quick estimate, and is never a substitute for a complete income approach to value appraisal. This estimate of current market value is determined by dividing net income by the capitalization rate from past experience.

Example: Mary wants to purchase an apartment building that is listed at the sales price of $960,000 and that has net operating income of $120,000 annually. Joe, her appraiser, tells Mary that, from his experience, this type of building in this area has a capitalization rate of about 12%. Therefore, Mary's quick estimate of value, before she receives Joe's complete appraisal, is $1,000,000 ($120,000 divided by 12% (0.12)). Mary may use this estimate in making a decision about proposing an offer to buy without waiting for a more accurate estimate.

A **gross rent multiplier** (GRM), based on monthly market rent, is typically used in the appraisal of a rental house. To determine the gross rent multiplier, an appraiser will determine the gross monthly rent of recently sold properties and then divide each property's sales price by the gross monthly rent.

Example: Building A produces monthly rent of $4,000 and sold recently for $400,000. Building B produces monthly rent of $3,200 and sold recently for $350,000. The GRM for Building A is $400,000 divided by $4,000, or 100. The GRM for Building B is $350,000 divided by $3,200, or 109.375. After analyzing several more properties, the appraiser concludes that a GRM of 100 is appropriate for the subject property. Applying that multiple to the subject property's monthly rent of $3,700, the appraiser reaches an estimate of value by this method of $370,000.

Cost Approach

When the property is not an income-producing property and it is difficult to find comparables, the cost approach to value is often used. This approach is most often used with unique properties and public service buildings (churches, a college campus, or a state capitol building).

The appraiser begins by estimating the replacement cost of the improvements. **Replacement cost** is the cost, at today's prices and using today's methods of construction, for an improvement having the same or equivalent usefulness as the subject property. Or, the appraiser may estimate the **reproduction cost**, the cost of creating an exact replica of the improvements. This would show the value of a new building. Because the subject property is not new, adjustments must be made for depreciation. There are three types of depreciation:

1. **Physical deterioration**—the effect of the elements and ordinary wear and tear. Generally curable.
2. **Functional obsolescence**—features that are no longer considered desirable in design, manner of construction, or layout. A house with four bedrooms and only one bathroom suffers from functional obsolescence. Can be curable or incurable.
3. **Economic obsolescence**—results from factors outside of the property over which the owner has no control, such as economic, locational, or environmental influences. Generally incurable.

The **value of the land** must be considered in determining value by the cost approach. The value of the land is established as though it were vacant, using the market data approach. While land value can decrease, land does not depreciate.

Here is the formula for determining value using the cost approach:

value = replacement or reproduction cost − accrued depreciation + land value

Example: An appraiser has determined that the reproduction cost of a building is $500,000. There is $60,000 of accrued depreciation and the land is valued at $200,000. The market value would be determined by taking $500,000 (the replacement cost) and subtracting $60,000 (the accrued depreciation) and then adding $200,000 (the land value). The appraiser would estimate the value to be $640,000.

Fair Housing/Consumer Protection

Basic Concepts

Federal and state fair housing laws were enacted to allow all people an equal opportunity to enjoy the benefits of owning real property.

A **protected class** is any group of people designated as such by the Department of Housing and Urban Development (HUD) in consideration of federal and state civil rights legislation. Protected classes currently include color, race, religion or creed, ancestry or national origin, gender, handicap, and familial status. It is prohibited to discriminate against someone in a protected class, perceived to be in a protected class, or because of his or her association with a protected class.

A **complainant** alleging a violation of fair housing laws may file a complaint with HUD or the office of the U.S. Attorney General. After receiving a complaint, **testers** may be sent out to confirm the validity of the complaint. When testers are used, one set of testers is matched to the same protected class as the complainant. Care is taken to ensure that the test is legitimate and not entrapment. The **respondent** in the complaint can be a property owner, real estate agent or agency, or management company.

Federal Civil Rights Act of 1866

The **Civil Rights Act of 1866** prohibits discrimination on the basis of race in the sale, lease, or other transfer of real or personal property. This act has no exceptions. It applies to individual home sellers as well as to real estate agencies.

Federal Fair Housing Act of 1968 (Title VIII)

The **Federal Fair Housing Act (Title VIII of the Civil Rights Act of 1968)** and its amendments broadened the prohibitions against discrimination in housing to include sex, race, color, religion, national origin, handicap (mental and physical), and familial status in connection with the sale or rental of housing or vacant land offered for residential construction or use. The law specifically prohibits the following discriminatory acts:

- refusing to sell to, rent to, or negotiate with any person who is a member of a protected class, or otherwise making a dwelling unavailable to such a person
- changing terms, conditions, or services for different individuals as a means of discrimination against a member of a protected class
- practicing discrimination through any statement or advertisement that restricts the sale or rental of residential property
- representing to any person, as a means of discrimination, that a dwelling is unavailable for sale or rental
- **blockbusting**—making a profit by inducing owners of housing to sell or rent by representing that persons of a protected class are moving into the neighborhood
- **redlining**—altering the terms or conditions of a home loan to any person, or otherwise denying such a loan as a means of discrimination
- denying persons membership or limiting their participation in any multiple-listing service, real estate broker's organization, or other facility related to the sale or rental of dwellings
- **steering**—the practice of directing home seekers to or away from particular neighborhoods based on protected class. Steering includes both efforts to exclude minorities from one area of a city and efforts to direct minorities to minority or changing areas.
- attributing an impact on value due to any of the prohibited practices previously listed in an appraisal report
- making notations indicating discriminatory preferences
- coercing, intimidating, or interfering with any person in the exercise of his or her rights

Familial status includes prohibiting discriminations against children (those under 18), families with children (whether headed by a parent or guardian), persons who are in the process of obtaining custody of a child, and pregnant women.

The Fair Housing Amendment prohibits the following discriminations against a handicapped person:

- refusal to make reasonable accommodations in policies
- refusal to permit reasonable modifications of existing premises at the handicapped person's expense

After 1991, all new (or rehab) four-family homes or larger must be designed so the first floor units include handicapped accessibility. If upper floors are serviced by elevators, these units must have accessibility, too.

The 1968 Fair Housing Act covers only residential property. Any type of residential property is covered under the act if the sale is handled by a real estate agent (depending on the type of property, liability may be only for the broker), or if discriminatory advertising is used or any written notice or statement that indicates a discriminatory preference.

A single-family house is also covered under fair housing laws if one of the following is true:

- It is not privately owned (corporate).
- It is owned by a private individual who owns more than three houses (a dealer) or who, in any two-year period, sells more than one property.

A multifamily dwelling is covered if one of the following is true:

- It consists of five units or more.
- It consists of two to four units, and the owner does not reside in one of the units.

Title VIII does not cover:

- The sale or rental of a single-family home by a private individual who owns three or fewer properties as long as he or she sells without a broker, with no discriminatory advertising and have not sold another house in two years.
- The rental of rooms or units in owner-occupied multifamily dwellings of two to four units, as long as discriminatory advertising and the services of a real estate agent are not used.
- The sale, rental, or occupancy of dwellings owned or operated by a religious organization for a noncommercial purpose to persons of the same religion, as long as membership in that religion is not restricted on account of race, color, or national origin.
- The rental or occupancy of lodgings operated by a private club for its members for other than commercial purposes.
- Housing for the elderly that meets certain HUD guidelines.

A person who believes he or she has been discriminated against can file a written complaint with HUD and/or file a civil action directly in a U.S. District Court or state or local court. An **administrative law judge** may hear the case and can award damages.

The burden of proof is on the person filing the complaint. A person found guilty of a fair housing violation may face:

- civil penalties of up to $10,000 for the first offense, up to $25,000 for the second offense within a five-year period, and up to $50,000 for the third offense within a seven-year period
- monetary fines for actual and/or punitive damages caused by the discrimination
- an injunction to stop the sale or rental of the property to someone else, making it available to the complainant
- court costs

- criminal penalties against those who coerce, intimidate, threaten, or interfere with a person's buying, renting, or selling of housing
- state penalties, including the loss of the real estate license

Lead Paint Law

Homes built prior to 1979 may contain lead paint (it was banned for use in residential property in 1978). Both Connecticut law and the federal Residential Property Hazard Reduction Act of 1972 ("Title X") require that:

- Prospective homeowners and tenants be provided with a HUD/EPA pamphlet entitled *Protect Your Family from Lead in Your Home.*
- Prospective homeowners and tenants be provided with written disclosure of any known lead hazards and records regarding the property.
- A lead warning statement be included in a sales agreement and be provided to be signed as a separate document in all other cases.
- Federally assisted or owned property has additional abatement requirements.
- The owner and his or her licensee must disclose the age of the home and any known lead hazards to prospective buyers. Buyers have a ten-day period to inspect the property for lead.
- Housing with children under six years of age are at special risk and subject to special regulations.

Connecticut Real Estate Agency License Law

The Connecticut Real Estate Commission has created three publications to summarize Connecticut law governing the licensure and conduct of real estate brokers and salespersons:

1. *Connecticut Real Estate Commission Policy on Agency*
2. *Connecticut Laws and Regulations Concerning the Conduct of Real Estate Brokers and Salespersons*
3. *Guidelines and Interpretations of Connecticut Real Estate Licensing Law*

These publications may be viewed on the website for the Real Estate Commission at www.ct.gov/dcp/cwp/view.asp?a=1624&Q=276028&dcpNav_GID=1543&dcpNav=.

Duties and Powers of the Real Estate Commission

There are eight members of the Connecticut Real Estate Commission (the "Commission"), all appointed as volunteers by the governor. Three of the members are to be licensed real estate brokers, two are to be licensed real estate salespersons, and three are to be members of the general public. The governor also appoints one of the members to be the chairperson. The Commission holds at least four meetings a year.

The Commission has the power to:

- promulgate (announce) and administer Connecticut license law
- conduct examinations
- examine records

- hold hearings and appeals to enforce the license law
- suspend, revoke, refuse to renew, and reinstate licenses

There are many ways for agents to lose their licenses either temporarily or permanently. According to Connecticut license law, the Commission may suspend, revoke, or refuse to renew a license on the following grounds:

- violating any of the laws governing Connecticut real estate salespersons, brokers, or real estate agencies
- making any material misrepresentation
- making a false promise likely to influence, persuade, or induce
- acting as a representative of more than one person in a transaction without the knowledge and consent of all concerned
- representing or attempting to represent more than one broker at the same time without the permission of both brokers
- failure to account for or remit client funds within a reasonable time
- being a party to a listing agreement with automatic renewal periods that does not have a specific ultimate ending date
- paying a commission to an unlicensed person
- failure to give copies of important documents to the proper parties
- conviction of certain crimes
- collecting advance compensation but not accounting for the same to the client
- any act of dishonesty, fraud, or improper dealing
- commingling a client's funds with the licensee's funds
- failing to disclose any information required by law for the licensee to disclose
- falsifying license application or renewal application

When the Commission holds a hearing regarding a person's license, the Commission may summon witnesses and records. The licensee must receive reasonable written notice of the hearing (including a statement of the grounds and a copy of the complaint or charges). The licensee has the right to appear personally and by counsel and to cross-examine witnesses and to produce evidence. A licensee may file an appeal to the decision of the Commission with the Connecticut Superior Court within 45 days after the decision is issued.

Licensing Requirements

The following activities, when performed for another person and for a fee, regarding real estate or real property interests, require a real estate license in the state of Connecticut:

- sales
- exchanges
- purchases
- rentals/leases
- negotiations

- offers
- listings
- options
- advertising as a real estate agency
- apartment searches
- offers or attempts to do any of the above

Types of Licenses

A **real estate broker** is any person who, for another person and for a fee, performs any of the previously mentioned activities.

A **real estate salesperson** also has the right to perform any of the previously mentioned activities, except he or she cannot complete negotiations. A salesperson cannot be self-employed and must act under and be supervised by a **sponsoring broker** who is responsible for the salesperson's actions.

When a business entity applies for a broker's license, at least one of its officers, members, or partners shall be the firm's **designated broker**. The designated broker also needs an individual broker's license in his or her own name. (Note: It is easy to confuse the terms *designated broker* used here and *designated agent*, which is an alternative to conventional, straight dual agency.) At least 51% of the entity must be owned and controlled by licensed Connecticut real estate brokers.

A Connecticut salesperson has no valid license at all unless a licensed broker agrees to act as the **sponsoring broker** for the salesperson. Without a sponsoring broker, a salesperson cannot be engaged in the real estate sales business and cannot renew his or her license. A Connecticut real estate broker is licensed to act independently on his or her own without another sponsoring broker.

A **nonresident** can hold a Connecticut real estate license; however, the nonresident must file an irrevocable consent appointing the chairman of the Commission to accept service of process of any legal proceedings against the nonresident concerning the nonresident's real estate professional conduct.

Eligibility for Licensing

In order to receive a **salesperson's** license, a person must:

- be at least 18 years old
- complete 60 hours of classroom instruction
- be of good moral character
- pass the exam
- have a licensed sponsoring broker

To receive a **broker's** license, a person must:

- be licensed as a salesperson and actively employed by a licensed real estate broker for at least two years
- complete 60 hours of additional classroom instruction
- pass the broker's exam

Real estate licenses are valid for one year. All broker licenses expire on April 30. All salesperson licenses expire on May 31. A person must take 12 hours of continuing education classes within the two-year period prior to renewing either a salesperson or broker license in every even-numbered year. If licensees do not complete their continuing education requirements, they may not renew their license.

There are some people who do not need a real estate license. These include:

- any individual acting for him- or herself
- a salaried employee or property manager employed by the property owner and living on the premises involved
- a trustee
- a public official or public employee performing official duties
- a person acting as an attorney-in-fact under a power of attorney
- an attorney performing legal duties for a client
- a court appointee

Requirements Governing Activities of Licensees

The following are the statutory requirements regarding **advertising**:

- A broker shall not advertise in any way that is false or misleading. All advertised information must be accurate.
- **Blind advertising**—Brokers may not advertise real property to purchase, sell, rent, mortgage, or exchange through classified advertisement or otherwise unless they affirmatively disclose that they are a real estate broker. All advertisements shall include the name, address, and telephone number of the real estate broker.
- **Salespersons are prohibited from advertising** the purchase, sale, rental, or exchange of any real property under their own names.
- No broker shall advertise to purchase, sell, rent, mortgage, or exchange any real property in any manner that indicates directly or indirectly unlawful **discrimination** against any individual or group.

A real estate salesperson can be hired by a real estate broker as an **employee** or as an **independent contractor**. A salesperson cannot be self-employed. He or she must be affiliated with a broker (and only one broker at a time). A salesperson cannot accept a payment, fee, or commission from a client or anyone else except a licensed Connecticut real estate broker or salesperson. The broker is responsible for the actions of his or her agents, whether they are employees or independent contractors. Because a salesperson works for a broker, he or she cannot sue a principal him- or herself. Only the employing broker can sue a principal. A salesperson can sue a broker.

A **commission** is a fee for brokerage services that is negotiated between the principal and broker.

Licensees must disclose any involvement of themselves, their business associates, or their family members in any property in which the licensees act as agents. This involvement must be disclosed in writing to all other parties, and the other parties need to acknowledge the disclosure in writing. In most states, licensees must disclose this involvement in all advertisements, agreements, and signage.

All offers submitted to an agent must be conveyed as soon as possible to the owner of the property. Agents also have a responsibility to give copies of the real estate contract to all of the parties in the transaction.

One of the fiduciary responsibilities agents owe their clients is accountability of all funds. This means that all deposits (for both purchases and rentals) need to be placed immediately into the broker's escrow account. The broker is accountable for all money held in the escrow account and must return the deposit at either the closing on the property or the termination of the sale. The broker needs to keep records of all funds deposited in his or her escrow account, including all information pertinent to the transaction.

Salespersons must promptly turn deposits over to their broker. Connecticut law requires all deposits to be placed in the broker's trust account within three banking business days after the last required signature is placed upon the contract or other document under which the deposit is paid. Interest earned on these funds is paid to the Connecticut Housing Finance Authority to assist low-income mortgage loan applicants. The broker must pay interest on these funds to the client if so requested by the client.

A **net listing** offers the property owner a guaranteed sales price, with the listing broker taking any part of the purchase price over that amount. Net listings are illegal in Connecticut.

The broker-owner must maintain a usual place of business and notify the Commission of any change of location. The broker also needs to notify the Commission of the relationship of all licensees affiliated with the company, and notify the Commission when a new agent joins the office or an agent leaves the office. Each broker and salesperson must display a copy of his or her license in a conspicuous location that can be seen by the general public.

Agents are prohibited from advising against the use of an attorney in any real property transaction.

Customers versus Clients

Connecticut real estate brokers or salespersons can have only a limited relationship with someone with whom he or she communicates that is not yet his or her client (i.e., a **customer**). The licensee owes the customer the duty of fair, honest, nondiscriminatory dealings. The licensee can discuss properties, the real estate market, the licensee's qualifications and experience, and the licensee's broker firm and business practices. The licensee cannot show the customer properties listed by the licensee's broker firm (in-house properties) unless the licensee either (1) completes and delivers for signature to the customer the "Notice to Unrepresented Parties" form, or (2) enters into a buyer agency agreement with the customer (in which case a matter of dual agency may result). This clarifies who (if anyone) represents the customer and that the licensee represents the seller of the listed property.

Until a customer becomes a client, a licensee cannot negotiate or advocate on behalf of the customer nor obtain any confidential information from the customer.

If the customer does become a client and is interested in a property listed by the licensee's broker firm, both the listing seller and this new client must give **written, informed consent to dual agency**. Connecticut has two approaches to this dual agency:

1. **Conventional (straight) dual agency**—All parties sign a dual agency agreement. The firm's broker and all salespersons in the firm are dual agents representing both sides of the transaction equally. The licensees act primarily as conduits to pass information and offers between the buyer and seller, but can provide little other assistance. The salesperson representing both the buyer and the seller are all dual agents.

2. **Designated agency**—All parties sign a designated agency agreement in which the broker appoints both a **designated seller's agent** and a **designated buyer's agent**. The broker remains a dual agent, but the designated agents no longer have any dual agency obligations or duties. They represent their respective clients independently.

If the customer becomes a client by signing a listing or buyer agency agreement, the licensee can show the new client the available property of any other real estate broker. If the customer does not become a client and does not sign a listing or buyer agency agreement with the licensee, the licensee cannot show this customer the property listed by any other broker firm except the licensee's firm. At least technically, this licensee can become the temporary subagent of the other firm's broker and seller, but the use of buyer agency agreements has made this form of representation obsolete in Connecticut.

Disclosures

A Connecticut licensee must disclose all **material facts** known to the licensee about a property to prospective buyers and sellers. These include all substantial facts that would make a meaningful difference in the transaction to the parties. The licensee must also disclose certain facts that cause a property to be **psychologically impacted** (felonies and unexplained deaths) if the client so requests. However, the licensee may NOT disclose nor inquire about the status of any person connected with the property regarding AIDS or HIV status.

A seller of one- to four-family Connecticut residential property must complete and submit to a prospective buyer a **Residential Property Condition Disclosure Report** form. This must be presented before an offer is received. Failure to provide this form subjects the seller to a $300 penalty at closing. Whether the seller provides an accurate and complete disclosure form or not, the listing licensee has an independent obligation to disclose material facts.

Real Estate Guaranty Fund

The Commission maintains a **Real Estate Guaranty Fund** (the Fund) to assist in compensation to victims of improper professional conduct by Connecticut real estate salespersons and brokers. The Fund receives money from the following sources:

1. One-time fee of $20 paid the first time any person receives a license from the Real Estate Commission
2. $3 from each license renewal fee is collected by the Commission and paid to the fund
3. Fines and penalties
4. Interest and repayments from the involved licensee (who loses his or her license) until the Fund is repaid

The Fund may collect and hold up to $500,000. Any excess monies are paid to the Connecticut State Treasures of the Connecticut General Fund. If the Fund ever runs out of money, it issues an IOU to the aggrieved party until it can pay.

A person who sues a licensee in court for professional misconduct and wins a judgment may apply to the Fund for up to $25,000 in compensation (if the judgment is not paid). If such funds are paid, the licensee loses his or her license until the funds are repaid.

Miscellaneous

A licensee can neither accept from nor pay to anyone a referral fee for new business except a licensed Connecticut real estate broker or salesperson.

Promotional Sales of Out-of-State Real Property

No broker shall offer for sale in Connecticut an interest in real property that is located in a land development of another state unless the owner or developer of such land development **registers property with the Commission**. It must be registered on the form and the fee paid as prescribed by the Commission. Such registration shall be renewed annually.

The Commission may **inspect** any out-of-state real property developments seeking registration or registered with it. The owner or developer must pay for the costs of any inspection. Following an inspection, the Commission shall issue a written report. This report must be kept on file both with the Commission and in the owner or developer's files while the development is registered with the Commission and for one year following the termination or expiration of the registration.

Once the Commission registers an out-of-state real property development, the owner or developer must note the fact of the registration in all its advertisements in the state.

No interest in any real property located in an out-of-state real property development shall be subject to any promotional advertisement, offering for sale, or sold in Connecticut unless it is offered for sale and sold by a licensed Connecticut broker. Promotional advertising as used herein means any advertising material offered through any means of communication in Connecticut.

Properties that are registered and qualified under the federal Interstate Land Sales Full Disclosure Act are exempt from most Connecticut registration requirements.

Apartment Rentals

Brokers and salespersons engaged in renting real property, whether by written agreement or not, shall provide each prospective tenant with a written notice that states whether the prospective tenant will pay any fee for such service, the amount of such fee, the manner and time in which it is to be paid, and whether or not any fee or any portion thereof will be payable by the tenant if a tenancy is not created. This written notice must be given by the real estate broker or salesperson at the first personal meeting between the broker or salesperson and a prospective tenant. It must be signed by the real estate broker or salesperson, contain the license number of such broker or salesperson, be signed by the prospective tenant, and contain the date such notice was given by the broker or salesperson to the prospective tenant. Where a prospective tenant declines to sign such written notice, the real estate broker or salesperson must note on such written notice the tenant's name and the refusal to sign such notice.

Any advertisement concerning the availability of an apartment shall disclose in print no smaller than that for the apartment itself that "the apartment advertised may no longer be available for rental."

No real estate broker shall charge any fee to a prospective tenant unless a tenancy is created or in those cases where no tenancy in real property is created unless the prospective tenant has agreed in writing to pay such a fee.

5 ▶ Real Estate Math Review

CHAPTER SUMMARY

Real estate mathematics accounts for almost 10% of the Connecticut Real Estate Sales Exam, so you should take this topic seriously. But even if math is not your favorite subject, this chapter will help you do your best. It not only covers arithmetic, algebra, geometry, and word problems, but also has practice problems for each of the real estate math topics.

ERE ARE THE types of math questions you will encounter on the exam:

- Percents
- Areas
- Property Tax
- Loan-to-Value Ratios
- Points
- Equity
- Qualifying Buyers
- Prorations
- Commissions

- Sale Proceeds
- Transfer Tax/Conveyance Tax/Revenue Stamps
- Competitive Market Analyses (CMA)
- Income Properties
- Depreciation

Keep in mind that although the math topics are varied, you will be using the same math skills to complete each question. But before you review your math skills, take a look at some helpful strategies for doing your best.

▶ Strategies for Math Questions

Answer Every Question

You should answer every single question, even if you don't know the answer. There is no penalty for a wrong answer, and you have a 25% chance of guessing correctly. If one or two answers are obviously wrong, the odds of selecting the correct one may be even higher.

Bring a Calculator

You are allowed to bring a calculator to your exam. **You must check with your exam center to find out exactly what type of calculator is permitted.** In general, permissible calculators are battery operated, do not print, are not programmable, and do not have a keypad with letters. As a precaution, you should bring an extra battery with you to your exam. Try not to rely entirely on the calculator. Although using one can prevent simple adding and subtracting errors, it may take longer for you to use the calculator than to figure it out yourself.

Use Scratch Paper

Resist the temptation to "save time" by doing all your work on your calculator. The main pitfall with calculators is the temptation to work the problem all the way through to the end on the calculator. At this point, if none of the answers provided is correct, there is no way to know where the mistake lies. Use scratch paper to avoid this problem.

Check Your Work

Checking your work is always good practice, and it's usually quite simple. Even if you come up with an answer that is one of the answer choices, you should check your work. Test writers often include answer choices that are the results of common errors, which you may have made.

▶ Real Estate Math Review

Here's a quick review of some basic arithmetic, algebra, geometry, and word problem skills you will need for your exam.

Arithmetic Review

Symbols of Multiplication

When two or more numbers are being multiplied, they are called **factors**. The answer that results is called the **product**.

> *Example:*
> $5 \times 6 = 30$ 5 and 6 are **factors** and 30 is the **product**.

There are several ways to represent multiplication in the above mathematical statement.

- A dot between factors indicates multiplication:

$5 \cdot 6 = 30$

- Parentheses around one or more factors indicates multiplication:

$(5)6 = 30, 5(6) = 30$, and $(5)(6) = 30$

- Multiplication is also indicated when a number is placed next to a variable:

$5a = 30$ In this equation, 5 is being multiplied by a.

Divisibility

Like multiplication, division can be represented in a few different ways:

$8 \div 3$ $3\overline{)8}$ $\frac{8}{3}$

In each of the above, 3 is the **divisor** and 8 is the **dividend**.

If the number after the one you need to round to is 5 or more, make the preceding number one higher. If it is less than 5, drop it and leave the preceding number the same. (Information about rounding is usually provided in the exam instructions or in the exam bulletin.)

Example:

0.0135 = .014 or .01

Decimals

The most important thing to remember about decimals is that the first place value to the right begins with tenths. The place values are as follows:

1	2	6	8	•	3	4	5	7
THOUSANDS	HUNDREDS	TENS	ONES	DECIMAL POINT	TENTHS	HUNDREDTHS	THOUSANDTHS	TEN THOUSANDTHS

In expanded form, this number can also be expressed as:

$$1{,}268.3457 = (1 \times 1{,}000) + (2 \times 100) + (6 \times 10) + (8 \times 1) + (3 \times .1) + (4 \times .01) + (5 \times .001) + (7 \times .0001)$$

Fractions

To do well when working with fractions, it is necessary to understand some basic concepts. Here are some math rules for fractions using variables:

$$\frac{a}{b} \times \frac{c}{d} = \frac{a \times c}{b \times d}$$

$$\frac{a}{b} + \frac{c}{b} = \frac{a + c}{b}$$

$$\frac{a}{b} \div \frac{c}{d} = \frac{a}{b} \times \frac{d}{c} = \frac{a \times d}{b \times c}$$

$$\frac{a}{b} + \frac{c}{d} = \frac{ad + bc}{bd}$$

Multiplication of Fractions

Multiplying fractions is one of the easiest operations to perform. To multiply fractions, simply multiply the numerators and the denominators, writing each in the respective place over or under the fraction bar.

Example:

$\frac{4}{5} \times \frac{6}{7} = \frac{24}{35}$

Division of Fractions

Dividing fractions is the same thing as multiplying fractions by their **reciprocals**. To find the reciprocal of any number, flip its numerator and denominator. For example, the reciprocals of the following numbers are:

$\frac{1}{3} \rightarrow \frac{3}{1} = 3$

$x \rightarrow \frac{1}{x}$

$\frac{4}{5} \rightarrow \frac{5}{4}$

$5 \rightarrow \frac{1}{5}$

When dividing fractions, simply multiply the dividend (the number being divided) by the divisor's (the number doing the dividing) reciprocal to get the answer.

Example:

$\frac{12}{21} \div \frac{3}{4} = \frac{12}{21} \times \frac{4}{3} = \frac{48}{63} = \frac{16}{21}$

Adding and Subtracting Fractions

To add or subtract fractions with like denominators, just add or subtract the numerators and leave the denominator as it is. For example,

$\frac{1}{7} + \frac{5}{7} = \frac{6}{7}$ and $\frac{5}{8} - \frac{2}{8} = \frac{3}{8}$

To add or subtract fractions with unlike denominators, you must find the **least common denominator**, or LCD.

For example, if given the denominators 8 and 12, 24 would be the LCD because $8 \times 3 = 24$, and $12 \times 2 = 24$. In other words, the LCD is the smallest number divisible by each of the denominators.

Once you know the LCD, convert each fraction to its new form by multiplying both the numerator and denominator by the necessary number to get the LCD, and then add or subtract the new numerators.

Example:

$\frac{1}{3} + \frac{2}{5} = \frac{5(1)}{5(3)} + \frac{3(2)}{3(5)} = \frac{5}{15} + \frac{6}{15} = \frac{11}{15}$

Percent

A **percent** is a measure of a part to a whole, with the whole being equal to 100.

- To change a decimal to a percentage, move the decimal point two units to the right and add a percentage symbol.

  Example:
  .45 = 45%   .07 = 7%   .9 = 90%

- To change a fraction to a percentage, first change the fraction to a decimal. To do this, divide the numerator by the denominator. Then change the decimal to a percentage.

  Example:
  $\frac{4}{5} = .80 = 80\%$

  $\frac{2}{5} = .4 = 40\%$

  $\frac{1}{8} = .125 = 12.5\%$

- To change a decimal to a percentage, move the decimal point two units to the right and add a percentage symbol.
- To change a percentage to a decimal, simply move the decimal point two places to the left and eliminate the percentage symbol.

  Example:
  64% = .64   87% = .87   7% = .07

- To change a percentage to a fraction, divide by 100 and reduce.

  Example:
  $64\% = \frac{64}{100} = \frac{16}{25}$

  $75\% = \frac{75}{100} = \frac{3}{4}$

  $82\% = \frac{82}{100} = \frac{41}{50}$

- Keep in mind that any percentage that is 100 or greater will need to reflect a whole number or mixed number when converted.

  Example:
  $125\% = 1.25$ or $1\frac{1}{4}$
  $350\% = 3.5$ or $3\frac{1}{2}$

Here are some conversions you should be familiar with:

Fraction	Decimal	Percentage
$\frac{1}{2}$	.5	50%
$\frac{1}{4}$	.25	25%
$\frac{1}{3}$	.333 . . .	$33.\overline{3}$%
$\frac{2}{3}$	.666 . . .	$66.\overline{6}$%
$\frac{1}{10}$	.1	10%
$\frac{1}{8}$	.125	12.5%
$\frac{1}{6}$	.1666 . . .	$16.\overline{6}$%
$\frac{1}{5}$	.2	20%

Algebra Review

Equations

An **equation** is solved by finding a number that is equal to an unknown variable.

Simple Rules for Working with Equations

1. The equal sign separates an equation into two sides.
2. Whenever an operation is performed on one side, the same operation must be performed on the other side.
3. Your first goal is to get all of the variables on one side and all of the numbers on the other.
4. The final step often will be to divide each side by the coefficient, leaving the variable equal to a number.

Checking Equations

To check an equation, substitute the number equal to the variable in the original equation.

Example:

To check the following equation, substitute the number 10 for the variable *x*.

$$\frac{x}{6} = \frac{x + 10}{12}$$

$$\frac{10}{6} = \frac{10 + 10}{12}$$

$$\frac{10}{6} = \frac{20}{12}$$

$$1\frac{2}{3} = 1\frac{2}{3}$$

$$\frac{10}{6} = \frac{10}{6}$$

Because this statement is true, you know the answer $x = 10$ must be correct.

Special Tips for Checking Equations

1. If time permits, be sure to check all equations.
2. Be careful to answer the question that is being asked. Sometimes, this involves solving for a variable and then performing an operation.

Example:

If the question asks the value of $x - 2$, and you find $x = 2$, the answer is not 2, but $2 - 2$. Thus, the answer is 0.

Algebraic Fractions

Algebraic fractions are very similar to fractions in arithmetic.

Example:

Write $\frac{x}{5} - \frac{x}{10}$ as a single fraction.

Solution:

Just like in arithmetic, you need to find the LCD of 5 and 10, which is 10. Then change each fraction into an equivalent fraction that has 10 as a denominator.

$$\frac{x}{5} - \frac{x}{10} = \frac{x(2)}{5(2)} - \frac{x}{10}$$

$$= \frac{2x}{10} - \frac{x}{10}$$

$$= \frac{x}{10}$$

Geometry Review

Area	the space inside a two-dimensional figure
Circumference	the distance around a circle
Perimeter	the distance around a figure
Radius	the distance from the center point of a circle to any point on the arc of a circle

Area

Area is the space inside of the lines defining the shape.

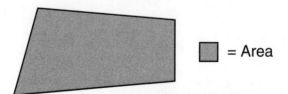

This geometry review will focus on the area formula for three main shapes: circles, rectangles/squares, and triangles.

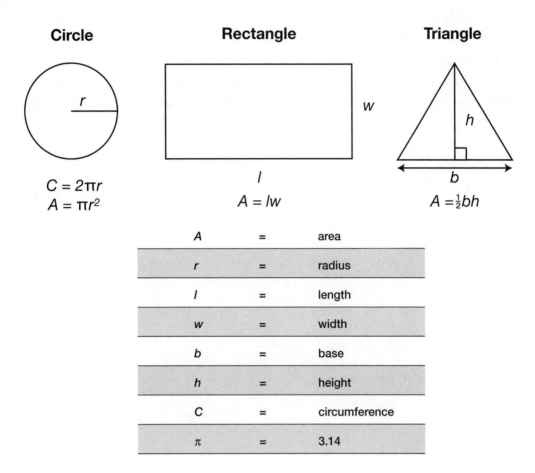

| Circle | Rectangle | Triangle |

$$C = 2\pi r$$
$$A = \pi r^2$$

$$A = lw$$

$$A = \tfrac{1}{2}bh$$

A	=	area
r	=	radius
l	=	length
w	=	width
b	=	base
h	=	height
C	=	circumference
π	=	3.14

Perimeter

The perimeter of an object is simply the sum of all of its sides.

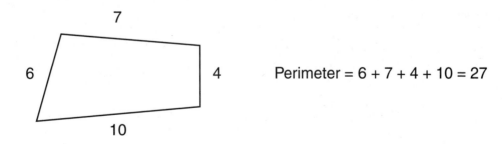

Perimeter = 6 + 7 + 4 + 10 = 27

The circumference is the perimeter of a circle.

$$C = 2\pi r$$

Word Problem Review

Because many of the math problems on the Connecticut Real Estate Sales Exam will be word problems, pay extra attention to the following review.

Translating Words into Numbers

The most important skill needed for word problems is being able to translate words into mathematical operations. The following will assist you by giving you some common examples of English phrases and their mathematical equivalents.

- "Increase" means add.

  Example:
  A number increased by five = $x + 5$.

- "Less than" means subtract.

  Example:
  10 less than a number = $x - 10$.

- "Times" or "product" means multiply.

  Example:
  Three times a number = $3x$.

- "Times the sum" means to multiply a number by a quantity.

  Example:
  Five times the sum of a number and three = $5(x + 3)$.

- Two variables are sometimes used together.

  Example:
  A number y exceeds five times a number x by ten.
  $y = 5x + 10$

- "Of" means multiply.

  Example:
  10% of 100 is 10 = $10\% \times 100 = 10$.

- "Is" means equals.

Example:
15 is 14 plus 1 becomes $15 = 14 + 1$.

Assigning Variables in Word Problems

It may be necessary to create and assign variables in a word problem. To do this, first identify an unknown and a known. You may not actually know the exact value of the "known," but you will know at least something about its value.

Examples:
Max is three years older than Ricky.
Unknown = Ricky's age = x.
Known = Max's age is three years older.
Therefore,
Ricky's age = x and Max's age = $x + 3$.

Heidi made twice as many cookies as Rebecca.
Unknown = number of cookies Rebecca made = x.
Known = number of cookies Heidi made = $2x$.

Jessica has five more than three times the number of books that Becky has.
Unknown = the number of books Becky has = x.
Known = the number of books Jessica has = $3x + 5$.

Percentage Problems

There is one formula that is useful for solving the three types of percentage problems:

$$\frac{\overset{\#}{\text{part}}}{\text{whole}} = \frac{\overset{\%}{}}{100}$$

When reading a percentage problem, substitute the necessary information into the above formula based on the following:

- 100 is always written in the denominator of the percentage sign column.
- If given a percentage, write it in the numerator position of the number column. If you are not given a percentage, then the variable should be placed there.
- The denominator of the number column represents the number that is equal to the whole, or 100%. This number always follows the word *of* in a word problem.

- The numerator of the number column represents the number that is the percent.
- In the formula, the equal sign can be interchanged with the word *is*.

Examples:

- Finding a percentage of a given number:

What number is equal to 40% of 50?

$$\overset{\#}{\underset{50}{x}} = \overset{\%}{\underset{100}{40}}$$

Cross multiply:

$100(x) = (40)(50)$

$100x = 2{,}000$

$\frac{100x}{100} = \frac{2{,}000}{100}$

$x = 20$ Therefore, 20 is 40% of 50.

- Finding a number when a percentage is given:

40% of what number is 24?

$$\overset{\#}{\underset{x}{24}} = \overset{\%}{\underset{100}{40}}$$

Cross multiply:

$(24)(100) = (40)(x)$

$2{,}400 = 40x$

$\frac{2{,}400}{40} = \frac{40x}{40}$

$60 = x$ Therefore, 40% of 60 is 24.

- Finding what percentage one number is of another:

What percentage of 75 is 15?

$$\overset{\#}{\underset{75}{15}} = \overset{\%}{\underset{100}{x}}$$

$$\text{Rate} = \frac{x \text{ units}}{y \text{ units}}$$

A percentage problem simply means that y units are equal to 100. It is important to remember that a percentage problem may be worded using the word *rate*.

Cross multiply:

$15(100) = (75)(x)$

$1{,}500 = 75x$

$\frac{1{,}500}{75} = \frac{75x}{75}$

$20 = x$ Therefore, 20% of 75 is 15.

Rate Problems

You may encounter a couple of different types of rate problems on the Connecticut Real Estate Sales Exam: cost per unit, interest rate, and tax rate. Rate is defined as a comparison of two quantities with different units of measure.

$$\textbf{Rate} = \frac{x \text{ units}}{y \text{ units}}$$

Examples: $\frac{\text{dollars}}{\text{square foot}}, \frac{\text{interest}}{\text{year}}$

Cost Per Unit

Some problems on your exam may require that you calculate the cost per unit.

Example:

If 100 square feet cost $1,000, how much does 1 square foot cost?

Solution:

$\frac{\text{Total Cost}}{\text{\# of square feet}} = \frac{1{,}000}{100} = \$10$ per square foot

Interest Rate

The formula for simple interest is Interest = Principal × Rate × Time, or $I = PRT$. If you know certain values, but not others, you can still find the answer using algebra. In simple interest problems, the value of T is usually 1, as in 1 year. There are three basic kinds of interest problems, depending on which number is missing.

Equivalencies

Here are some equivalencies you may need to use to complete some questions. Generally, any equivalencies you will need to know for your exam are provided to you.

Equivalencies

12 inches (in. or ") = 1 foot (ft. or ')

3 feet or 36 inches = 1 yard (yd.)

1,760 yards = 1 mile (mi)

5,280 feet = 1 mile

144 square inches (sq. in. or in.^{2}) = 1 square foot (sq. ft. or ft.^{2})

9 square feet = 1 square yard

43,560 feet = 1 acre

640 acres = 1 square mile

Percents

You may be asked a basic percentage problem.

Example:

What is 86% of 1,750?

Solution:

Start by translating words into math terms.

$x = (86\%)(1,750)$

Change the percent into a decimal by moving the decimal point two spaces to the left.

$86\% = .86$

Now you can solve.

$x = (.86)(1,750)$

$x = 1,505$

Other percentage problems you may find on the Connecticut Real Estate Sales Exam will come in the form of rate problems. Keep reading for more examples of these problems.

Interest Problems

Let's take a look at a problem in which you have to calculate the interest rate (R). Remember, the rate is the same as the percentage.

Example:

Mary Valencia borrowed $5,000, for which she is paying $600 interest per year. What is the rate of interest being charged?

Solution:

Start with the values you know.

Principal = $5,000

Interest = $600

Rate = x

Time = 1 year

Using the formula $I = PRT$, insert the values you know, and solve for x.

$600 = 5,000(x)(1)$

$600 = 5,000x$

$\frac{600}{5,000} = \frac{x}{5,000}$

$.12 = x$

To convert .12 to a percent, move the decimal point two places to the right.

$.12 = 12\%$

Area

Some of the problems on your exam may ask you to calculate the area of a piece of land, a building, or some other figure. Here are some formulas and how to use them.

Rectangles

Remember the formula: Area = (length)(width).

Example:

A man purchased a lot that is 50 feet by 10 feet for a garden. How many square feet of land does he have?

Solution:

Using the formula, Area = (length)(width), you have:

$A = (50)(10) = 500$ square feet

Example:

The Meyers bought a piece of land for a summer home that was 2.75 acres. The lake frontage was 150 feet. What was the length of the lot?

Solution:

When you take your sales exam, you may be provided with certain equivalencies. You will need to refer to the "Equivalencies" list on the previous page to answer this question. First, find the area of the land in square feet.

$(2.75)(43,560) = 119,790$ square feet

In the previous example, you were given the length and the width. In this example, you are given the area and the width, so you are solving for the length. Because you know the area and the width of the lot, use the formula to solve.

Area = (length)(width)

$119,790 = (x)(150)$

Divide both sides by 150.

$\frac{119,790}{150} = \frac{(x)(150)}{150}$

$x = \frac{119,790}{150}$

$x = 798.6$ feet

Triangles

Although it may not be as common, you may be asked to find the area of a triangle. If you don't remember the formula, see the section on Area.

Example:

The Baroms are buying a triangular piece of land for a gas station. It is 200 feet at the base, and the side perpendicular to the base is 200 feet. They are paying $2 per square foot for the property. What will it cost?

Solution:

Start with the formula Area $= \frac{1}{2}$(base)(height).

Now, write down the values you know.

Area $= x$

Base $= 200$

Height $= 200$

If it's easier, you can change $\frac{1}{2}$ to a decimal.

$\frac{1}{2} = .5$

Now you can plug these values into the formula.

$x = (.5)(200)(200)$

$x = (.5)(40,000)$

$x = 20,000$ square feet

Don't forget that the question is not asking for the number of square feet, but for the *cost* of the property per square foot. This is a rate problem, so you need to complete one more step:

(20,000 square feet)($2 per square foot) = $40,000

Example:

Victor and Evelyn Robinson have an outlot that a neighbor wants to buy. The side of the outlot next to their property is 86 feet. The rear line is perpendicular to their side lot, and the road frontage is 111 feet. Their plat shows they own 3,000 square feet in the outlot. What is the length of the rear line of the outlot? Round your answer to the nearest whole number.

Solution:

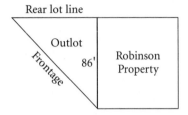

It helps to draw the figure to conceive shapes. The rear lot line is perpendicular to the side lot line. This makes the side lot line the base and the rear lot line the height (altitude).

Area = $\frac{1}{2}$(base)(height)

Area = 3,000 square feet

Base = 86 feet

Height = x

If it's easier, you can change $\frac{1}{2}$ to a decimal.

$\frac{1}{2}$ = .5

Now you can plug these values into the formula.

3,000 = (.5)(86)(x)

3,000 = (43)(x)

Divide both sides by 43.

$\frac{3,000}{43} = \frac{(43)(x)}{43}$

x = 69.767 feet

Don't forget the question says to round your answer to the nearest whole number. The answer is 70 feet.

Circles

Remember the formula Area = πr^2.

Example:

Murray Brodman, a contractor, has been awarded the job to put up a circular bandstand in the town square. The radius of the circular area for the bandstand is 15 feet. What is the area of the bandstand? Use 3.14 for π.

Solution:

Area = πr^2

Start with the values you know.

Area = x

π = 3.14

radius = 15

Now plug these values into the formula.

Area = (3.14)(15)(15) = 706.5 sq. ft.

▶ Property Tax

To solve property tax questions, you will be using percents and rates.

Example:

The tax rate in your county is $4.17 per hundred of assessed valuation, and Mr. Brown, a possible client, has told you his taxes are $1,100. What is his property assessment? (Round your answer to the nearest ten cents.)

Solution:

Start off with the values you know.

Taxes = $1,100

Assessment = x

Tax rate = $4.17 per hundred (%)

If you remember the definition of percent as being an amount per hundred, then $4.17 per hundred is actually 4.17%. To make this equation more manageable, convert this percent to a decimal by moving the decimal point two spaces to the left. Now the tax rate is .0417.

.0417 of the assessed value of the house is $1,100. Translate the words into math terms. This means: $(.0417)(x) = 1,100$.

To solve the equation, divide both sides by .0417.

$$\frac{.0417x}{.0417} = \frac{1,100}{.0417}$$

x = $26,378.896

Remember, the question asks you to round to the nearest ten cents. That means that .896 needs to be rounded up to 90. So the answer is $26,378.90.

Example:

Mr. Smith knew his own taxes were $975 and his property assessment was $17,000 for the house and $6,000 for the land. He wanted to know the tax rate (%).

Tip

Note that you may be asked for monthly amounts in certain problems. Most calculations are on an annual basis—unless you divide by 12.

Solution:

Start with the values you know.

Tax = $975

Assessment for house = $17,000 plus assessment for land = $6,000. Therefore, total = $23,000.

Rate (%) = x

According to the question, $23,000 at a rate of x is $975. Convert this statement into an equation.

($23,000)($x$) = 975.

Solve the equation by dividing both sides by 23,000.

$$\frac{23,000x}{23,000} = \frac{975}{23,000}$$

x = .0423913

To make this equation more simple, round the answer to .0424.

Remember that you are looking for the rate. Therefore, you need to convert this decimal to a percent by moving the decimal point two places to the right. The rate is 4.24%. (This can also be expressed as $4.24 per hundred.)

Loan-to-Value Ratios

These problems often deal with percentages.

Example:

A mortgage loan for 10% is at a 75% loan-to-value ratio. The interest on the original balance for the first year is $6,590. What is the value of the property securing the loan? Round to the nearest one cent.

Solution:

First, find out the loan amount.

$6,590 is 10% of the loan amount. Let x equal the loan amount. Now, translate these words into math terms.

$6,590 = (10%)($x$)

Change 10% into a decimal by moving the decimal point two places to the left.

10% = .1

Now you have:

$6,590 = (.1)($x$)

Divide both sides by (.1).

x = $65,900

Now that you know the loan amount ($65,900), use this information to find the value of the property.

Write down the values you know.

Loan amount = $65,900

Loan-to-value ratio = 75%

Value = x

We know that 75% of the value is $65,900.

Translate this into math terms.

$(75\%)(x) = \$65,900$

Change the percent into a decimal (75% = .75) and solve.

$(.75)(x) = 65,900$

Divide both sides by .75.

$$\frac{(.75)(x)}{(.75)} = \frac{65,900}{(.75)}$$

$x = 87,866.66666$

When rounded to the nearest one cent, the answer is $87,866.67.

Points

Loan discounts are often called **points**, or loan placement fees, *one point* meaning 1% of the face amount of the loan. The service fee of 1% paid by buyers of government-backed loans is called a **loan origination fee**.

Example:

A homebuyer may obtain a $50,000 FHA mortgage loan, provided the seller pays a discount of five points. What is the amount of the discount?

Solution:

The definition of one point is 1% of the face amount of the loan.

Therefore, 5 points = 5% of the face of the loan. First, change the percent to a decimal.

5% = .05

Now you can use these values to solve.

Amount of discount = x

Points = .05

Amount of loan = $50,000

So, $x = (.05)(50,000)$.

$x = \$2,500$

Example:

A property is listed at $74,000. An offer is made for $72,000, provided the seller pays three points on a loan for 80% of the purchase price. The brokerage commission rate is 7%. How much less will the seller receive if he accepts the offer than he would have received if he sold at all cash at the original terms?

Solution:

Here are the values you know:

Sold for original terms—price	$74,000	
Less 7% commission	− 5,180	(.07)(74,000) = 5,180
Seller's net	$68,820	

This question becomes more difficult, because in order to find the seller's net on the offered price, you must calculate the discount. The provision is that the seller pays three points (or .03) on a loan for 80% (or .8) of the price.
Start by finding 80% of the price.
(.8)(72,000) = $57,600
Now, the points are applied to this amount. This means .03 of $57,600 is the discount.
So, (.03)(57,600) = discount = 1,728.

You know these values:

Sold at offered terms—price	$72,000	
Less 7% commission	− 5,040	(.07)(72,000) = 5,040
Less discount	1,728	
Seller's net	$65,232	

$72,000	Sales price		Net at original	$68,820
× .80	Loan-to-value ratio		Net at offered	− 65,232
$57,600	Loan amount		Difference	$3,588
× .03	Points			
$1,728	Discount			

Equity

Example:

If a homeowner has a first mortgage loan balance of $48,350, a second mortgage loan balance of $18,200, and $26,300 equity, what is the value of her home?

Solution:

In this case, the value of the home is determined by the total loan balance plus the equity. Add the three numbers to find the value of the home.
$48,350 loan balance + $18,200 loan balance + $26,300 = value of the home
$92,850 = value of the home

Qualifying Buyers

Example:

A buyer is obtaining a conventional loan that requires 29/33 ratios. He earns $66,000 a year, and has a $1,350 car payment. What is his maximum PITI payment?

  a. $1,612.50

  b. $1,812.50

  c. $465

  d. $2,475

Solution:

$66,000 divided by 12 = $5,500 monthly income

($5,500)(.29) = $1,595 front end qualifier

($5,500)(.33) = $1,815 – $1,350 debt = $465 back end qualifier

Maximum PITI (Principal, Interest, Taxes, and Insurance) is the lower of these two qualifiers, $465.

Prorations

At the time of settlement, there must be a reconciliation or adjustment of any monies owed by either party as of that date. The important fact to bear in mind is that *the party who used the service pays for it.* If you will keep this firmly in mind, you will not have any difficulty deciding who to credit and who to debit.

Example:

Mr. Seller's taxes are $1,200 a year paid in advance on a calendar year. He is settling on the sale of his house to Mr. Buyer on August 1. Which of them owes how much to the other?

Solution:

Ask yourself some questions:

How many months has the seller paid for?	12	($1,200)
How many months has the seller used?	7	($700)
How many months should the seller be reimbursed for?	5	($500)
How many months will the buyer use?	5	($500)
How many months has he paid for?	0	($0)
How many months should he reimburse the seller for?	5	($500)

Credit Mr. Seller $500

Debit Mr. Buyer $500

What would the answer be if the taxes were paid in arrears? In other words, the seller has used the service for seven months but hasn't paid anything. The buyer will have to pay it all at the end of the year. In that case, the seller owes the buyer for seven months, or $700.

In working proration problems, be sure you have the right dates when you subtract. Sometimes, the termination date for the policy is not given, and the tendency is to subtract the date the policy was written from the date of settlement. This will not give you the unused portion. You must subtract the date of settlement from the date of termination of the policy, which will be exactly the same date one, three, or five years after written, depending on the term of the policy. Most problems use either a one- or three-year term.

Remember!

Use a 30-day month and a 360-day year in all calculations unless you are told otherwise. Assume a calendar year, unless a fiscal or school year is specified.

Commissions

Let's look at a commission problem. They are typically rate (percentage) problems.

Example:

Broker Jones sold the Smith house for $65,000. The total commission came to $4,000. What was Jones's commission rate? Round to the nearest whole percent.

Solution:

You see the word *rate* and decide this is solved using percentages.

Start with the values you know.

Price of house = 65,000

Commission rate = x

Commission = 4,000

Now, translate the word problem into an equation.

$65,000x = 4,000$

Divide both sides by 65,000.

$x = \frac{4,000}{65,000}$

$x = 0.061$

Convert the decimal to a percent by moving the decimal two places to the right. 0.061 becomes 6.1%.

Example:

An agent received a 3% commission on $\frac{1}{4}$ of her total sales. On the remainder, she received a 6% commission. What was her average commission for all of her sales?

Solution:

Start off by asking yourself: How many fourths (parts) were there? Four, naturally.

3%   6%   6%   6%

To find the average, you add up all the numbers, and divide by the number of items you add together. In this case, there are four numbers.

So, $3 + 6 + 6 + 6 = 21$.

And $21\% \div 4 = 5.25\%$.

Sale Proceeds

Example:

Salesman Garcia was trying to list a house. The owner said he wanted to clear (net) $12,000 from the sale of the house. The balance of the mortgage was $37,000. It would cost about $1,200 to fix up the house to sell. How much would the owner have to sell the house for if the 7% commission was included? (Round your answer to the nearest cent.)

Solution:

Use a chart to clarify the problem.

Expenses	In Dollars	In Percents
Seller's net	$12,000	
Loan balance	$37,000	
Repairs	$1,200	
Commission		%
	$50,200	7%

If the sales price is 100% and the commission is 7% of the sales price, all the remaining items added together must make 93% of the sales price. The place where most people go wrong is in not including the seller's net when they add the expenses. The seller's net has to come out of the sales price. (Where else would it come from?) Therefore, it is part of the remaining 93%. You now have a percentage problem. As always, convert your percents to decimals.

Start with the values you know:

Expenses = $50,200

Sales price = x

Seller's net, loan balance, repairs = .93 of sales price

.93 of the sales price is $50,200.

Convert this statement into an equation.

$(.93)(x) = \$50,200$

Divide both sides by .93.

$\frac{(.93)(x)}{.93} = \frac{\$50,200}{.93}$

$x = \frac{\$50,200}{.93}$

$x = \$53,978.4945$

Don't forget to round to the nearest cent!

$x = \$53,978.49$

Transfer Tax/Conveyance Tax/Revenue Stamps

Here is a transfer tax question.

Example:

A property is sold for $135,800 in cash. The transfer tax is $441.35. If transfer taxes are calculated per $200 of value, what was the rate (per $200) of the transfer tax?

Solution:

Start with the values you know.

Selling price = $135,800

Transfer tax rate = x per $200

Transfer tax = $441.35

It's probably easiest to begin by dividing by $200 because the rate is calculated per $200 of value.

So, $\frac{\$135,800}{\$200} = \$679$.

You know that $441.35 is produced by multiplying $679 by some rate. Translate this into math terms.

$\$441.35 = (x)(\$679)$

Divide both sides by $679.

$\frac{\$441.35}{(\$679)} = \frac{(x)(\$679)}{(\$679)}$

$.65 = x$

Therefore, the transfer tax rate is $.65 per $200.

Competitive Market Analyses (CMA)

To solve these problems, you will use measurements and other hypothetical features of the comparable property to arrive at a value. Remember, a CMA is not an appraisal.

Example:

If Building A measures 52' by 106' and Building B measures 75' by 85', how much will B cost if A costs $140,000 and both cost the same per square foot to build?

Solution:

Area = (length)(width)

Area of Building A = (52)(106) = 5,512 square feet

Area of Building B = (75)(85) = 6,375 square feet

Cost of Building A per square foot = $\frac{140,000}{5,512}$ = $25.40

Cost of Building B = (6,375)($25.40) = $161,925

Example:

Carson's house (B), which is being appraised, is an exact twin of the houses on either side of it, built by the same builder at the same time. House A was appraised for $45,000, but it has a 14 × 20 foot garage, which was added at a cost of about $18 per square foot. House C was recently sold for $43,000, with central air valued at $3,000. What would be a fair estimate of the value of Carson's house?

Solution:

Comparable C	$43,000
– Air Conditioning	– 3,000
	40,000

Comparable A	$45,000	Garage: 14' × 20' = 280 sq. ft.
– Cost of Garage	– 5,040	280 sq. ft. × $18 = $5,040
	$39,960	

Answer: $40,000

Income Properties

Example:

An investor is considering the purchase of an income property generating a gross income of $350,000. Operating expenses constitute 70% of gross income. If the investor wants a return of 14%, what is the maximum he can pay?

Solution:

Gross income = $350,000

Expenses = 70% of gross income

Net income = Gross income – Expenses

Desired return = 14%

Maximum buyer can pay = x

This is a multistep problem. Start by calculating the expenses, but remember, you will need to stop to calculate the net income. First, change the percent to a decimal.

70% = .70

Now, you know that expenses are 70% of the gross income of $350,000. Change the words to mathematical terms.

Expenses = $(.7)(350,000) = \$245,000$

Gross income – Expenses = Net income

$350,000 - \$245,000 = \$105,000$

The buyer wants the net income ($105,000) to be 14% of what he pays for the property.

Change the percent to a decimal (14% = .14) and then convert this statement to an equation.

$105,000 = (.14)(x)$

Divide both sides by .14.

$$\frac{\$105,000}{.14} = \frac{(.14)(x)}{.14}$$

$105,000 \div .14 = x$

$750,000 = x$

Depreciation

There are several methods of depreciation, but the only one you are likely to meet on your exam is the straight-line method. This method spreads the total depreciation over the useful life of the building in equal annual amounts. It is calculated by dividing the replacement cost by the years of useful life left.

$$\frac{\text{replacement cost}}{\text{years of useful life}} = \text{annual depreciation}$$

The depreciation rate may be given or may have to be calculated by the straight-line method. This means dividing the total depreciation (100%) by the estimated useful life given for the building.

$$\frac{100\%}{\text{years of useful life}} = \text{depreciated rate}$$

If a building has 50 years of useful life left, the depreciation rate would be computed as follows:

$$\frac{100\%}{50} = 2\%$$

In other words, it has a 2% depreciation rate annually.

Example:

The replacement cost of a building has been estimated at $80,000. The building is 12 years old and has an estimated 40 years of useful life left. What can be charged to annual depreciation? What is the total depreciation for 12 years? What is the present value of this building?

Solution:

Calculate the annual depreciation.

$$\frac{\text{replacement cost}}{\text{years of useful life}} = \text{annual depreciation}$$

$$\frac{\$80,000}{40} = \$2,000$$

Find the total depreciation over the 12 years.

Annual depreciation of $2,000 × 12 years = $24,000.

Find the current value: replacement – depreciation = current value.

$80,000 – $24,000 = $56,000

▶ Summary

Hopefully, with this review, you have realized that real estate math is not as bad as it seems. If you feel you need more practice, check out LearningExpress's *Practical Math Success in 20 Minutes a Day* or *1001 Math Problems.* Use the exams in the books to practice even more real estate math.

6 ▶ Real Estate Glossary

CHAPTER SUMMARY

One of the most basic components in preparing for the Connecticut Real Estate Sales Exam is making sure you know all the terminology. This glossary provides a list of the most commonly used real estate terms and their definitions.

THESE TERMS WILL help you not only as you study for your real estate exam, but also after you pass your exam and are practicing in the field. The terms are listed in alphabetical order for easy reference.

▶ A

abandonment the voluntary surrender of a right, claim, or interest in a piece of property without naming a successor as owner or tenant.

abstract of title a certified summary of the history of a title to a particular parcel of real estate that includes the original grant and all subsequent transfers, encumbrances, and releases.

abutting sharing a common boundary; adjoining.

acceleration clause a clause in a note, mortgage, or deed of trust that permits the lender to declare the entire amount of principal and accrued interest due and payable immediately in the event of default.

acceptance the indication by a party receiving an offer that they agree to the terms of the offer. In most states, the offer and acceptance must be reduced to writing when real property is involved.

accretion the increase or addition of land resulting from the natural deposit of sand or soil by streams, lakes, or rivers.

accrued depreciation (1) the amount of depreciation, or loss in value, that has accumulated since initial construction; (2) the difference between the current appraised value and the cost to replace the building new.

accrued items a list of expenses that have been incurred but have not yet been paid, such as interest on a mortgage loan, which are included on a closing statement.

acknowledgment a formal declaration before a public official, usually a notary public, by a person who has signed a deed, contract, or other document that the execution was a voluntary act.

acre a measure of land equal to 43,560 square feet or 4,840 square yards.

actual eviction the result of legal action brought by a landlord against a defaulted tenant, whereby the tenant is physically removed from rented or leased property by a court order.

actual notice the actual knowledge that a person has of a particular fact.

addendum any provision added to a contract, or an addition to a contract that expands, modifies, or enhances the clarity of the agreement. To be a part of the contract and legally enforceable, an addendum must be referenced within the contract.

adjacent lying near to but not necessarily in actual contact with.

adjoining contiguous or attached; in actual contact with.

adjustable-rate mortgage (ARM) a mortgage in which the interest changes periodically, according to corresponding fluctuations in an index. All ARMs are tied to indexes. For example, a seven-year, adjustable-rate mortgage is a loan where the rate remains fixed for the first seven years, then fluctuates according to the index to which it is tied.

adjusted basis the original cost of a property, plus acquisition costs, plus the value of added improvements to the property, minus accrued depreciation.

adjustment date the date the interest rate changes on an adjustable-rate mortgage.

administrator a person appointed by a court to settle the estate of a person who has died without leaving a will.

ad valorem tax tax in proportion to the value of a property.

adverse possession a method of acquiring title to another person's property through court action after taking actual, open, hostile, and continuous possession for a statutory period of time; may require payment of property taxes during the period of possession.

affidavit a written statement made under oath and signed before a licensed public official, usually a notary public.

agency the legal relationship between principal and agent that arises out of a contract wherein an agent is employed to do certain acts on behalf of the principal who has retained the agent to deal with a third party.

agent one who has been granted the authority to act on behalf of another.

agreement of sale a written agreement between a seller and a purchaser whereby the purchaser agrees to buy a certain piece of property from the seller for a specified price.

air rights the right to use the open space above a particular property.

alienation the transfer of ownership of a property to another, either voluntarily or involuntarily.

alienation clause the clause in a mortgage or deed of trust that permits the lender to declare all unpaid principal and accrued interest due and payable if the borrower transfers title to the property.

allodial system in the United States, a system of land ownership in which land is held free and clear of any rent or services due to the government; commonly contrasted with the feudal system, in which ownership is held by a monarch.

amenities features or benefits of a particular property that enhance the property's desirability and value, such as a scenic view or a pool.

amortization the method of repaying a loan or debt by making periodic installment payments composed of both principal and interest. When all principal has been repaid, it is considered fully amortized.

amortization schedule a table that shows how much of each loan payment will be applied toward principal and how much toward interest over the lifespan of the loan. It also shows the gradual decrease of the outstanding loan balance until it reaches zero.

amortize to repay a loan through regular payments that are composed of principal and interest.

annual percentage rate (APR) the total or effective amount of interest charged on a loan, expressed as a percentage, on a yearly basis. This value is created according to a government formula intended to reflect the true annual cost of borrowing.

anti-deficiency laws laws used in some states to limit the claim of a lender on default on payment of a purchase money mortgage on owner-occupied residential property to the value of the collateral.

antitrust laws laws designed to protect free enterprise and the open marketplace by prohibiting certain business practices that restrict competition. In reference to real estate, these laws would prevent such practices as price-fixing or agreements by brokers to limit their areas of trade.

apportionments adjustment of income, expenses, or carrying charges related to real estate, usually computed to the date of closing so that the seller pays all expenses to date, then the buyer pays all expenses beginning on the closing date.

appraisal an estimate or opinion of the value of an adequately described property, as of a specific date.

appraised value an opinion of a property's fair market value, based on an appraiser's knowledge, experience, and analysis of the property, based on comparable sales.

appraiser an individual qualified by education, training, and experience to estimate the value of real property. Appraisers may work directly for mortgage lenders, or they may be independent contractors.

appreciation an increase in the market value of a property.

appurtenance something that transfers with the title to land even if not an actual part of the property, such as an easement.

arbitration the process of settling a dispute in which the parties submit their differences to an impartial third party, on whose decision on the matter is binding.

ARELLO the Association of Real Estate License Law Officials.

assessed value the value of a property used to calculate real estate taxes.

assessment the process of assigning value on property for taxation purposes.

assessor a public official who establishes the value of a property for taxation purposes.

asset items of value owned by an individual. Assets that can be quickly converted into cash are considered "liquid assets," such as bank accounts and stock portfolios. Other assets include real estate, personal property, and debts owed.

assignment the transfer of rights or interest from one person to another.

assumption of mortgage the act of acquiring the title to a property that has an existing mortgage and agreeing to be liable for the payment of any debt still existing on that mortgage. However, the lender must accept the transfer of liability for the original borrower to be relieved of the debt.

attachment the process whereby a court takes custody of a debtor's property until the creditor's debt is satisfied.

attest to bear witness by providing a signature.

attorney-in-fact a person who is authorized under a power of attorney to act on behalf of another.

avulsion the removal of land from one owner to another when a stream or other body of water suddenly changes its channel.

▶ B

balloon mortgage a loan in which the periodic payments do not fully amortize the loan, so that a final payment (a balloon payment) is substantially larger than the amount of the periodic payments that must be made to satisfy the debt.

balloon payment the final, lump-sum payment that is due at the termination of a balloon mortgage.

bankruptcy an individual or individuals can restructure or relieve themselves of debts and liabilities by filing in federal bankruptcy court. There are many types of bankruptcies, and the most common for an individual is "Chapter 7 No Asset," which relieves the borrower of most types of debts.

bargain and sale deed a deed that conveys title, but does not necessarily carry warranties against liens or encumbrances.

base line one of the imaginary east-west lines used as a reference point when describing property with the rectangular or government survey method of property description.

bench mark a permanently marked point with a known elevation, used as a reference by surveyors to measure elevations.

beneficiary (1) one who benefits from the acts of another; (2) the lender in a deed of trust.

bequest personal property given by provision of a will.

betterment an improvement to property that increases its value.

bilateral contract a contract in which each party promises to perform an act in exchange for the other party's promise also to perform an act.

bill of sale a written instrument that transfers ownership of personal property. A bill of sale cannot be used to transfer ownership of real property, which is passed by deed.

binder an agreement, accompanied by an earnest money deposit, for the purchase of a piece of real estate to show the purchaser's good faith intent to complete a transaction.

biweekly mortgage a mortgage in which payments are made every two weeks instead of once a month. Therefore, instead of making 12 monthly payments during the year, the borrower makes the equivalent of 13 monthly payments. The extra payment reduces the principal, thereby reducing the time it takes to pay off a 30-year mortgage.

blanket mortgage a mortgage in which more than one parcel of real estate is pledged to cover a single debt.

blockbusting the illegal and discriminatory practice of inducing homeowners to sell their properties by suggesting or implying the introduction of members of a protected class into the neighborhood.

bona fide in good faith, honest.

bond evidence of personal debt secured by a mortgage or other lien on real estate.

boot money or property provided to make up a difference in value or equity between two properties in an exchange.

branch office a place of business secondary to a principal office. The branch office is a satellite office generally run by a licensed broker, for the benefit of the broker running the principal office, as well as the associate broker's convenience.

breach of contract violation of any conditions or terms in a contract without legal excuse.

broker the term *broker* can mean many things, but in terms of real estate, it is the owner-manager of a business that brings together the parties to a real estate transaction for a fee. The roles of brokers and brokers' associates are defined by state law. In the mortgage industry, *broker* usually refers to a company or individual who does not lend the money for the loans directly, but that brokers loan to larger lenders or investors.

brokerage the business of bringing together buyers and sellers or other participants in a real estate transaction.

broker's price opinion (BPO) a broker's opinion of value based on a competitive market analysis, rather than a certified appraisal.

building code local regulations that control construction, design, and materials used in construction that are based on health and safety regulations.

building line the distance from the front, rear, or sides of a building lot beyond which no structures may extend.

building restrictions limitations listed in zoning ordinances or deed restrictions on the size and type of improvements allowed on a property.

bundle of rights the concept that ownership of a property includes certain rights regarding the property, such as possession, enjoyment, control of use, and disposition.

buydown usually refers to a fixed-rate mortgage where the interest rate is "bought down" for a temporary period, usually one to three years. After that time and for the remainder of the term, the borrower's payment is calculated at the note rate. In order to buy down the initial rate for the temporary payment, a lump sum is paid and held in an account used to supplement the borrower's monthly payment. These funds usually come from the seller as a financial incentive to induce someone to buy his or her property.

buyer's broker real estate broker retained by a prospective buyer; this buyer becomes the broker's client to whom fiduciary duties are owed.

bylaws rules and regulations adopted by an association—for example, a condominium.

▶ C

cancellation clause a provision in a lease that confers on one or all parties to the lease the right to terminate the parties' obligations, should the occurrence of the condition or contingency set forth in the clause happen.

canvassing the practice of searching for prospective clients by making unsolicited phone calls and/or visiting homes door to door.

cap the limit on fluctuation rates regarding adjustable-rate mortgages. Limitations, or caps, may apply to how much the loan may adjust over a six-month period, an annual period, and over the life of the loan. There is also a limit on how much that payment can change each year.

capital money used to create income, or the net worth of a business as represented by the amount by which its assets exceed its liabilities.

capital expenditure the cost of a betterment to a property.

capital gains tax a tax charged on the profit gained from the sale of a capital asset.

capitalization the process of estimating the present value of an income-producing piece of property by dividing anticipated future income by a capitalization rate.

capitalization rate the rate of return a property will generate on an owner's investment.

cash flow the net income produced by an investment property, calculated by deducting operating and fixed expenses from gross income.

caveat emptor a phrase meaning "let the buyer beware."

CC&R covenants, conditions, and restrictions of a cooperative or condominium development.

certificate of discharge a document used when the security instrument is a mortgage.

certificate of eligibility a document issued by the Veterans Administration that certifies a veteran's eligibility for a VA loan.

certificate of reasonable value (CRV) once the appraisal has been performed on a property being bought with a VA loan, the Veterans Administration issues a CRV.

certificate of sale the document given to a purchaser of real estate that is sold at a tax foreclosure sale.

certificate of title a report stating an opinion on the status of a title, based on the examination of public records.

chain of title the recorded history of conveyances and encumbrances that affect the title to a parcel of land.

chattel personal property, as opposed to real property.

chattel mortgage a loan in which personal property is pledged to secure the debt.

city a large municipality governed under a charter and granted by the state.

clear title a title that is free of liens and legal questions as to ownership of a property that is a requirement for the sale of real estate; sometimes referred to as *just title*, *good title*, or *free and clear*.

closing the point in a real estate transaction when the purchase price is paid to the seller and the deed to the property is transferred from the seller to the buyer.

closing costs there are two kinds: (1) nonrecurring closing costs and (2) prepaid items. Nonrecurring closing costs are any items paid once as a result of buying the property or obtaining a loan. Prepaid items are items that recur over time, such as property taxes and homeowners insurance. A lender makes an attempt to estimate the amount of nonrecurring closing costs and prepaid items on the good faith estimate, which is issued to the borrower within three days of receiving a home loan application.

closing date the date on which the buyer takes over the property.

closing statement a written accounting of funds received and disbursed during a real estate transaction. The buyer and seller receive separate closing statements.

cloud on the title an outstanding claim or encumbrance that can affect or impair the owner's title.

clustering the grouping of home sites within a subdivision on smaller lots than normal, with the remaining land slated for use as common areas.

codicil a supplement or addition to a will that modifies the original instrument.

coinsurance clause a clause in an insurance policy that requires the insured to pay a portion of any loss experienced.

collateral something of value hypothecated (real property) or pledged (personal property) by a borrower as security for a debt.

collection when a borrower falls behind, the lender contacts the borrower in an effort to bring the loan current. The loan goes to "collection."

color of title an instrument that gives evidence of title, but may not be legally adequate to actually convey title.

commercial property property used to produce income, such as an office building or a restaurant.

commingling the illegal act of an agent mixing a client's monies, which should be held in a separate escrow account, with the agent's personal monies; in some states, it means placing funds that are separate property in an account containing funds that are community property.

commission the fee paid to a broker for services rendered in a real estate transaction.

commitment letter a pledge in writing affirming an agreement.

common areas portions of a building, land, and amenities owned (or managed) by a planned unit development or condominium project's homeowners association or a cooperative project's cooperative corporation. These areas are used by all of the unit owners, who share in the common expenses of their operation and maintenance. Common areas may include swimming pools, tennis courts, and other recreational facilities, as well as common corridors of buildings, parking areas, and lobbies.

common law the body of laws derived from local custom and judicial precedent.

community property a system of property ownership in which each spouse has equal interest in property acquired during the marriage; recognized in nine states.

comparable sales recent sales of similar properties in nearby areas that are used to help estimate the current market value of a property.

competent parties people who are legally qualified to enter a contract, usually meaning that they are of legal age, of sound mind, and not under the influence of drugs or other mind-altering substances.

competitive market analysis (CMA) an analysis intended to assist a seller or buyer in determining a property's range of value.

condemnation the judicial process by which the government exercises its power of eminent domain.

condominium a form of ownership in which an individual owns a specific unit in a multiunit building and shares ownership of common areas with other unit owners.

condominium conversion changing the ownership of an existing building (usually a multi-dwelling rental unit) from single ownership to condominium ownership.

conformity an appraisal principle that asserts that property achieves its maximum value when a neighborhood is homogeneous in its use of land; the basis for zoning ordinances.

consideration something of value that induces parties to enter into a contract, such as money or services.

construction mortgage a short-term loan used to finance the building of improvements to real estate.

constructive eviction action or inaction by a landlord that renders a property uninhabitable, forcing a tenant to move out with no further liability for rent.

constructive notice notice of a fact given by making the fact part of the public record. All persons are responsible for knowing the information, whether or not they have actually seen the record.

contingency a condition that must be met before a contract is legally binding. A satisfactory home inspection report from a qualified home inspector is an example of a common type of contingency.

contract an agreement between two or more legally competent parties to do or to refrain from doing some legal act in exchange for a consideration.

contract for deed a contract for the sale of a parcel of real estate in which the buyer makes periodic payments to the seller and receives title to the property only after all, or a substantial part, of the purchase price has been paid, or regular payments have been made for one year or longer.

conventional loan a loan that is neither insured nor guaranteed by an agency of government.

conversion option an option in an adjustable-rate mortgage to convert it to a fixed-rate mortgage.

convertible ARM an adjustable-rate mortgage that allows the borrower to change the ARM to a fixed-rate mortgage at a specific time.

conveyance the transfer of title from the grantor to the grantee.

cooperative a form of property ownership in which a corporation owns a multiunit building and stockholders of the corporation may lease and occupy individual units of the building through a proprietary lease.

corporation a legal entity with potentially perpetual existence that is created and owned by shareholders who appoint a board of directors to direct the business affairs of the corporation.

cost approach an appraisal method whereby the value of a property is calculated by estimating the cost of constructing a comparable building, subtracting depreciation, and adding land value.

counteroffer an offer submitted in response to an offer. It has the effect of overriding the original offer.

credit an agreement in which a borrower receives something of value in exchange for a promise to repay the lender.

credit history a record of an individual's repayment of debt.

cul-de-sac a dead-end street that widens at the end, creating a circular turnaround area.

curtesy the statutory or common law right of a husband to all or part of real estate owned by his deceased wife, regardless of will provisions, recognized in some states.

curtilage area of land occupied by a building, its outbuildings, and yard, either actually enclosed or considered enclosed.

▶ **D**

damages the amount of money recoverable by a person who has been injured by the actions of another.

datum a specific point used in surveying.

DBA the abbreviation for "doing business as."

debt an amount owed to another.

decedent a person who dies.

dedication the donation of private property by its owner to a governmental body for public use.

deed a written document that, when properly signed and delivered, conveys title to real property from the grantor to the grantee.

deed-in-lieu a foreclosure instrument used to convey title to the lender when the borrower is in default and wants to avoid foreclosure.

deed of trust a deed in which the title to property is transferred to a third-party trustee to secure repayment of a loan; three-party mortgage arrangement.

deed restriction an imposed restriction for the purpose of limiting the use of land, such as the size or type of improvements to be allowed. Also called a *restrictive covenant*.

default the failure to perform a contractual duty.

defeasance clause a clause in a mortgage that renders it void where all obligations have been fulfilled.

deficiency judgment a personal claim against a borrower when mortgaged property is foreclosed and sale of the property does not produce sufficient funds to pay off the mortgage. Deficiency judgments may be prohibited in some circumstances by anti-deficiency protection.

delinquency failure to make mortgage or loan payments when payments are due.

density zoning a zoning ordinance that restricts the number of houses or dwelling units that can be built per acre in a particular area, such as a subdivision.

depreciation a loss in value due to physical deterioration, functional, or external obsolescence.

descent the transfer of property to an owner's heirs when the owner dies intestate.

devise the transfer of title to real estate by will.

devisee one who receives a bequest of real estate by will.

devisor one who grants real estate by will.

directional growth the direction toward which certain residential sections of a city are expected to grow.

discount point 1% of the loan amount charged by a lender at closing to increase a loan's effective yield and lower the fare rate to the borrower.

discount rate the rate that lenders pay for mortgage funds—a higher rate is passed on to the borrower.

dispossess to remove a tenant from property by legal process.

dominant estate (tenement) property that includes the right to use an easement on adjoining property.

dower the right of a widow in the property of her husband upon his death in noncommunity property states.

down payment the part of the purchase price that the buyer pays in cash and is not financed with a mortgage or loan.

dual agency an agent who represents both parties in a transaction.

due-on-sale clause a provision in a mortgage that allows the lender to demand repayment in full if the borrower sells the property that serves as security for the mortgage.

duress the use of unlawful means to force a person to act or to refrain from an action against his or her will.

▶ E

earnest money down payment made by a buyer of real estate as evidence of good faith.

easement the right of one party to use the land of another for a particular purpose, such as to lay utility lines.

easement by necessity an easement, granted by law and requiring court action, that is deemed necessary for the full enjoyment of a parcel of land. An example would be an easement allowing access from land-locked property to a road.

easement by prescription a means of acquiring an easement by continued, open, and hostile use of someone else's property for a statutorily defined period of time.

easement in gross a personal right granted by an owner with no requirement that the easement holder own adjoining land.

economic life the period of time over which an improved property will generate sufficient income to justify its continued existence.

effective age an appraiser's estimate of the physical condition of a building. The actual age of a building may be different from its effective age.

emblements cultivated crops; generally considered to be personal property.

eminent domain the right of a government to take private property for public use upon payment of its fair market value. Eminent domain is the basis for condemnation proceedings.

encroachment a trespass caused when a structure, such as a wall or fence, invades another person's land or air space.

encumbrance anything that affects or limits the title to a property, such as easements, leases, mortgages, or restrictions.

equitable title the interest in a piece of real estate held by a buyer who has agreed to purchase the property, but has not yet completed the transaction; the interest of a buyer under a contract for deed.

equity the difference between the current market value of a property and the outstanding indebtedness due on it.

equity of redemption the right of a borrower to stop the foreclosure process.

erosion the gradual wearing away of land by wind, water, and other natural processes.

escalation clause a clause in a lease allowing the lessor to charge more rent based on an increase in costs; sometimes called a *pass-through clause.*

escheat the claim to property by the state when the owner dies intestate and no heirs can be found.

escrow the deposit of funds and/or documents with a disinterested third party for safekeeping until the terms of the escrow agreement have been met.

escrow account a trust account established to hold escrow funds for safekeeping until disbursement.

escrow analysis annual report to disclose escrow receipts, payments, and current balances.

escrow disbursements money paid from an escrow account.

estate an interest in real property. The sum total of all the real property and personal property owned by an individual.

estate for years a leasehold estate granting possession for a definite period of time.

estate tax federal tax levied on property transferred upon death.

estoppel certificate a document that certifies the outstanding amount owed on a mortgage loan, as well as the rate of interest.

et al. abbreviation for the Latin phrase *et alius,* meaning "and another."

et ux. abbreviation for Latin term *et uxor,* meaning "and wife."

et vir. Latin term meaning "and husband."

eviction the lawful expulsion of an occupant from real property.

evidence of title a document that identifies ownership of property.

examination of title a review of an abstract to determine current condition of title.

exchange a transaction in which property is traded for another property, rather than sold for money or other consideration.

exclusive agency listing a contract between a property owner and one broker that gives only the broker the right to sell the property for a fee within a specified period of time but does not obligate the owner to pay the broker a fee if the owner produces his own buyer without the broker's assistance. The owner is barred only from appointing another broker within this time period.

exclusive right to sell a contract between a property owner and a broker that gives the broker the right to collect a commission regardless of who sells the property during the specified period of time of the agreement.

executed contract a contract in which all obligations have been fully performed.

execution the signing of a contract.

executor/executrix a person named in a will to administer an estate. The court will appoint an administrator if no executor is named. "Executrix" is the feminine form.

executory contract a contract in which one or more of the obligations have yet to be performed.

express contract an oral or written contract in which the terms are expressed in words.

extension agreement an agreement between mortgagor and mortgagee to extend the maturity date of the mortgage after it is due.

external obsolescence a loss in value of a property due to factors outside the property, such as a change in surrounding land use.

▶ **F**

fair housing law a term used to refer to federal and state laws prohibiting discrimination in the sale or rental of residential property.

fair market value the highest price that a buyer, willing but not compelled to buy, would pay, and the lowest a seller, willing but not compelled to sell, would accept.

Federal Housing Administration (FHA) an agency within the U.S. Department of Housing and Urban Development (HUD) that insures mortgage loans by FHA-approved lenders to make loans available to buyers with limited cash.

Federal National Mortgage Association (Fannie Mae) a privately owned corporation that buys existing government-backed and conventional mortgages.

Federal Reserve System the central banking system of the United States, which controls the monetary policy and, therefore, the money supply, interest rates, and availability of credit.

fee simple the most complete form of ownership of real estate.

FHA-insured loan a loan insured by the Federal Housing Administration.

fiduciary relationship a legal relationship with an obligation of trust, as that of agent and principal.

finder's fee a fee or commission paid to a mortgage broker for finding a mortgage loan for a prospective borrower.

first mortgage a mortgage that has priority to be satisfied over all other mortgages.

fixed-rate loan a loan with an interest rate that does not change during the entire term of the loan.

fixture an article of personal property that has been permanently attached to the real estate so as to become an integral part of the real estate.

foreclosure the legal process by which a borrower in default of a mortgage is deprived of interest in the mortgaged property. Usually, this involves a forced sale of the property at public auction, where the proceeds of the sale are applied to the mortgage debt.

forfeiture the loss of money, property, rights, or privileges due to a breach of legal obligation.

franchise in real estate, an organization that lends a standardized trade name, operating procedures, referral services, and supplies to member brokerages.

fraud a deliberate misstatement of material fact or an act or omission made with deliberate intent to deceive (active fraud) or gross disregard for the truth (constructive fraud).

freehold estate an estate of ownership in real property.

front foot a measurement of property taken by measuring the frontage of the property along the street line.

functional obsolescence a loss in value of a property due to causes within the property, such as faulty design, outdated structural style, or inadequacy to function properly.

future interest ownership interest in property that cannot be enjoyed until the occurrence of some event; sometimes referred to as a *household* or *equitable interest*.

▶ G

general agent an agent who is authorized to act for and obligate a principal in a specific range of matters, as specified by their mutual agreement.

general lien a claim on all property, real and personal, owned by a debtor.

general warranty deed an instrument in which the grantor guarantees the grantee that the title being conveyed is good and free of other claims or encumbrances.

government-backed mortgage a mortgage that is insured by the Federal Housing Administration (FHA) or guaranteed by the Department of Veterans Affairs (VA) or the Rural Housing Service (RHS). Mortgages that are not government loans are identified as conventional loans.

Government National Mortgage Association (Ginnie Mae) a government-owned corporation within the U.S. Department of Housing and Urban Development (HUD). Ginnie Mae manages and liquidates government-backed loans and assists HUD in special lending projects.

government survey system a method of land description in which meridians (lines of longitude) and base lines (lines of latitude) are used to divide land into townships and sections.

graduated lease a lease that calls for periodic, stated changes in rent during the term of the lease.

grant the transfer of title to real property by deed.

grant deed a deed that includes three warranties: (1) that the owner has the right to convey title to the property, (2) that there are no encumbrances other than those noted specifically in the deed, and (3) that the owner will convey any future interest that he or she may acquire in the property.

grantee one who receives title to real property.

grantor one who conveys title to real property; the present owner.

gross income the total income received from a property before deducting expenses.

gross income multiplier a rough method of estimating the market value of an income property by multiplying its gross annual rent by a multiplier discovered by dividing the sales price of comparable properties by their annual gross rent.

gross lease a lease in which a tenant pays only a fixed amount for rental and the landlord pays all operating expenses and taxes.

gross rent multiplier similar to *gross income multiplier*, except that it looks at the relationship between sales price and monthly gross rent.

ground lease a lease of land only, on which a tenant already owns a building or will construct improvements.

guaranteed sale plan an agreement between a broker and a seller that the broker will buy the seller's property if it does not sell within a specified period of time.

guardian one who is legally responsible for the care of another person's rights and/or property.

▶ **H**

habendum **clause** the clause in a deed, beginning with the words *to have and to hold*, that defines or limits the exact interest in the estate granted by the deed.

hamlet a small village.

heir one who is legally entitled to receive property when the owner dies intestate.

highest and best use the legally permitted use of a parcel of land that will yield the greatest return to the owner in terms of money or amenities.

holdover tenancy a tenancy where a lessee retains possession of the property after the lease has expired, and the landlord, by continuing to accept rent, agrees to the tenant's continued occupancy.

holographic will a will that is entirely handwritten, dated, and signed by the testator.

home equity conversion mortgage (HECM) often called a *reverse-annuity mortgage*; instead of making payments to a lender, the lender makes payments to you. It enables older homeowners to convert the equity they have in their homes into cash, usually in the form of monthly payments. Unlike traditional home equity loans, a borrower does not qualify on the basis of income but on the value of his or her home. In addition, the loan does not have to be repaid until the borrower no longer occupies the property.

home equity line of credit a mortgage loan that allows the borrower to obtain cash drawn against the equity of his or her home, up to a predetermined amount.

home inspection a thorough inspection by a professional that evaluates the structural and mechanical condition of a property. A satisfactory home inspection is often included as a contingency by the purchaser.

homeowners insurance an insurance policy specifically designed to protect residential property owners against financial loss from common risks such as fire, theft, and liability.

homeowners warranty an insurance policy that protects purchasers of newly constructed or pre-owned homes against certain structural and mechanical defects.

homestead the parcel of land and improvements legally qualifying as the owner's principal residence.

HUD an acronym for the Department of Housing and Urban Development, a federal agency that enforces federal fair housing laws and oversees agencies such as FHA and GNMA.

▶ **I**

implied contract a contract where the agreement of the parties is created by their conduct.

improvement human-made addition to real estate.

income capitalization approach a method of estimating the value of income-producing property by dividing its expected annual net operating income of the property by a capitalization rate.

income property real estate developed or improved to produce income.

incorporeal right intangible, nonpossessory rights in real estate, such as an easement or right of way.

independent contractor one who is retained by another to perform a certain task and is not subject to the control and direction of the hiring person with regard to the end result of the task. Individual contractors receive a fee for their services, but pay their own expenses and taxes and receive no employee benefits.

index a number used to compute the interest rate for an adjustable-rate mortgage (ARM). The index is a published number or percentage, such as the average yield on Treasury bills. A margin is added to the index to determine the interest rate to be charged on the ARM. This interest rate is subject to any caps that are associated with the mortgage.

industrial property buildings and land used for the manufacture and distribution of goods, such as a factory.

inflation an increase in the amount of money or credit available in relation to the amount of goods or services available, which causes an increase in the general price level of goods and services.

initial interest rate the beginning interest rate of the mortgage at the time of closing. This rate changes for an adjustable-rate mortgage (ARM).

installment the regular, periodic payment that a borrower agrees to make to a lender, usually related to a loan.

installment contract see *contract for deed.*

installment loan borrowed money that is repaid in periodic payments, known as *installments.*

installment sale a transaction in which the sales price is paid to the seller in two or more installments over more than one calendar year.

insurance a contract that provides indemnification from specific losses in exchange for a periodic payment. The individual contract is known as an insurance policy, and the periodic payment is known as an *insurance premium.*

insurance binder a document that states that temporary insurance is in effect until a permanent insurance policy is issued.

insured mortgage a mortgage that is protected by the Federal Housing Administration (FHA) or by private mortgage insurance (PMI). If the borrower defaults on the loan, the insurer must pay the lender the insured amount.

interest (1) a fee charged by a lender for the use of the money loaned; (2) a share of ownership in real estate.

interest accrual rate the percentage rate at which interest accrues on the mortgage.

interest rate the rent or rate charged to use funds belonging to another.

interest rate buydown plan an arrangement where the property seller (or any other party) deposits money to an account so that it can be released each month to reduce the mortgagor's monthly payments during the early years of a mortgage. During the specified period, the mortgagor's effective interest rate is "bought down" below the actual interest rate.

interest rate ceiling the maximum interest rate that may be charged for an adjustable-rate mortgage (ARM), as specified in the mortgage note.

interest rate floor the minimum interest rate for an adjustable-rate mortgage (ARM), as specified in the mortgage note.

interim financing a short-term loan made during the building phase of a project; also known as a *construction loan.*

intestate to die without having authored a valid will.

invalid not legally binding or enforceable.

investment property a property not occupied by the owner.

▶ **J**

joint tenancy co-ownership that gives each tenant equal interest and equal rights in the property, including the right of survivorship.

joint venture an agreement between two or more parties to engage in a specific business enterprise.

judgment a decision rendered by a court determining the rights and obligations of parties to an action or lawsuit.

judgment lien a lien on the property of a debtor resulting from a court judgment.

judicial foreclosure a proceeding that is handled as a civil lawsuit and conducted through court; used in some states.

jumbo loan a loan that exceeds Fannie Mae's mortgage amount limits. Also called a *nonconforming loan.*

junior mortgage any mortgage that is inferior to a first lien and that will be satisfied only after the first mortgage; also called a *secondary mortgage.*

▶ **L**

laches a doctrine used by a court to bar the assertion of a legal claim or right, based on the failure to assert the claim in a timely manner.

land the earth from its surface to its center, and the air space above it.

landlocked property surrounded on all sides by property belonging to another.

lease a contract between a landlord and a tenant wherein the landlord grants the tenant possession and use of the property for a specified period of time and for a consideration.

leased fee the landlord's interest in a parcel of leased property.

leasehold a tenant's right to occupy a parcel of real estate for the term of a lease.

lease option a financing option that allows homebuyers to lease a home with an option to buy. Each month's rent payment may consist of rent, plus an additional amount that can be applied toward the down payment on an already specified price.

legal description a description of a parcel of real estate specific and complete enough for an independent surveyor to locate and identify it.

lessee the one who receives that right to use and occupy the property during the term of the leasehold estate.

lessor the owner of the property who grants the right of possession to the lessee.

leverage the use of borrowed funds to purchase an asset.

levy to assess or collect a tax.

license (1) a revocable authorization to perform a particular act on another's property; (2) authorization granted by a state to act as a real estate broker or salesperson.

lien a legal claim against a property to secure payment of a financial obligation.

life estate a freehold estate in real property limited in duration to the lifetime of the holder of the life estate or another specified person.

life tenant one who holds a life estate.

liquidity the ability to convert an asset into cash.

lis pendens a Latin phrase meaning "suit pending"; a public notice that a lawsuit has been filed that may affect the title to a particular piece of property.

listing agreement a contract between the owner and a licensed real estate broker where the broker is employed to sell real estate on the owner's terms within a given time, for which service the owner agrees to pay the broker an agreed-upon fee.

listing broker a broker who contracts with a property owner to sell or lease the described property; the listing agreement typically may provide for the broker to make property available through a multiple-listing system.

littoral rights landowner's claim to use water in large, navigable lakes and oceans adjacent to property; ownership rights to land-bordering bodies of water up to the high-water mark.

loan a sum of borrowed money, or principal, that is generally repaid with interest.

loan officer or *lender*, serves several functions and has various responsibilities, such as soliciting loans; a loan officer both represents the lending institution and represents the borrower to the lending institution.

lock-in an agreement in which the lender guarantees a specified interest rate for a certain amount of time.

lock-in period the time period during which the lender has guaranteed an interest rate to a borrower.

lot and block description a method of describing a particular property by referring to a lot and block number within a subdivision recorded in the public record.

▶ **M**

management agreement a contract between the owner of an income property and a firm or individual who agrees to manage the property.

margin the difference between the interest rate and the index on an adjustable-rate mortgage. The margin remains stable over the life of the loan, while the index fluctuates.

marketable title title to property that is free from encumbrances and reasonable doubts and that a court would compel a buyer to accept.

market data approach a method of estimating the value of a property by comparing it to similar properties recently sold and making monetary adjustments for the differences between the subject property and the comparable property.

market value the amount that a seller may expect to obtain for merchandise, services, or securities in the open market.

mechanic's lien a statutory lien created to secure payment for those who supply labor or materials for the construction of an improvement to land.

metes and bounds a method of describing a parcel of land using direction and distance.

mill one-tenth of one cent; used by some states to express or calculate property tax rates.

minor a person who has not attained the legal age of majority.

misrepresentation a misstatement of fact, either deliberate or unintentional.

modification the act of changing any of the terms of the mortgage.

money judgment a court order to settle a claim with a monetary payment, rather than specific performance.

month-to-month tenancy tenancy in which the tenant rents for only one month at a time.

monument a fixed, visible marker used to establish boundaries for a survey.

mortgage a written instrument that pledges property to secure payment of a debt obligation as evidenced by a promissory note. When duly recorded in the public record, a mortgage creates a lien against the title to a property.

mortgage banker an entity that originates, funds, and services loans to be sold into the secondary money market.

mortgage broker an entity that, for a fee, brings borrowers together with lenders.

mortgage lien an encumbrance created by recording a mortgage.

mortgagee the lender who benefits from the mortgage.

mortgagor the borrower who pledges the property as collateral.

multi-dwelling units properties that provide separate housing units for more than one family that secure only a single mortgage. Apartment buildings are also considered multi-dwelling units.

multiple-listing system (MLS—also multiple-listing service) the method of marketing a property listing to all participants in the MLS.

mutual rescission an agreement by all parties to a contract to release one another from the obligations of the contract.

► N

negative amortization occurs when an adjustable-rate mortgage is allowed to fluctuate independently of a required minimum payment. A gradual increase in mortgage debt happens when the monthly payment is not large enough to cover the entire principal and interest due. The amount of the shortfall is added to the remaining balance to create negative amortization.

net income the income produced by a property, calculated by deducting operating expenses from gross income.

net lease a lease that requires the tenant to pay maintenance and operating expenses, as well as rent.

net listing a listing in which the broker's fee is established as anything above a specified amount to be received by the seller from the sale of the property.

net worth the value of all of a person's assets.

no cash-out refinance a refinance transaction in which the new mortgage amount is limited to the sum of the remaining balance of the existing first mortgage.

nonconforming use a use of land that is permitted to continue, or grandfathered, even after a zoning ordinance is passed that prohibits the use.

nonliquid asset an asset that cannot easily be converted into cash.

notarize to attest or certify by a notary public.

notary public a person who is authorized to administer oaths and take acknowledgments.

note a written instrument acknowledging a debt, with a promise to repay, including an outline of the terms of repayment.

note rate the interest rate on a promissory note.

notice of default a formal written notice to a borrower that a default has occurred on a loan and that legal action may be taken.

novation the substitution of a new contract for an existing one; the new contract must reference the first and indicate that the first is being replaced and no longer has any force and effect.

▶ O

obligee person on whose favor an obligation is entered.

obligor person who is bound to another by an obligation.

obsolescence a loss in the value of a property due to functional or external factors.

offer to propose as payment; bid on property.

offer and acceptance two of the necessary elements for the creation of a contract.

open-end mortgage a loan containing a clause that allows the mortgagor to borrow additional funds from the lender, up to a specified amount, without rewriting the mortgage.

open listing a listing contract given to one or more brokers in which a commission is paid only to the broker who procures a sale. If the owner sells the house without the assistance of one of the brokers, no commission is due.

opinion of title an opinion, usually given by an attorney, regarding the status of a title to property.

option an agreement that gives a prospective buyer the right to purchase a seller's property within a specified period of time for a specified price.

optionee one who receives or holds an option.

optionor one who grants an option; the property owner.

ordinance a municipal regulation.

original principal balance the total amount of principal owed on a loan before any payments are made; the amount borrowed.

origination fee the amount charged by a lender to cover the cost of assembling the loan package and originating the loan.

owner financing a real estate transaction in which the property seller provides all or part of the financing.

ownership the exclusive right to use, possess, control, and dispose of property.

▶ **P**

package mortgage a mortgage that pledges both real and personal property as collateral to secure repayment of a loan.

parcel a lot or specific portion of a large tract of real estate.

participation mortgage a type of mortgage in which the lender receives a certain percentage of the income or resale proceeds from a property, as well as interest on the loan.

partition the division of property held by co-owners into individual shares.

partnership an agreement between two parties to conduct business for profit. In a partnership, property is owned by the partnership, not the individual partners, so partners cannot sell their interest in the property without the consent of the other partners.

party wall a common wall used to separate two adjoining properties.

payee one who receives payment from another.

payor one who makes payment to another.

percentage lease a lease in which the rental rate is based on a percentage of the tenant's gross sales. This type of lease is most often used for retail space.

periodic estate tenancy that automatically renews itself until either the landlord or tenant gives notice to terminate it.

personal property (hereditaments) all items that are not permanently attached to real estate; also known as *chattels*.

physical deterioration a loss in the value of a property due to impairment of its physical condition.

PITI principal, interest, taxes, and insurance—components of a regular mortgage payment.

planned unit development (PUD) a type of zoning that provides for residential and commercial uses within a specified area.

plat a map of subdivided land showing the boundaries of individual parcels or lots.

plat book a group of maps located in the public record showing the division of land into subdivisions, blocks, and individual parcels or lots.

plat number a number that identifies a parcel of real estate for which a plat has been recorded in the public record.

PMI private mortgage insurance.

point a point is 1% of the loan.

point of beginning the starting point for a survey using the "metes and bounds" method of description.

police power the right of the government to enact laws, ordinances, and regulations to protect the public health, safety, welfare, and morals.

power of attorney a legal document that authorizes someone to act on another's behalf. A power of attorney can grant complete authority or can be limited to certain acts and/or certain periods of time.

preapproval condition where a borrower has completed a loan application and provided debt, income, and savings documentation that an underwriter has reviewed and approved. A preapproval is usually done at a certain loan amount, making assumptions about what the interest rate will actually be at the time the loan is actually made, as well as estimates for the amount that will be paid for property taxes, insurance, and so on.

prepayment amount paid to reduce the outstanding principal balance of a loan before the due date.

prepayment penalty a fee charged to a borrower by a lender for paying off a debt before the term of the loan expires.

prequalification a lender's opinion on the ability of a borrower to qualify for a loan, based on furnished information regarding debt, income, and available capital for down payment, closing costs, and prepaids. Prequalification is less formal than preapproval.

prescription a method of acquiring an easement to property by prolonged, unauthorized use.

primary mortgage market the financial market in which loans are originated, funded, and serviced.

prime rate the short-term interest rate that banks charge to their preferred customers. Changes in prime rate are used as the indexes in some adjustable-rate mortgages, such as home equity lines of credit.

principal (1) one who authorizes another to act on his or her behalf; (2) one of the contracting parties to a transaction; (3) the amount of money borrowed in a loan, separate from the interest charged on it.

principal meridian one of the 36 longitudinal lines used in the rectangular survey system method of land description.

probate the judicial procedure of proving the validity of a will.

procuring cause the action that brings about the desired result. For example, if a broker takes actions that result in a sale, the broker is the procuring cause of the sale.

promissory note details the terms of the loan and is the debt instrument.

property management the operating of an income property for another.

property tax a tax levied by the government on property, real or personal.

prorate to divide ongoing property costs such as taxes or maintenance fees proportionately between buyer and seller at closing.

pur autre vie a phrase meaning "for the life of another." In a life estate *pur autre vie*, the term of the estate is measured by the life of a person other than the person who holds the life estate.

purchase agreement a written contract signed by the buyer and seller stating the terms and conditions under which a property will be sold.

purchase money mortgage a mortgage given by a buyer to a seller to secure repayment of any loan used to pay part or all of the purchase price.

▶ Q

qualifying ratios calculations to determine whether a borrower can qualify for a mortgage. There are two ratios. The "top" ratio is a calculation of the borrower's monthly housing costs (principal, taxes, insurance, mortgage insurance, homeowners association fees) as a percentage of monthly income. The "bottom" ratio includes housing costs as well as all other monthly debt.

quitclaim deed a conveyance where the grantor transfers without warranty or obligations whatever interest or title he or she may have.

▶ R

range an area of land six miles wide, numbered east or west from a principal meridian in the rectangular survey system.

ready, willing, and able one who is able to pay the asking price for a property and is prepared to complete the transaction.

real estate land, the earth below it, the air above it, and anything permanently attached to it.

real estate agent a real estate broker who has been appointed to market a property for and represent the property owner (listing agent), or a broker who has been appointed to represent the interest of the buyer (buyer's agent).

real estate board an organization whose members primarily consist of real estate sales agents, brokers, and administrators.

real estate broker a licensed person, association, partnership, or corporation who negotiates real estate transactions for others for a fee.

Real Estate Settlement Procedures Act (RESPA) a consumer protection law that requires lenders to give borrowers advance notice of closing costs and prohibits certain abusive practices against buyers using federally related loans to purchase their homes.

real property the rights of ownership to land and its improvements.

REALTOR® a registered trademark for use by members of the National Association of REALTORS® and affiliated state and local associations.

recording entering documents, such as deeds and mortgages, into the public record to give constructive notice.

rectangular survey system a method of land description based on principal meridians (lines of longitude) and base lines (lines of latitude). Also called the *government survey system*.

redemption period the statutory period of time during which an owner can reclaim foreclosed property by paying the debt owed plus court costs and other charges established by statute.

redlining the illegal practice of lending institutions refusing to provide certain financial services, such as mortgage loans, to property owners in certain areas.

refinance transaction the process of paying off one loan with the proceeds from a new loan using the same property as security or collateral.

Regulation Z a Federal Reserve regulation that implements the federal Truth-in-Lending Act.

release clause a clause in a mortgage that releases a portion of the property upon payment of a portion of the loan.

remainder estate a future interest in an estate that takes effect upon the termination of a life estate.

remaining balance in a mortgage, the amount of principal that has not yet been repaid.

remaining term the original amortization term minus the number of payments that have been applied to it.

rent a periodic payment paid by a lessee to a landlord for the use and possession of leased property.

replacement cost the estimated current cost to replace an asset similar or equivalent to the one being appraised.

reproduction cost the cost of building an exact duplicate of a building at current prices.

rescission canceling or terminating a contract by mutual consent or by the action of one party on default by the other party.

restriction (restrict covenant) a limitation on the way a property can be used.

reverse annuity mortgage when a homeowner receives monthly checks or a lump sum with no repayment until property is sold; usually an agreement between mortgagor and elderly homeowners.

reversion the return of interest or title to the grantor of a life estate.

revision a revised or new version, as in a contract.

right of egress (or ingress) the right to enter or leave designated premises.

right of first refusal the right of a person to have the first opportunity to purchase property before it is offered to anyone else.

right of redemption the statutory right to reclaim ownership of property after a foreclosure sale.

right of survivorship in joint tenancy, the right of survivors to acquire the interest of a deceased joint tenant.

riparian rights the rights of a landowner whose property is adjacent to a flowing waterway, such as a river, to access and use the water.

▶ S

safety clause a contract provision that provides a time period following expiration of a listing agreement, during which the agent will be compensated if there is a transaction with a buyer who was initially introduced to the property by the agent.

sale-leaseback a transaction where the owner sells improved property and, as part of the same transaction, signs a long-term lease to remain in possession of its premises, thus becoming the tenant of the new owner.

sales contract a contract between a buyer and a seller outlining the terms of the sale.

salesperson one who is licensed to sell real estate in a given territory.

salvage value the value of a property at the end of its economic life.

satisfaction an instrument acknowledging that a debt has been paid in full.

secondary mortgage a mortgage that is in less than first lien position; see *junior mortgage.*

section as used in the rectangular survey system, an area of land measuring one square mile, or 640 acres.

secured loan a loan that is backed by property or collateral.

security property that is offered as collateral for a loan.

selling broker the broker who secures a buyer for a listed property; the selling broker may be the listing agent, a subagent, or a buyer's agent.

separate property property owned individually by a spouse, as opposed to community property.

servient tenement a property on which an easement or right-of-way for an adjacent (dominant) property passes.

setback the amount of space between the lot line and the building line, usually established by a local zoning ordinance or restrictive covenants; see *deed restrictions.*

settlement statement (HUD-1) the form used to itemize all costs related to closing of a residential transaction covered by RESPA regulations.

severalty the ownership of a property by only one legal entity.

special assessment a tax levied against only the specific properties that will benefit from a public improvement, such as a street or sewer; an assessment by a homeowners association for a capital improvement to the common areas for which no budgeted funds are available.

special warranty deed a deed in which the grantor guarantees the title only against the defects that may have occurred during the grantor's ownership and not against any defects that occurred prior to that time.

specific lien a lien, such as a mortgage, that attaches to one defined parcel of real estate.

specific performance a legal action in which a court compels a defaulted party to a contract to perform according to the terms of the contract, rather than awarding damages.

standard payment calculation the method used to calculate the monthly payment required to repay the remaining balance of a mortgage in equal installments over the remaining term of the mortgage at the current interest rate.

Statute of Frauds the state law that requires certain contracts to be in writing to be enforceable.

Statute of Limitations the state law that requires that certain actions be brought to court within a specified period of time.

statutory lien a lien imposed on property by statute, such as a tax lien.

steering the illegal practice of directing prospective homebuyers to or away from particular areas.

straight-line depreciation a method of computing depreciation by decreasing value by an equal amount each year during the useful life of the property.

subdivision a tract of land divided into lots as defined in a publicly recorded plat that complies with state and local regulations.

sublet the act of a lessee transferring part or all of his or her lease to a third party while maintaining responsibility for all duties and obligations of the lease contract.

subordinate to voluntarily accept a lower priority lien position than that to which one would normally be entitled.

subrogation the substitution of one party into another's legal role as the creditor for a particular debt.

substitution the principle in appraising that a buyer will be willing to pay no more for the property being appraised than the cost of purchasing an equally desirable property.

suit for possession a lawsuit filed by a landlord to evict a tenant who has violated the terms of the lease or retained possession of the property after the lease expired.

suit for specific performance a lawsuit filed for the purpose of compelling a party to perform particular acts to settle a dispute, rather than pay monetary damages.

survey a map that shows the exact legal boundaries of a property, the location of easements, encroachments, improvements, rights of way, and other physical features.

syndicate a group formed by a syndicator to combine funds for real estate investment.

▶ T

tax deed in some states, an instrument given to the purchaser at the time of sale.

tax lien a charge against a property created by law or statute. Tax liens take priority over all other types of liens.

tax rate the rate applied to the assessed value of a property to determine the property taxes.

tax sale the court-ordered sale of a property after the owner fails to pay *ad valorem* taxes owed on the property.

tenancy at sufferance the tenancy of a party who unlawfully retains possession of a landlord's property after the term of the lease has expired.

tenancy at will an indefinite tenancy that can be terminated by either the landlord or the tenant at any time by giving notice to the other party one rental period in advance of the desired termination date.

tenancy by the entirety ownership by a married couple of property acquired during the marriage with right of survivorship; not recognized by community property states.

tenancy in common a form of co-ownership in which two or more persons hold an undivided interest in property without the right of survivorship.

tenant one who holds or possesses the right of occupancy title.

tenement the space that may be occupied by a tenant under the terms of a lease.

testate to die having created a valid will directing the testator's desires with regard to the disposition of the estate.

"time is of the essence" a phrase in a contract that requires strict adherence to the dates listed in the contract as deadlines for the performance of specific acts.

time-sharing undivided ownership of real estate for only an allotted portion of a year.

title a legal document that demonstrates a person's right to, or ownership of, a property. **Note:** Title is *not* an instrument. The instrument, such as a deed, gives evidence of title or ownership.

title insurance an insurance policy that protects the holder from defects in a title, subject to the exceptions noted in the policy.

title search a check of public records to ensure that the seller is the legal owner of the property and that there are no liens or other outstanding claims.

Torrens system a system of registering titles to land with a public authority, who is usually called a *registrar*.

township a division of land, measuring 36 square miles, in the government survey system.

trade fixtures an item of personal property installed by a commercial tenant and removable upon expiration of the lease.

transfer tax a state or municipal tax payable when the conveyancing instrument is recorded.

trust an arrangement in which title to property is transferred from a grantor to a trustee, who holds title but not the right of possession for a third party, the beneficiary.

trustee a person who holds title to property for another person designated as the beneficiary.

Truth-in-Lending Law also known as *Regulation Z*; requires lenders to make full disclosure regarding the terms of a loan.

▶ U

underwriting the process of evaluating a loan application to determine the risk involved for the lender.

undivided interest the interest of co-owners to use an entire property despite the fractional interest owned.

unilateral contract a one-sided contract in which one party is obligated to perform a particular act completely, before the other party has any obligation to perform.

unsecured loan a loan that is not backed by collateral or security.

useful life the period of time a property is expected to have economic utility.

usury the practice of charging interest at a rate higher than that allowed by law.

▶ V

VA-guaranteed loan a mortgage loan made to a qualified veteran that is guaranteed by the Department of Veterans Affairs.

valid contract an agreement that is legally enforceable and binding on all parties.

valuation estimated worth.

variance permission obtained from zoning authorities to build a structure that is not in complete compliance with current zoning laws. A variance does not permit a nonconforming use of a property.

vendee a buyer.

vendor a seller; the property owner.

village an incorporated minor municipality usually larger than a hamlet and smaller than a town.

voidable contract a contract that appears to be valid but is subject to cancellation by one or both of the parties.

void contract a contract that is not legally enforceable; the absence of a valid contract.

▶ W

waiver the surrender of a known right or claim.

warranty deed a deed in which the grantor fully warrants a good clear title to the property.

waste the improper use of a property by a party with the right to possession, such as the holder of a life estate.

will a written document that directs the distribution of a deceased person's property, real and personal.

wraparound mortgage a mortgage that includes the remaining balance on an existing first mortgage plus an additional amount. Full payments on both mortgages are made to the wraparound mortgagee who then forwards the payments on the first mortgage to the first mortgagee.

writ of execution a court order to the sheriff or other officer to sell the property of a debtor to satisfy a previously rendered judgment.

▶ Z

zone an area reserved by authorities for specific use that is subject to certain restrictions.

zoning ordinance the exercise of regulating and controlling the use of a property in a municipality.

7 ▶ Connecticut Real Estate Sales Exam 2

CHAPTER SUMMARY

This is the second of the four practice tests in this book. Because you have taken one practice test already, you should feel more confident with your test-taking skills. Use this test to see how knowing what to expect can make you feel better prepared.

L IKE THE FIRST exam in this book, this test is based on the Connecticut Real Estate Sales Exam. If you are following the advice in this book, you have done some studying between the first exam and this one. This second exam will give you a chance to see how much you've improved. The answer sheet follows this page, and the test is followed by the answer key and explanations.

► Connecticut Real Estate Sales Exam 2 Answer Sheet

1.	ⓐ	ⓑ	ⓒ	ⓓ
2.	ⓐ	ⓑ	ⓒ	ⓓ
3.	ⓐ	ⓑ	ⓒ	ⓓ
4.	ⓐ	ⓑ	ⓒ	ⓓ
5.	ⓐ	ⓑ	ⓒ	ⓓ
6.	ⓐ	ⓑ	ⓒ	ⓓ
7.	ⓐ	ⓑ	ⓒ	ⓓ
8.	ⓐ	ⓑ	ⓒ	ⓓ
9.	ⓐ	ⓑ	ⓒ	ⓓ
10.	ⓐ	ⓑ	ⓒ	ⓓ
11.	ⓐ	ⓑ	ⓒ	ⓓ
12.	ⓐ	ⓑ	ⓒ	ⓓ
13.	ⓐ	ⓑ	ⓒ	ⓓ
14.	ⓐ	ⓑ	ⓒ	ⓓ
15.	ⓐ	ⓑ	ⓒ	ⓓ
16.	ⓐ	ⓑ	ⓒ	ⓓ
17.	ⓐ	ⓑ	ⓒ	ⓓ
18.	ⓐ	ⓑ	ⓒ	ⓓ
19.	ⓐ	ⓑ	ⓒ	ⓓ
20.	ⓐ	ⓑ	ⓒ	ⓓ
21.	ⓐ	ⓑ	ⓒ	ⓓ
22.	ⓐ	ⓑ	ⓒ	ⓓ
23.	ⓐ	ⓑ	ⓒ	ⓓ
24.	ⓐ	ⓑ	ⓒ	ⓓ
25.	ⓐ	ⓑ	ⓒ	ⓓ
26.	ⓐ	ⓑ	ⓒ	ⓓ
27.	ⓐ	ⓑ	ⓒ	ⓓ
28.	ⓐ	ⓑ	ⓒ	ⓓ
29.	ⓐ	ⓑ	ⓒ	ⓓ
30.	ⓐ	ⓑ	ⓒ	ⓓ
31.	ⓐ	ⓑ	ⓒ	ⓓ
32.	ⓐ	ⓑ	ⓒ	ⓓ
33.	ⓐ	ⓑ	ⓒ	ⓓ
34.	ⓐ	ⓑ	ⓒ	ⓓ
35.	ⓐ	ⓑ	ⓒ	ⓓ
36.	ⓐ	ⓑ	ⓒ	ⓓ
37.	ⓐ	ⓑ	ⓒ	ⓓ

38.	ⓐ	ⓑ	ⓒ	ⓓ
39.	ⓐ	ⓑ	ⓒ	ⓓ
40.	ⓐ	ⓑ	ⓒ	ⓓ
41.	ⓐ	ⓑ	ⓒ	ⓓ
42.	ⓐ	ⓑ	ⓒ	ⓓ
43.	ⓐ	ⓑ	ⓒ	ⓓ
44.	ⓐ	ⓑ	ⓒ	ⓓ
45.	ⓐ	ⓑ	ⓒ	ⓓ
46.	ⓐ	ⓑ	ⓒ	ⓓ
47.	ⓐ	ⓑ	ⓒ	ⓓ
48.	ⓐ	ⓑ	ⓒ	ⓓ
49.	ⓐ	ⓑ	ⓒ	ⓓ
50.	ⓐ	ⓑ	ⓒ	ⓓ
51.	ⓐ	ⓑ	ⓒ	ⓓ
52.	ⓐ	ⓑ	ⓒ	ⓓ
53.	ⓐ	ⓑ	ⓒ	ⓓ
54.	ⓐ	ⓑ	ⓒ	ⓓ
55.	ⓐ	ⓑ	ⓒ	ⓓ
56.	ⓐ	ⓑ	ⓒ	ⓓ
57.	ⓐ	ⓑ	ⓒ	ⓓ
58.	ⓐ	ⓑ	ⓒ	ⓓ
59.	ⓐ	ⓑ	ⓒ	ⓓ
60.	ⓐ	ⓑ	ⓒ	ⓓ
61.	ⓐ	ⓑ	ⓒ	ⓓ
62.	ⓐ	ⓑ	ⓒ	ⓓ
63.	ⓐ	ⓑ	ⓒ	ⓓ
64.	ⓐ	ⓑ	ⓒ	ⓓ
65.	ⓐ	ⓑ	ⓒ	ⓓ
66.	ⓐ	ⓑ	ⓒ	ⓓ
67.	ⓐ	ⓑ	ⓒ	ⓓ
68.	ⓐ	ⓑ	ⓒ	ⓓ
69.	ⓐ	ⓑ	ⓒ	ⓓ
70.	ⓐ	ⓑ	ⓒ	ⓓ
71.	ⓐ	ⓑ	ⓒ	ⓓ
72.	ⓐ	ⓑ	ⓒ	ⓓ
73.	ⓐ	ⓑ	ⓒ	ⓓ
74.	ⓐ	ⓑ	ⓒ	ⓓ

75.	ⓐ	ⓑ	ⓒ	ⓓ
76.	ⓐ	ⓑ	ⓒ	ⓓ
77.	ⓐ	ⓑ	ⓒ	ⓓ
78.	ⓐ	ⓑ	ⓒ	ⓓ
79.	ⓐ	ⓑ	ⓒ	ⓓ
80.	ⓐ	ⓑ	ⓒ	ⓓ
81.	ⓐ	ⓑ	ⓒ	ⓓ
82.	ⓐ	ⓑ	ⓒ	ⓓ
83.	ⓐ	ⓑ	ⓒ	ⓓ
84.	ⓐ	ⓑ	ⓒ	ⓓ
85.	ⓐ	ⓑ	ⓒ	ⓓ
86.	ⓐ	ⓑ	ⓒ	ⓓ
87.	ⓐ	ⓑ	ⓒ	ⓓ
88.	ⓐ	ⓑ	ⓒ	ⓓ
89.	ⓐ	ⓑ	ⓒ	ⓓ
90.	ⓐ	ⓑ	ⓒ	ⓓ
91.	ⓐ	ⓑ	ⓒ	ⓓ
92.	ⓐ	ⓑ	ⓒ	ⓓ
93.	ⓐ	ⓑ	ⓒ	ⓓ
94.	ⓐ	ⓑ	ⓒ	ⓓ
95.	ⓐ	ⓑ	ⓒ	ⓓ
96.	ⓐ	ⓑ	ⓒ	ⓓ
97.	ⓐ	ⓑ	ⓒ	ⓓ
98.	ⓐ	ⓑ	ⓒ	ⓓ
99.	ⓐ	ⓑ	ⓒ	ⓓ
100.	ⓐ	ⓑ	ⓒ	ⓓ
101.	ⓐ	ⓑ	ⓒ	ⓓ
102.	ⓐ	ⓑ	ⓒ	ⓓ
103.	ⓐ	ⓑ	ⓒ	ⓓ
104.	ⓐ	ⓑ	ⓒ	ⓓ
105.	ⓐ	ⓑ	ⓒ	ⓓ
106.	ⓐ	ⓑ	ⓒ	ⓓ
107.	ⓐ	ⓑ	ⓒ	ⓓ
108.	ⓐ	ⓑ	ⓒ	ⓓ
109.	ⓐ	ⓑ	ⓒ	ⓓ
110.	ⓐ	ⓑ	ⓒ	ⓓ

▶ Connecticut Real Estate Sales Exam 2

1. The period of time over which an asset is expected to remain economically viable is called
   a. salvage value.
   b. cost basis.
   c. useful life.
   d. accelerated life.

2. A listing in which an owner instructs an agent NOT to sell to a woman would be classified as
   a. an easement.
   b. illegal.
   c. avulsion.
   d. demise.

3. All new residential construction in Connecticut must have
   a. a water filtration system.
   b. fire detectors.
   c. radon mitigation systems.
   d. carbon monoxide detectors.

4. The equity in a property valued at $450,000 and owned free and clear would be
   a. $0
   b. $250,000
   c. $450,000
   d. none of the above

5. The term *cloud on the title* means
   a. the title is free and clear.
   b. the seller must pay the broker's commission.
   c. the title is encumbered.
   d. a title search does not have to be done.

6. Which of the following is NOT considered an element of value?
   a. comparison
   b. utility
   c. scarcity
   d. demand

7. Qualifying the buyer for a mortgage is the job of the
   a. broker.
   b. principal.
   c. mortgagor.
   d. mortgagee.

8. In Connecticut, the real estate tax is essentially a(n)
   a. *ad hoc* tax.
   b. state tax.
   c. *ad valorem* tax.
   d. title lien.

9. Broker Tom received an offer of $195,000 on a property listed with him for $200,000. Before he has a chance to present the offer to the seller, he receives a second offer for $202,000. What must Broker Tom do?
   a. Call the first buyer and reject the offer of $195,000.
   b. Present only the highest offer.
   c. Present both offers.
   d. Go back to both buyers and tell them to bring in their highest and best offers.

10. In order for a deed to be recorded in Connecticut, it must
   a. be signed by the mortgagor.
   b. be signed by the grantor and acknowledged.
   c. be signed by the grantee and acknowledged.
   d. both **b** and **c**

11. A mortgage in which the seller will deliver a deed upon receipt of the final is known as a(n)
   a. purchase money mortgage.
   b. secondary mortgage.
   c. land contract.
   d. equity mortgage.

12. What is the purpose of a closing statement?
   a. to show the title search
   b. to record the financial obligations of the buyer and seller
   c. to show the liabilities of the lessee
   d. none of the above

13. If a landlord failed to provide water and the tenants moved out for their own protection, this would be considered
   a. constructive eviction.
   b. actual eviction.
   c. eminent domain.
   d. illegal.

14. If a large manufacturing company was allowed to construct a new plant near a new subdivision, the depreciation for the subdivision would be considered
   a. substitution.
   b. physical.
   c. functional.
   d. economic.

15. Janet, a Connecticut salesperson, advertised a property in the paper. She included her name, her office address, and her phone number. What required piece of information was missing?
   a. her service area
   b. her areas of specialty
   c. her experience
   d. her broker's and agency's names

16. Regardless of who sells the house during the listing period, the broker will get paid. This type of listing agreement is called a(n)
   a. open listing.
   b. exclusive agency listing.
   c. exclusive right to sell listing.
   d. net listing.

17. Mary is eager to sell her house quickly and asks her listing agent to offer a bonus to the agent who sells the house. What should the listing agent tell her?
   a. "That's great! It will sell much faster."
   b. "No, it's illegal to offer a bonus."
   c. "We can only offer a bonus to the selling agency; agents can only collect a bonus from their broker."
   d. "I don't think it is a good idea."

18. The buyer of a cooperative receives shares of stock in the corporation and a
   a. proprietary lease.
   b. bargain and sale deed.
   c. warranty deed.
   d. quitclaim deed.

19. While the objective in the cost approach is to estimate the value of both land and improvements, the land is typically appraised using the
   a. income approach.
   b. gross rent multiplier approach.
   c. market data approach.
   d. option approach.

20. In Connecticut, real estate commissions or fees are
   a. set by the Real Estate Commission.
   b. negotiated between the client and the agency.
   c. determined by the MLS.
   d. set by law.

21. Sam decides to send an e-mail to all of the families of his son's Little League team telling them about his new listing. In this e-mail, he is legally required to include
   a. the name of his broker.
   b. the last date on which the information was updated.
   c. the list price of the property.
   d. This form of simple advertising has no requirements.

22. Martha has entered into an exclusive agency listing. She
   a. is guaranteed a commission if the property sells during the term of her listing.
   b. must agree to split the commission 50/50 with other agents.
   c. has to put the listing on the MLS.
   d. is required by law to make a diligent effort to sell the property.

23. In Connecticut, a buyer agency contract
   a. must be on the required form.
   b. must be in writing to be legal and enforceable.
   c. is required whenever an agent works with a buyer.
   d. can't require the buyer to pay the commission.

24. Mary wants to look at a house listed with Acme Realty, but she does not want to sign a buyer agency agreement. Joan, an agent with Acme Realty, can show her the property if
   a. Mary verbally agrees to a buyer agency relationship.
   b. the seller gives written permission.
   c. Joan gives Mary a Disclosure for Unrepresented Persons stating that she works for the seller.
   d. Mary signs a Consent to Dual Agency.

25. The economic characteristics of land that affect value include
   a. construction and labor costs.
   b. proximity to landfills.
   c. relative scarcity, improvements, and area preference.
   d. eminent domain.

26. When an appraiser has completed all three appraisal approaches, the appraiser then
   a. summarizes them.
   b. compares them.
   c. reconciles them.
   d. assesses them.

27. In an FHA mortgage, if the appraised value is less than the selling price, the borrower must
   a. pay the difference in cash.
   b. cancel the loan.
   c. apply for a new loan.
   d. obtain a second mortgage.

28. A second mortgage can be obtained from all of the following EXCEPT
   a. the sellers.
   b. the buyer's aunt.
   c. another bank.
   d. Fannie Mae.

29. In a property tax sale in Connecticut, which of the following is true?
   a. The owner retains title to the property.
   b. The purchaser has a six-month right of redemption.
   c. If the seller was in residence at the time of the foreclosure, he or she has a six-month statutory right of redemption.
   d. There is no right of redemption.

30. The earnest money deposit in the settlement statement is
   a. not shown.
   b. debited to the buyer.
   c. an expense for the seller.
   d. credited to the buyer.

31. Which of the following happens at the closing?
   a. The buyer and seller sign the deed.
   b. The deed is executed and delivered by the seller.
   c. The deed is recorded.
   d. The broker must be present.

32. The maximum amount of money in the Real Estate Guaranty Fund at any one time can NOT exceed
   a. $250,000
   b. $500,000
   c. $750,000
   d. $1,000,000

33. If Mr. and Mrs. Smith, the sellers, signed a purchase and sale agreement with Mr. and Mrs. Jones, and then for no apparent reason refused to go through with the transaction, the buyers could sue for
   a. adverse possession.
   b. an adverse easement.
   c. dower and curtesy.
   d. specific performance.

34. When a principal hires an agent to work on the principal's behalf, this creates
   a. an agency.
   b. a fiduciary relationship.
   c. an obligation of faith and loyalty for both parties.
   d. all of the above

35. The agent who produces a ready, willing, and able buyer is known as the
   a. fiduciary.
   b. procuring cause.
   c. buyer's agent.
   d. none of the above

36. The seller tells the agent that the seller wants to net $300,000. The agent can keep anything over that amount. In Connecticut, that would be
   a. an exclusive listing.
   b. illegal.
   c. advantageous to the seller.
   d. advantageous to the agent.

37. All Connecticut real estate salespersons' licenses
   a. are granted in perpetuity.
   b. do not need to be renewed unless previously revoked.
   c. expire annually on March 31.
   d. expire annually on May 31.

38. To renew a Connecticut license in even-numbered years, a salesperson or broker must
   a. have completed 12 hours of continuing education.
   b. pay a fee of $300.
   c. be active in the real estate business.
   d. all of the above

39. A person must have a real estate license in Connecticut if that person is
   a. selling a house.
   b. buying a house for investment.
   c. engaging in the real estate business.
   d. constructing houses.

40. Engaging in the real estate business means that for another person and for a fee or other valuable compensation, a person
   a. assists in the purchase of real estate.
   b. assists in the rental of real estate.
   c. assists in the exchange of real estate.
   d. all of the above

41. An asphalt company gives a property owner an estimated cost of $15 per cubic foot to install a driveway that is 40 feet long by 20 feet wide with a thickness of 3 inches of asphalt over the driveway. What would be the cost to install the driveway?
   a. $1,200
   b. $1,500
   c. $3,000
   d. $18,000

42. In order to practice real estate in Connecticut, all salespersons must
   a. be affiliated with a broker.
   b. join a multiple-listing service.
   c. become a REALTOR®.
   d. obtain an appraiser's license.

43. A property owner's rights to sell, lease, encumber, use, enjoy, and exclude would be described as a
   a. fee simple.
   b. bundle of rights.
   c. devise.
   d. littoral.

44. Luis Mendez rented a building for the purpose of having a Mexican restaurant. He installed booths in the space for his patrons to sit in. These booths would be considered
   a. fixtures.
   b. real property.
   c. *cosas nutrales*.
   d. trade fixtures.

45. John and Mary Smith are selling their home. The buyers, who have two children under the age of six, had the property tested for lead and the inspector found defective lead paint. John and Mary have a four-year-old daughter. Under these circumstances,
   a. the inspector must report his or her findings to the Connecticut Department of Public Health.
   b. the inspector need only report to the buyers who hired him or her.
   c. the sellers must remediate the lead paint before the home can be legally sold.
   d. the buyers would be prohibited from going ahead with the purchase because of the risk to their children.

46. Janet inherits a home from her parents by will. This is an example of a(n)
   a. escheat.
   b. devise.
   c. demise.
   d. life estate.

47. Jesse, John's tenant, was arrested for getting into a fight at a local bar. John wants to end the tenancy. What can John do?
   a. He can remove Jesse's belongings and change the locks.
   b. He can stop providing services.
   c. He can serve Jesse with a 30-Day Notice to Quit.
   d. He can ask Jesse to leave, but Jesse can refuse.

48. If a married man willed all of his property to his children with nothing to his wife, upon his death, what rights would his wife have if they lived in Connecticut?
   a. none
   b. curtesy
   c. dower
   d. a statutory right to a life estate equal to one-third of his property

49. You have been asked to determine the value of a three-family house. What do you need to know in order to determine the value?
   a. net operating income and capitalization rates
   b. sale prices of nearby homes
   c. property assessment
   d. the current mortgage payments

50. ABC Realty represents both buyer and seller in the same transaction and they have agreed to designated agency. John has been designated to represent the buyers and Mary is representing the sellers. In this situation,
   a. ABC Realty is in violation of Connecticut law.
   b. all of the agents of ABC Realty are dual agents.
   c. all of the agents of ABC Realty are dual agents except for John and Mary, who each represent their respective clients as single agents.
   d. John and Mary cannot advise their clients about negotiation.

51. Under Connecticut law, a partnership or association would be granted a real estate license only if
   a. the broker of record has a current license.
   b. at least 51% of the owners hold a broker's license.
   c. all papers are filed with and approved by the Secretary of State.
   d. the brokerage business agrees to pay an annual fee to the Real Estate Guaranty Fund.

52. Janet, an agent with XYZ Realty, wants to represent buyers who are looking for homes in her area. She wants to be able to show them all of the properties currently available. In order to do this, Connecticut law requires that she enter into a(n)
   a. oral agency agreement with the buyers.
   b. written agency agreement with the buyers.
   c. dual agency agreement with the buyers.
   d. co-brokerage agreement.

53. Alice has been designated by her firm to represent the buyers in a transaction in which her company works for both the buyers and sellers. As a designated agent, Alice
   a. cannot advise her clients about an offering price.
   b. has to be fair to both the buyers and the sellers.
   c. can tell the buyers anything she learned about the sellers after she was appointed as the buyers' designated agent.
   d. is not allowed to talk to the seller's agent.

54. A person bought a house with an agreement that he or she could not keep commercial vehicles on the property. This is an example of
   a. restrictive covenant.
   b. a discriminatory agreement.
   c. a dominant estate.
   d. a serviant estate.

55. Bob has a listing with Hal Seller. Betty Buyer hires Bob as a buyer agent to help her find a home. Betty decides to make an offer on Hal's property. What should Bob do?
   a. He can be a designated agent for one of his clients and have someone else in the firm be the designated agent for the other.
   b. He can be a dual agent.
   c. He can't represent either party because of his conflict of interest.
   d. Either **a** or **b** is possible with the client's agreement.

56. Juan, who is looking for a home to buy, signs a six-month exclusive right to represent buyer agency agreement with Lucy. Two weeks later, Juan finds a for sale by owner that he really likes and he buys it with no help from Lucy. Based on these facts, which of the following is true?
   a. Juan automatically owes Lucy a commission.
   b. Juan owes Lucy a commission only if his buyer representation agreement specifically said that Juan would pay Lucy's fee.
   c. Lucy can't collect a commission under any circumstances because she wasn't the "procuring cause of sale."
   d. Lucy has violated Connecticut license law.

57. Fred is hosting an open house and Barbara shows up to see the property. She tells Fred that she has been working with Brenda and has signed a buyer agreement with her, but doesn't really like or trust her. After Barbara sees the property, she tells Fred that she wants to make an offer and doesn't want Brenda to know. What should Fred do?
   a. Take the offer because that is in the seller's best interest and tell Brenda about it later.
   b. Refuse to take the offer.
   c. Take the offer and not worry about Barbara's relationship with Brenda.
   d. Tell Barbara how to get out of her agreement with Brenda.

58. The Connecticut property condition disclosure
   a. should be completed by the seller.
   b. should be completed by the listing agent.
   c. is optional, not mandatory.
   d. is necessary only for properties valued in excess of $500,000.

59. Happy Acres subdivision has a deed restriction that prohibits owners from having more than two dogs. Gretchen discovers that her neighbor Ethel has four dogs and they all bark at night. Ethel refuses to do anything about it. In order to enforce the deed restriction, Gretchen should
   a. call the police.
   b. file a report with the local zoning commission.
   c. hire an attorney and file an injunction against Ethel.
   d. call the animal control office.

60. Gertrude is taking a listing in January. The sellers tell her that part of the reason that they are selling is that during the summer, the lights and noise from the baseball fields next door are very unpleasant. In this situation, Gertrude should
   a. try to get the property closed before the baseball season starts.
   b. keep quiet about the problem because it isn't caused by anything on the property that is for sale.
   c. be sure that any prospective buyers know about the situation before they make an offer.
   d. none of the above

61. Harry is a buyer's agent and knows that it is very important to the buyers that they are able to pasture their four horses at the home they buy. The buyers really like one listing in particular and want to make an offer. Harry should
   a. check with the town officials to verify that they can have four horses on the property.
   b. suggest that the buyers check with the town officials to verify that they can have the horses.
   c. not worry about the horses because they can always get a variance if they need it.
   d. none of the above

62. In the state of Connecticut, the seller pays
   a. a local conveyance tax.
   b. a local conveyance tax and a state conveyance tax.
   c. a local conveyance tax, a state conveyance tax, and a federal conveyance tax.
   d. Conveyance taxes are paid by the buyer.

63. Sonya recently purchased a home and has discovered that there is an underground oil tank that the sellers never disclosed. Which of the following is NOT true about her situation?
   a. Sonya may be liable for cleanup costs if the tank leaks.
   b. Sonya may be required to remove the tank if she tries to sell the property.
   c. Sonya would have to disclose the presence of the tank if she tries to sell the property.
   d. Sonya can rescind the purchase of the property and get her money back.

64. The Smith to Jones closing is taking place today. All of the closing statements and prorations will have been calculated by the
   a. selling broker.
   b. buyer's agent.
   c. attorneys.
   d. mortgage lender.

65. Mary represents the Adams family and the Gable family, who are both interested in buying the same house. Before putting together his offer, Mr. Adams asks Mary what the Clarks are offering for the property. When is Mary allowed to tell Mr. Adams about the Clarks' offer?
   a. never
   b. after one of the offers is accepted
   c. after the mortgage commitment is received
   d. after the deed is recorded

66. Alfred is buying a house and asks his real estate agent to put the words *time is of the essence* into the purchase and sale agreement. This means that
    a. it would be a good idea to do everything on time.
    b. time frames don't matter with regard to this contract.
    c. this is a meaningless phrase and has no affect on the contract.
    d. with regard to this contract, everything must be done within the stated time frames.

67. Wear and tear on the property is an example of
    a. physical depreciation.
    b. functional obsolescence.
    c. environmental depreciation.
    d. neighborhood depreciation.

68. Effective gross income is
    a. gross income less the debt service.
    b. gross income less vacancy and credit losses.
    c. gross income less operating expenses.
    d. the same thing as cash flow.

69. Mark had a listing on the Smith property and it expired. Now, Mark has buyers who are interested in making an offer on the Smith property. Mark
    a. is a dual agent.
    b. can tell his buyers everything he knows about the property, including previous offers and the Smiths' motivation for selling.
    c. can tell his buyers any material facts he knows about the property, but nothing about the Smiths' finances or motivation.
    d. should turn the buyers over to another agent who has no relationship with the Smiths.

70. Alison has buyer clients who have just had their offer to purchase accepted by the sellers. They ask Alison who they should use for a home inspector. Alison should
    a. recommend her cousin who is a builder because he won't blow the sale by scaring the buyers.
    b. give them the names of three or more home inspectors who are licensed in Connecticut.
    c. suggest that they look in the yellow pages.
    d. save her clients some money by explaining that the house is only two years old, so they don't really need an inspection.

71. Anthony is going out on a listing presentation. The first thing he should do when he gets to the home is
    a. give the sellers a copy of his resume.
    b. have the sellers fill out the Connecticut property condition disclosure.
    c. show the sellers his market analysis.
    d. discuss agency with the sellers and explain that he doesn't represent them.

72. In order to be a subagent in Connecticut, you must get written permission from
    a. the seller.
    b. the listing agent.
    c. the Real Estate Commission.
    d. both **a** and **b**

73. Connecticut allows all types of agency relationships EXCEPT
    a. facilitators.
    b. buyer agents.
    c. dual agents.
    d. designated agents.

74. The buyer's agent should give the buyers a copy of the property condition disclosure
  a. when the property is first shown.
  b. before an offer is made.
  c. as soon as the offer is accepted.
  d. at the time of the home inspection.

75. In Connecticut, a buyer who wants to make an offer on a property should
  a. make a verbal offer.
  b. fill out a binder.
  c. execute a contract of sale.
  d. It could be any of the above, as practices vary throughout the state.

76. In Connecticut, a listing agreement must have all of the following EXCEPT
  a. a fixed expiration date.
  b. a description of the property being listed.
  c. the exact amount of the commission.
  d. a renewal clause.

77. The property condition disclosure is
  a. the seller's knowledge about the property.
  b. a written guarantee by the seller about the condition of the property.
  c. good to have, but not required.
  d. something the listing agent should fill out to the best of his or her ability.

78. A real estate broker takes a listing on a property where a violent murder took place. The agent
  a. must disclose the information about the murder to all prospective buyers.
  b. is prohibited from disclosing any information about the murder to buyers.
  c. shouldn't have taken the listing.
  d. should pass a request for information from a *bona fide* buyer about the murder on to the seller who can respond to the request or not.

79. All of the following are exempt from the property condition disclosure law EXCEPT
  a. new construction.
  b. foreclosures.
  c. a three-family building.
  d. a property gifted to a relative.

80. Ralph bought a house in June. In October, when he went to use the furnace for the first time, he found that it didn't work. Under these circumstances,
  a. he can force the sellers to pay for replacing the furnace.
  b. he can force the real estate agents to replace the furnace.
  c. he can do nothing unless he can prove that fraud was committed.
  d. he can recover the cost from the Real Estate Guaranty Fund.

81. Connie, an agent in Connecticut, has listed a property for sale on the MLS. Allen, who is an agent from a different firm, has a potential buyer for Connie's listing. Typically, Allen would be a
  a. subagent.
  b. buyer's agent.
  c. designated agent.
  d. facilitator.

82. Happy Homes Realty represents both the buyer and the seller in the same transaction. As the offer is being presented, the seller announces that she won't participate in dual or designated agency. Happy Homes Realty

    a. should inform the seller that she has no choice because she signed the dual agency disclosure when they took the listing.

    b. should inform the seller that she will owe a commission anyway.

    c. can't represent both sides unless they both agree in writing, so Happy Homes Realty will have to give up the buyer or the seller.

    d. is required to report the incident to the Real Estate Commission.

83. The listing broker must give an agency disclosure to

    a. the seller after the listing is signed.

    b. all buyers who view the property.

    c. any buyer who makes an offer on the property.

    d. an unrepresented buyer who wants to work through the listing broker.

84. Harold has listed a house for sale. He gets a phone call from Tony who wants to see the property. What should Harold do?

    a. Harold must have Tony sign a buyer representation agreement before showing the property.

    b. Harold can show the property, and if Tony is interested in making an offer, then Tony must sign a buyer representation agreement.

    c. Harold must have a conversation about agency with Tony before showing the property so that Tony can decide how they will work together regarding agency.

    d. Harold can't work with Tony because Harold already represents the seller.

85. In Connecticut, real estate commissions

    a. are negotiable between the agent and the client.

    b. are always between 3–7%.

    c. are established by the local associations of REALTORS®.

    d. are reviewed every six months by the Real Estate Commission.

86. The office administrator for a Connecticut real estate company coordinates the flow of documents, maintains the escrow account, prepares advertising copy, and supervises other clerical personnel. The administrator does not have a real estate license. Which of the following is true?

    a. She is in violation of Connecticut license law.

    b. She must have a broker's license to handle the escrow account.

    c. She must have at least a salesperson's license to do the job.

    d. She does not need a license to perform administrative duties.

87. In Connecticut, applications for a real estate license must

    a. be in writing.

    b. be completed before taking the real estate course.

    c. contain a photo of the applicant.

    d. include three sworn statements attesting to the character of the applicant.

88. Members of the Connecticut Real Estate Commission

    a. are elected.

    b. are appointed by the governor.

    c. are appointed by the attorney general.

    d. are full-time employees of the state.

89. Mary is applying to the state of Connecticut for a real estate license. She will have to prove
   a. that she is at least 21 years of age.
   b. that she has never been convicted of a felony.
   c. that she has completed the required licensing course.
   d. that she has successfully completed two years of college or the equivalent.

90. All Connecticut brokers' licenses expire on
   a. December 31 of every year.
   b. December 31 in even-numbered years.
   c. June 1 each year.
   d. March 31 each year.

91. In Connecticut, a real estate assistant without a license may do all of the following EXCEPT
   a. maintain transaction files.
   b. write real estate ads.
   c. explain simple contracts to clients.
   d. prepare flyers for an open house.

92. What continuing education requirements must be met by a salesperson?
   a. three hours of law/fair housing every year and nine hours of other approved courses
   b. three hours of law/fair housing every two years and nine hours of other approved courses
   c. 12 hours of approved continuing education every two years; the required courses can vary
   d. There are no educational requirements.

93. Mary was in a licensing class and not working in real estate when she started helping her friend Alfonse to sell his home. They found a home and negotiated an accepted offer before Mary passed her real estate exam. When the property closed, Mary had a license and was working as a salesperson for Green Acres Realty. Alfonse refused to pay her a commission because she wasn't licensed when the deal came together. Under these circumstances,
   a. Alfonse is correct.
   b. Mary is entitled to a commission because she had a license when it closed.
   c. Green Acres Realty could get in trouble because Mary was practicing real estate without a license.
   d. Mary is entitled to compensation because she did the job, but she can't call it a commission.

94. Jennifer wants to sell her own home. In Connecticut,
   a. she must have a real estate license to sell her house.
   b. she is required to get a Non-Licensed Seller's Permit from the Real Estate Commission.
   c. she can sell it herself if she hires an attorney to represent her in the negotiation phase of the transaction.
   d. there is no restriction on her selling her own home.

95. In order to activate a Connecticut salesperson's license, a person must have all of the following EXCEPT
   a. completed an approved Principles and Practices of Real Estate course.
   b. passed the state licensing exam.
   c. U.S. citizenship and be a resident of Connecticut.
   d. a sponsoring broker.

96. All Connecticut real estate licenses
a. are granted in perpetuity.
b. must be renewed each year on March 31.
c. must be renewed each year on May 31.
d. must be renewed every year.

97. If a person's license is revoked by the Real Estate Commission, he or she can appeal to
a. the governor.
b. the attorney general.
c. the local Superior Court.
d. the Department of Consumer Protection.

98. If a borrower has a loan with Private Mortgage Insurance and wants to eliminate it, he or she will usually need to pay the loan down to what percent of the property's value?
a. 90%
b. 80%
c. 70%
d. 60%

99. A Connecticut broker has been hired by a Florida developer to sell lots in Florida to Connecticut residents. The broker and developer will need to comply with
a. the dual agency laws.
b. the designated agency laws.
c. the Interstate Land Sales Full Disclosure Act.
d. the Installment Land Sales Contract Act.

100. At the closing, the mortgagee signs
a. the deed.
b. the promissory note.
c. the mortgage.
d. none of the above

101. At the closing, the deed is signed by
a. the grantor.
b. the grantee.
c. both the grantor and the grantee.
d. neither the grantor nor the grantee.

102. In order for a deed to be recorded in Connecticut, it must be
a. seasoned.
b. acknowledged.
c. inducted.
d. warranted.

103. A Connecticut landlord must do all of the following EXCEPT
a. pay interest on security deposits.
b. keep the security deposit in a separate bank account.
c. allow the tenant to use the security deposit for the last month's rent.
d. account for the security deposit within 30 days of the end of the lease.

104. The role of an appraiser is to
a. estimate value.
b. determine value.
c. establish value.
d. none of the above

105. An investor asks you for advice on the best way to take title. In Connecticut, the best advice would be
a. as a sole proprietorship.
b. ownership in trust.
c. a corporation to protect from liability.
d. to suggest that the client consult an attorney.

106. You have been associated with Hillside Realty and have decided to leave and join Green Acres Real Estate. In this circumstance, which of the following is NOT true?
   a. You must promptly give Hillside Realty a list of all your active clients and pending transactions.
   b. Hillside Realty must give you an accounting of how your clients and transactions will be treated.
   c. Green Acres Real Estate cannot contact any of your Hillside clients and solicit their business.
   d. You can take your clients with you when you leave Hillside Realty.

107. A tenant replaces a light fixture with a ceiling fan. The ceiling fan is
   a. the personal property of the tenant.
   b. a fixture belonging to the landlord.
   c. a trade fixture and can be removed by the tenant any time before the expiration of the lease.
   d. a fructus industrials.

108. An investor who is using selling prices and gross income to determine the value of property is most likely using
   a. the capitalization approach.
   b. a gross rent multiplier.
   c. the sales comparison approach.
   d. the cost approach.

109. One of the disadvantages of real estate as an investment is
   a. lack of appreciation.
   b. lack of leverage.
   c. lack of liquidity.
   d. lack of income.

110. In Connecticut, a broker
   a. must pay the client interest on escrow funds.
   b. must put client money in a separate escrow account.
   c. can use escrow money to pay the office rent as long as the money is put back before closing.
   d. must file a quarterly Escrow Funds Report with the Real Estate Commission.

► Answers

1. **c.** The period for which an asset is expected to remain economically viable is called its useful or economic life.

2. **b.** This would violate both Connecticut and federal fair housing laws.

3. **d.** Carbon monoxide detectors are required in all new homes.

4. **c.** The equity is $450,000.

5. **c.** It means that there is something that is wrong with the title.

6. **a.** The elements of value are demand, utility, scarcity, and transferability.

7. **d.** The mortgagee (lender) is responsible for qualifying the purchaser.

8. **c.** Property tax is *ad valorem* (according to value).

9. **c.** The broker must present all offers in a timely manner. The seller decides how to respond to them.

10. **b.** The deed must be signed by the grantor and the signature must be acknowledged.

11. **c.** This is a form of owner financing known as a *land contract* or *contract for deed*.

12. **b.** The closing statement shows the financial obligations of the buyer and seller.

13. **a.** If the landlord fails to maintain basic services, the tenants can move out and claim constructive eviction.

14. **d.** Depreciation that is caused by something off site is called *economic* or *neighborhood* or *environmental depreciation*.

15. **d.** All newspaper advertising must include the name of the broker and/or agency.

16. **c.** With an exclusive right to sell listing, the broker gets compensated regardless of who sells the property.

17. **c.** A salesperson must turn over all compensation he or she receives to the broker.

18. **a.** The buyer of a cooperative does not own real estate. He or she owns shares of stock in the corporation and has a proprietary lease on his or her unit.

19. **c.** The value of the land is usually arrived at using the market approach.

20. **b.** Commissions are not set by law and may be negotiable between the client and the broker.

21. **a.** A real estate salesperson must always include the name of his or her broker in any advertising.

22. **d.** An agent who takes any type of exclusive listing is required to make a diligent effort to market the property.

23. **b.** An agency agreement must be in writing to be enforceable.

24. **c.** An agent can show an in-house listing to an unrepresented buyer as long as he or she presents the buyer with the unrepresented person's disclosure.

25. **c.** In addition to relative scarcity, improvements, and area preference, the economic characteristics of land include permanence of investment.

26. **c.** The appraiser reconciles the three approaches to arrive at a final estimate of value.

27. **a.** The borrower must pay the difference. He or she could take out secondary financing to make that possible.

28. **d.** Fannie Mae does not make loans; it buys them in the secondary market.

29. **c.** A property tax foreclosure is the only type of foreclosure in Connecticut with a statutory right of redemption.

30. **d.** The earnest money is shown as a credit to the buyer.

31. **b.** Only the grantor (seller) signs the deed.

32. **b.** The maximum is $500,000. Anything collected over that amount goes into the General Fund.

33. **d.** A suit for specific performance forces an individual to carry through with his or her promises.

34. **d.** An agency relationship is a fiduciary relationship that calls for both parties to act in good faith and loyalty.

35. **b.** The agent who produces a ready, willing, and able buyer is usually the procuring cause of the sale.

36. **b.** Net listings are illegal in Connecticut.

37. **d.** Salespersons' licenses expire on May 31; brokers' licenses expire on March 31.

38. **a.** Brokers and salespeople must complete 12 hours of continuing education. Brokers pay $300; salespeople pay $225. Neither has to be active in real estate to renew a license.

39. **c.** A person must have a license to engage in the real estate business.

40. **d.** You are practicing real estate if, for a fee and for another person, you perform, offer, or attempt to perform the following activities: listing for sale, selling, exchanging, buying, renting, or collecting rent for the use of real estate or reselling a mobile home.

41. **c.** $40' \times 80' \times .25' = 200$ cubic feet of asphalt
$200 \times \$15 = \$3,000$

42. **a.** A salesperson must be affiliated with a broker in order to practice real estate.

43. **b.** These rights are known as the bundle of rights. A person who owns in fee simple usually, but not always, gets all of them.

44. **d.** Because they are used in a business, they are trade fixtures and can be removed by the tenant any time prior to the expiration of the lease.

45. **a.** The inspector must report to the Department of Public Health because there is a child in the home. The Department of Public Health could order abatement.

46. **b.** A gift of real estate by will is called a *devise*.

47. **d.** Jesse did not break the lease, so it is still binding and John has no legal right to evict him. If John did **a** or **b**, he would be breaking the law.

48. **d.** Connecticut has not recognized dower or curtesy since 1877. We do have a statute that gives a surviving spouse a life estate in the deceased spouse's estate equal to one-third of the value of the real and personal property.

49. **a.** This is an income property, so knowing the net operating income and capitalization rate would allow you to determine value using the income approach.

50. **c.** John and Mary are not dual agents. Everyone else in the firm is a dual agent.

51. **b.** At least 51% of the owners in a partnership or association must be brokers.

52. **b.** In order to be able to show the buyers properties that are not listed with her own firm, Janet must have a written buyer agency agreement.

53. **c.** A designated agent can't reveal any confidential information learned about the other side prior to being designated and must disclose anything learned after designation.

54. **a.** A restrictive covenant is a private agreement between property owners.

55. **d.** Either designated or dual agency is possible with the written agreement of the clients.

56. **b.** In order for Lucy to collect a commission from Juan, the buyer representation agreement would have to have had language that specifically obligated Juan to pay the fee.

57. **b.** Once Fred knows about the agency relationship between Brenda and Barbara, he can do nothing to interfere with it.

58. **a.** The seller should complete the report.

59. **c.** The only way to enforce deed restriction or restrictive covenant is with an injunction.

60. **c.** The problem of the noise and lights is a material fact that should be disclosed to any prospective buyers.

61. **b.** Having the buyers do the checking relieves Harry and his firm from liability if there is a future problem regarding the horses.

62. **b.** Conveyance taxes are collected for the town and the state.

63. **d.** Once the purchase was final, Sonya owned the property and all of its problems. She could consider suing the sellers and/or real estate agents for misrepresentation or fraud.

64. **c.** In Connecticut, the attorneys handle the settlement statements.

65. **d.** This information remains confidential until the deed is recorded and it becomes a matter of public record.

66. **d.** *Time is of the essence* is a very powerful phrase that means everyone must meet the time requirements or be liable for damages.

67. **a.** Wear and tear is physical depreciation.

68. **b.** *Gross income* minus an *allowance for vacancy and credit losses* equals *effective income.*

69. **c.** Mark cannot reveal any confidential information he learned when he was the Smiths' agent.

70. **b.** She should recommend three or more licensed home inspectors.

71. **d.** He needs to let the sellers know that nothing they tell him is confidential.

72. **d.** Both the seller and the listing agent must give written permission to create subagency.

73. **a.** Facilitators or transaction brokerage is not allowed in Connecticut.

74. **b.** The disclosure should be given before an offer is made. It is signed by the buyers and attached to the offer.

75. **d.** There is no one accepted way of making an offer in Connecticut. Practice varies widely across the state.

76. **d.** A renewal clause would be prohibited in Connecticut.

77. **a.** It is the sellers telling what they know. There is no guarantee involved.

78. **d.** Disclosure is not required, but if a *bona fide* buyer makes a request in writing for the information, the agent is required to pass the request along to the seller.

79. **c.** Connecticut General Statutes Section 20–327b requires sellers to give a property condition disclosure report to all prospective purchasers. As stated in the report itself, "These provisions apply to the transfer of residential real property of four dwelling units or less . . ." so a three-family building would NOT be exempt.

80. **c.** Once he owns the property, the problems with it are his.

81. **b.** Typically, when an agent has a buyer for another firm's listing, he or she will act as a buyer's agent.

82. **c.** An agency cannot represent both sides of a transaction without the written consent of both parties.

83. **d.** A disclosure must be given to an unrepresented party.

84. **c.** At the first face-to-face meeting with a potential client, agency must be discussed.

85. **a.** Commissions are set by the agent and the client and may be negotiable.

86. **d.** As long as the administrator is not working directly with clients and customers, no real estate license is needed.

87. **a.** Applications must be written.

88. b. Real estate commissioners are appointed by the governor.

89. c. She must have completed an approved Principles and Practices of Real Estate course approved by the state.

90. d. All brokers' licenses expire March 31.

91. c. Without a license, an assistant cannot interact with clients.

92. c. The required course will vary over time.

93. a. Mary did not have a license and was practicing real estate illegally. No commission is owed.

94. d. You can sell real estate you own with no licensing requirements.

95. c. You do not have to be a citizen of the United States or Connecticut to get a license.

96. d. Licenses are for one year only.

97. c. You can appeal to the local Superior Court.

98. b. PMI is usually required for a loan-to-value ration above 80%.

99. c. They must comply with two laws in this act: federal and Connecticut.

100. d. The mortgagee is the lender and he or she does not sign any of the documents.

101. a. Only the grantor signs the deed.

102. b. A deed must be acknowledged before it can be recorded.

103. c. A landlord does not have to allow the tenant to use the security deposit for rent.

104. a. The appraiser estimates value.

105. d. Advising clients about ownership options would be practicing law. They should be referred to legal counsel.

106. d. Your clients and pending transactions are the property of the agency and cannot be taken with you.

107. b. It is attached to the real estate and belongs to the landlord.

108. b. The gross rent multiplier uses gross rent and sale price to determine value.

109. c. Real estate cannot be converted to cash quickly.

110. b. Client money must be kept in a separate escrow account and cannot be used by the broker for any purpose.

▶ Scoring

Again, evaluate how you did on this practice exam by finding the number of questions you got right, disregarding, for the moment, the ones you got wrong or skipped. If you achieved a score of at least 77 questions correct, you will most likely pass the Connecticut Real Estate Sales Exam.

If you did not score as well as you would like, ask yourself the following: Did I run out of time before I could answer all the questions? Did I go back and change my answers from right to wrong? Did I get flustered and sit staring at a difficult question for what seemed like hours? If you had any of these problems, be sure to go over the LearningExpress Test Preparation System in Chapter 2 to review how best to avoid them.

You probably have seen improvement from your first two practice exam scores and this one; but if you didn't improve as much as you would like, following are some options:

If you scored below the passing score on each section, you should seriously consider whether you are ready for the exam at this time. A good idea would

be to take some brush-up courses in the areas you feel less sure of. If you don't have time for a course, you might try private tutoring.

If you scored close to the minimum passing score, you need to work as hard as you can to improve your skills. Go back to your real estate license course textbooks to review the knowledge you need to do well or use the LearningExpress book, *Practical Math Success in 20 Minutes a Day*. Also, reread and pay close attention to the information in Chapter 4, Real Estate Refresher Course; Chapter 5, Real Estate Math Review; and Chapter 6, Real Estate Glossary. It might be helpful, as well, to ask friends and family to make up mock test questions and quiz you on them.

Now, revise your study schedule according to the time you have left, emphasizing those parts that gave you the most trouble this time. Use the table on page 170 to see where you need more work, so that you can concentrate your preparation efforts. After working more on the subject areas that give you problems, take the third practice exam in Chapter 8 to see how much you have improved.

EXAM 2 FOR REVIEW

Connecticut Real Estate Sales Exam 2 Subject Areas	Question Numbers (Questions 1–110)
Property Ownership and Land Use Controls and Registrations	3, 8, 13, 18, 29, 43, 44, 47, 54, 59, 103, 107
Valuation and Market Analysis	1, 4, 6, 14, 19, 25, 26, 49, 67, 68, 104, 108
Financing	7, 11, 27, 28, 98
Laws of Agency	22, 23, 24, 34, 50, 52, 53, 55, 57, 72, 73, 82
Mandated Disclosures	45, 58, 60, 71, 74, 77, 78, 79, 83
Contracts	33, 66, 75, 76
Transfer of Property	5, 10, 12, 30, 31, 46, 48, 62, 64, 100, 101, 102
Practice of Real Estate	9, 35, 56, 61, 63, 65, 69, 70, 80, 81, 84, 94, 99, 105, 106, 109, 110
License Law/Rules and Regulations	15, 17, 20, 21, 32, 36, 37, 38, 39, 40, 42, 51, 85, 86, 87, 88, 89, 90, 91, 92, 93, 95, 96, 97
Real Estate Math	41
Fair Housing	2

8 ▶ Connecticut Real Estate Sales Exam 3

CHAPTER SUMMARY

This is the third of the four practice tests in this book. Use this test to identify which types of questions are still giving you problems.

YOU ARE NOW MORE familiar with the content and format of the Connecticut Real Estate Sales Exam, and most likely, you feel more confident than you did at first. However, your practice test-taking experience will help you most if you create a situation as close as possible to the real one. For this exam, try to simulate real testing conditions. Find a quiet place where you will not be disturbed. Make sure you have two sharpened pencils and a good eraser. You should have plenty of time to answer all of the questions when you take the real exam, but you will want to practice working quickly without rushing. Be sure to leave enough time to complete the test in one sitting. Remember, you will have four hours for the actual exam. Use a timer or a stopwatch and see if you can work through all the test questions in the allotted time.

As before, the answer sheet you should use is on the next page. Following the exam you will find the answer key and explanations. These explanations, along with the table at the end of this chapter, will help you see where you need further study.

► Connecticut Real Estate Sales Exam 3 Answer Sheet

1.	(a)	(b)	(c)	(d)
2.	(a)	(b)	(c)	(d)
3.	(a)	(b)	(c)	(d)
4.	(a)	(b)	(c)	(d)
5.	(a)	(b)	(c)	(d)
6.	(a)	(b)	(c)	(d)
7.	(a)	(b)	(c)	(d)
8.	(a)	(b)	(c)	(d)
9.	(a)	(b)	(c)	(d)
10.	(a)	(b)	(c)	(d)
11.	(a)	(b)	(c)	(d)
12.	(a)	(b)	(c)	(d)
13.	(a)	(b)	(c)	(d)
14.	(a)	(b)	(c)	(d)
15.	(a)	(b)	(c)	(d)
16.	(a)	(b)	(c)	(d)
17.	(a)	(b)	(c)	(d)
18.	(a)	(b)	(c)	(d)
19.	(a)	(b)	(c)	(d)
20.	(a)	(b)	(c)	(d)
21.	(a)	(b)	(c)	(d)
22.	(a)	(b)	(c)	(d)
23.	(a)	(b)	(c)	(d)
24.	(a)	(b)	(c)	(d)
25.	(a)	(b)	(c)	(d)
26.	(a)	(b)	(c)	(d)
27.	(a)	(b)	(c)	(d)
28.	(a)	(b)	(c)	(d)
29.	(a)	(b)	(c)	(d)
30.	(a)	(b)	(c)	(d)
31.	(a)	(b)	(c)	(d)
32.	(a)	(b)	(c)	(d)
33.	(a)	(b)	(c)	(d)
34.	(a)	(b)	(c)	(d)
35.	(a)	(b)	(c)	(d)
36.	(a)	(b)	(c)	(d)
37.	(a)	(b)	(c)	(d)

38.	(a)	(b)	(c)	(d)
39.	(a)	(b)	(c)	(d)
40.	(a)	(b)	(c)	(d)
41.	(a)	(b)	(c)	(d)
42.	(a)	(b)	(c)	(d)
43.	(a)	(b)	(c)	(d)
44.	(a)	(b)	(c)	(d)
45.	(a)	(b)	(c)	(d)
46.	(a)	(b)	(c)	(d)
47.	(a)	(b)	(c)	(d)
48.	(a)	(b)	(c)	(d)
49.	(a)	(b)	(c)	(d)
50.	(a)	(b)	(c)	(d)
51.	(a)	(b)	(c)	(d)
52.	(a)	(b)	(c)	(d)
53.	(a)	(b)	(c)	(d)
54.	(a)	(b)	(c)	(d)
55.	(a)	(b)	(c)	(d)
56.	(a)	(b)	(c)	(d)
57.	(a)	(b)	(c)	(d)
58.	(a)	(b)	(c)	(d)
59.	(a)	(b)	(c)	(d)
60.	(a)	(b)	(c)	(d)
61.	(a)	(b)	(c)	(d)
62.	(a)	(b)	(c)	(d)
63.	(a)	(b)	(c)	(d)
64.	(a)	(b)	(c)	(d)
65.	(a)	(b)	(c)	(d)
66.	(a)	(b)	(c)	(d)
67.	(a)	(b)	(c)	(d)
68.	(a)	(b)	(c)	(d)
69.	(a)	(b)	(c)	(d)
70.	(a)	(b)	(c)	(d)
71.	(a)	(b)	(c)	(d)
72.	(a)	(b)	(c)	(d)
73.	(a)	(b)	(c)	(d)
74.	(a)	(b)	(c)	(d)

75.	(a)	(b)	(c)	(d)
76.	(a)	(b)	(c)	(d)
77.	(a)	(b)	(c)	(d)
78.	(a)	(b)	(c)	(d)
79.	(a)	(b)	(c)	(d)
80.	(a)	(b)	(c)	(d)
81.	(a)	(b)	(c)	(d)
82.	(a)	(b)	(c)	(d)
83.	(a)	(b)	(c)	(d)
84.	(a)	(b)	(c)	(d)
85.	(a)	(b)	(c)	(d)
86.	(a)	(b)	(c)	(d)
87.	(a)	(b)	(c)	(d)
88.	(a)	(b)	(c)	(d)
89.	(a)	(b)	(c)	(d)
90.	(a)	(b)	(c)	(d)
91.	(a)	(b)	(c)	(d)
92.	(a)	(b)	(c)	(d)
93.	(a)	(b)	(c)	(d)
94.	(a)	(b)	(c)	(d)
95.	(a)	(b)	(c)	(d)
96.	(a)	(b)	(c)	(d)
97.	(a)	(b)	(c)	(d)
98.	(a)	(b)	(c)	(d)
99.	(a)	(b)	(c)	(d)
100.	(a)	(b)	(c)	(d)
101.	(a)	(b)	(c)	(d)
102.	(a)	(b)	(c)	(d)
103.	(a)	(b)	(c)	(d)
104.	(a)	(b)	(c)	(d)
105.	(a)	(b)	(c)	(d)
106.	(a)	(b)	(c)	(d)
107.	(a)	(b)	(c)	(d)
108.	(a)	(b)	(c)	(d)
109.	(a)	(b)	(c)	(d)
110.	(a)	(b)	(c)	(d)

► Connecticut Real Estate Sales Exam 3

1. If a Connecticut broker lies to a lender about the sales price, the
   a. broker has done nothing wrong as long as the appraisal confirms the price.
   b. broker has simply followed the client's instructions and that is legal.
   c. buyer should go along with it because it is in his or her best interest.
   d. broker has broken the law and the buyer could be liable as well.

2. In Connecticut, in order to become a broker, a person must do all of the following EXCEPT
   a. complete 60 hours of Principles and Practices of Real Estate.
   b. take 120 hours of approved classes.
   c. had a salesperson's license for at least two years.
   d. participated in six real estate transactions.

3. If an investment property was purchased for $300,000 and the annual depreciation was $3,000 and the owner owned the property for 12 years, then the book value of the property would be
   a. $300,000
   b. $270,000
   c. $264,000
   d. $ 36,000

4. One of the disadvantages of real estate as an investment is
   a. lack of liquidity.
   b. appreciation.
   c. revocation.
   d. blockbusting.

5. A real estate broker deposits the buyer's earnest money in the real estate firm's business operating account and then uses it to pay the rent. This would be an example of
   a. commingling.
   b. commingling and conversion.
   c. a legal business expenditure.
   d. a legal personal expenditure.

6. A minor signed a two-year lease for an apartment. This would be an example of a(n)
   a. valid contract.
   b. void contract.
   c. voidable contract.
   d. unenforceable contract.

7. The owner of a health-food store in a shopping mall wants you to sell his business. What kind of license do you need in Connecticut?
   a. a salesperson's license
   b. a broker's license
   c. a commercial license
   d. No license is needed.

8. Most appraisals require the use of
   a. one approach.
   b. more than one approach.
   c. the plat.
   d. city planning.

9. The government organization concerned with social and economic needs of the community is the
   a. Planning Commission.
   b. Zoning Commission.
   c. Chamber of Commerce.
   d. Board of Health.

10. What gives a municipal government the authority to regulate and control the use of land for the protection of public health, safety, and the general welfare of its citizens?

   a. environmental protection laws

   b. the master plan

   c. police power

   d. the Board of Registration

11. A gas station is located in an area that never had zoning and now it has been zoned residential. The gas station can continue to operate in the residential zone because of

   a. nonconforming use.

   b. a variance.

   c. a conditional use permit.

   d. cluster zoning.

12. A woman willed her estate as follows: 63% to her husband, 10% to her son, 12% to her daughter, and the remainder to her college. If the college received $30,000, how much did her daughter receive?

   a. $10,000

   b. $15,000

   c. $20,000

   d. $24,000

13. A lease is an estate that

   a. will expire.

   b. has the landlord's consent.

   c. involves a novation.

   d. is intestate.

14. Leading prospective homebuyers to or away from certain neighborhoods because of who lives in those neighborhoods would be considered

   a. redlining.

   b. steering.

   c. a good business practice.

   d. a violation of RESPA.

15. A person buys a property for $500,000 with a 10% down payment and pays two points. The amount of the points would be

   a. $10,000

   b. $9,000

   c. $5,000

   d. $4,500

16. The Federal Housing Administration (FHA)

   a. lends money to banks.

   b. buys mortgages from banks.

   c. insures loans to qualified buyers.

   d. sets the federal discount rate.

17. If a home is 44 feet long and is being built on a lot that has 50 foot setbacks on the sidelines, what frontage must that lot have to build this house?

   a. at least 1,232 square feet

   b. at least 44 feet

   c. at least 94 feet

   d. at least 144 feet

18. A town has a tax rate of 16.5 mils. A property is assessed at a value of $935,980. How much are the annual real estate taxes?

   a. $14,443.67

   b. $24,443.67

   c. $18,998.02

   d. $15,443.67

19. An acre contains approximately
   a. 5,270 square yards.
   b. 40,000 square feet.
   c. 43,560 square feet.
   d. 42,560 square feet.

20. Mary, a Connecticut salesperson, placed an ad in the yellow pages that said "Mary Smith, Real Estate Salesperson, Service Is My Specialty." In her ad, Mary must also include
   a. her real estate license number.
   b. the expiration date of her license.
   c. her street address.
   d. the name of her broker.

21. In order for a broker to put a sign on a property, the broker must first
   a. get the written permission of the owner.
   b. get the written permission of the neighbors.
   c. have a listing on the property.
   d. get the permission of the zoning authority.

22. The agency relationship with a buyer must be discussed and decided
   a. at the first contact.
   b. at the first substantive meeting at which real estate is discussed.
   c. before a purchase and sale agreement is executed.
   d. before the closing.

23. The four government powers that can affect real estate do NOT include
   a. police power.
   b. reconciliation power.
   c. eminent domain.
   d. escheat.

24. Which of the following is an advantage of a biweekly mortgage?
   a. The borrower pays less each month in return for a longer term.
   b. It is the equivalent to 12 monthly payments per year.
   c. The interest rates are lower.
   d. The loan gets paid off faster.

25. A real estate salesperson decides to rent an apartment in his or her home without using a broker. When advertising the apartment, the salesperson
   a. must place the ad in the name of the employing broker.
   b. must disclose the fact that he or she is a licensee.
   c. does not need to do anything different from a private citizen.
   d. none of the above

26. The act of transferring property from one owner to another owner is known as
   a. ownership.
   b. alienation.
   c. subordination.
   d. deeding.

27. Real estate license laws are enacted to
   a. track prospective and existing real estate licensees.
   b. set standards and promote professionalism to protect the public.
   c. stop consumers from collecting referral fees.
   d. create a source of revenue for the state government.

28. If a consumer declines to sign the Disclosure for Unrepresented Persons, then
  a. the agent cannot work with the consumer.
  b. the consumer has agreed to an agency relationship.
  c. the agent should complete the form indicating that it was presented to the consumer.
  d. the agent has done his or her job and can work with the consumer.

29. The U.S. Supreme Court case of *Jones v. Mayer* reaffirmed
  a. the Civil Rights Act of 1866.
  b. Title IX.
  c. the Anti-Discriminatory Acts of 1957.
  d. the Civil Protections Act of 1840.

30. In Connecticut, the commissions charged by agents are
  a. set by law.
  b. set by the Connecticut Real Estate Commission on January 1 of each year.
  c. determined by the local association of REALTORS® for their market areas.
  d. negotiated between the client and the broker.

31. Jonathan had his property taken by eminent domain for the new highway. This would be an example of
  a. an Act of Dedication.
  b. an involuntary transfer.
  c. an Act for the Public Domain.
  d. partitioning of land.

32. Darrell and Wanda bought a house as a principal residence for a cost of $200,000. Six years later, they sold the home for $653,499. The capital gains tax that they owe on the profits of this sale are
  a. $153,499
  b. $215,654.57
  c. $149,654.57
  d. $98,024.85

33. A legally enforceable agreement is called a(n)
  a. nonbinding agreement.
  b. offer.
  c. contract.
  d. voluntary act.

34. An earnest money deposit received by a broker on behalf of a principal must be deposited in the broker's escrow account within
  a. three banking days of obtaining the offer.
  b. three banking days of the last signature going on the contract.
  c. five working days of obtaining the offer.
  d. There is no specific time frame. It must be done within a reasonable time.

35. Commingling of funds refers to
  a. the funds gathered at the closing table.
  b. mixing client money with the broker's own funds.
  c. co-brokering with another firm.
  d. obtaining interest on funds deposited with a bank.

36. Which of the following best describes the functions of mortgage brokers?
  a. They use depositors' money to make mortgage loans.
  b. They make mortgage loans and sell them on the secondary market.
  c. They are intermediaries who bring borrowers and lenders together and take a small fee off the top.
  d. They often keep loans in their own portfolio.

37. Maureen Gromley, a Connecticut broker, received an earnest money deposit check in the amount of $6,500 from a client and she immediately cashed it. At the closing, Maureen gave the seller a personal check for the $6,500 plus interest. Maureen
  a. behaved properly in this instance.
  b. didn't need to pay interest as long as the money went into the proper hands at closing.
  c. should have deposited the money in her escrow account within three banking days of the contract being signed.
  d. should have given the interest to the Connecticut Housing Finance Authority (CHFA).

38. Frederick Brimstone established an interest-bearing escrow account for client funds. When it came time for the closings, Frederick would write a check for the amount of the deposit and keep the interest for himself. Frederick
  a. should have set up the account so that the interest automatically went to the Connecticut Housing Financial Authority.
  b. should have given the interest to the client because it was his or her money that earned it.
  c. should have told the client up front that he was keeping the interest to cover his processing costs.
  d. didn't do anything wrong.

39. An appraisal is an unbiased
  a. determination of value.
  b. professional opinion of value.
  c. written opinion of value.
  d. estimate of market value.

40. All of the following must appear in a listing agreement EXCEPT
  a. the complete legal description of the property.
  b. a fixed expiration date.
  c. the required statement that broker compensation is not fixed by law.
  d. a statement saying that the agreement is subject to Connecticut's fair housing laws.

41. An exclusive seller's agent is an agent who represents
  a. sellers on a client basis and buyers as customers.
  b. both sellers and buyers as clients.
  c. sellers as customers and buyers as clients.
  d. both buyers and sellers as customers.

42. The buyer gives the seller $5,000. The seller signs a document agreeing that the buyer can purchase the property any time between now and July 1 of next year for a price of $375,000. This type of transaction is known as
  a. a lease with option to purchase.
  b. a purchase contract with delayed settlement.
  c. an option.
  d. a limited purchase and sale agreement.

43. Adolf signs a listing agreement with Juan. One of the clauses in the agreement says, "This listing is for six months, and if the property has not closed at the end of that period, the listing will automatically extend for another six months." According to Connecticut statutes, this listing
    a. is illegal.
    b. is legal because the listing is for less than eight months, as required by law.
    c. will continue in full effect until the property closes.
    d. is allowed because it has a specific time limit of six months.

44. Title VIII of the Civil Rights Act of 1968 makes it illegal to discriminate in housing based on
    a. gender, religion, health, and age.
    b. race, color, age, and gender.
    c. race, color, religion, and national origin.
    d. race, color, age, and familial status.

45. The federal law that requires the licensing of appraisers is known as
    a. FIRREA.
    b. USPAP.
    c. MAI.
    d. RESPA.

46. An investor decides to depreciate a residential building over $27\frac{1}{2}$ years. If the value of the property is $750,000 and the ratio of building to land value is 80/20, what is the annual depreciation?
    a. $21,828.18
    b. $20,625
    c. $41,250
    d. $5,454.55

47. The maximum amount of money that can be kept in the Connecticut Real Estate Guaranty Fund is
    a. $250,000
    b. $500,000
    c. $750,000
    d. $1,000,000

48. One of the functions of the DVA is to
    a. make loans.
    b. insure loans.
    c. guarantee loans.
    d. buy loans.

49. The duties a real estate agent owes to a client includes all of the following EXCEPT
    a. obedience to carry out the client's lawful instructions pertaining to real estate.
    b. accountability for all money handled for the client.
    c. loyalty to act in the best interests of the client at all times.
    d. disclosure of everything he or she knows about the transaction.

50. According to Connecticut statutes, an agent who takes a listing is required to
    a. give the seller a copy of the agreement at the time he or she signs it.
    b. create a numbered listing file in compliance with the record-keeping regulations.
    c. place the property on the MLS within 48 hours.
    d. advertise the property in the local newspapers in a timely manner.

51. An agent's false statements about a property are called

   a. duress.

   b. puffery.

   c. reality.

   d. misrepresentation.

52. The Fergussons listed their house for sale with Amy. The listing agreement was for nine months, but at the end of five months, the Fergussons notified Amy that they were terminating the agreement and listing with another agency. Under these circumstances,

   a. the seller has cancelled the agreement and there is nothing Amy can do about it.

   b. the seller has withdrawn the authority to market the property, but the listing contract is still in effect.

   c. the seller is required by law to leave the property on the market until the end of the agreed upon nine months.

   d. the Connecticut Commission will decide the consequences.

53. A closing takes place when

   a. a purchase and sale agreement is signed.

   b. as the final step in the transfer of title.

   c. the real estate agent decides.

   d. a willing buyer meets a willing seller.

54. A person who believes that he or she has been illegally discriminated against may file a complaint with the Connecticut

   a. Association of REALTORS®.

   b. Real Estate Commission.

   c. Consumer Protection Agency.

   d. Commission on Human Rights and Opportunities.

55. The area of a building is usually measured by

   a. length × width = square feet.

   b. length × width × height = cubic feet.

   c. cubic yards.

   d. length × width = square meters.

56. A Connecticut homeowner who has AIDS lists his home for sale. A prospective buyer asks her agent if there is anything she should know about the property. Should the agent disclose the fact that someone with AIDS has lived in the house?

   a. Yes, this is a material fact that should be disclosed.

   b. No, the law says the buyer should do his or her own due diligence.

   c. No, because the agent works for the seller.

   d. No, because it would be a violation of Connecticut and Federal Fair Housing Laws.

57. A 50,000 square foot building has an annual income of $250,000 on a triple net basis. What is the annual rent per square foot?

   a. not enough information is available

   b. $5 per square foot

   c. $2.50 per square foot

   d. $0.20 per square foot

58. The owner of a two-family home in Connecticut is living in one of the units and wants to rent out the other one. The landlord is not using a real estate agent and is looking for a tenant strictly by word of mouth. A person with a disability wants to rent the apartment and will need to install a wheelchair ramp and special hardware in the home. The property owner

   a. must install the ramp and hardware for the tenant.

   b. must rent to the tenant, but can require the tenant to put in the ramp and hardware at his or her own expense and take them out when he or she leaves.

   c. does not have to rent to the tenant.

   d. All rental residences are required to be handicap accessible.

59. A buyer's agent represents

   a. both sellers and buyers on the same property.

   b. a buyer client in a transaction.

   c. the seller, but works with the buyer.

   d. the buyer and is a subagent of the seller.

60. A Connecticut salesperson may legally collect real estate–related compensation from

   a. buyers or sellers.

   b. anybody involved in the transaction.

   c. his or her employing broker only.

   d. a licensed real estate broker only.

61. A Connecticut salesperson may work for more than one broker at the same time if

   a. the office sales manager agrees.

   b. the brokers are in different parts of the state.

   c. the Connecticut Real Estate Commission gives written permission.

   d. the written consent of the brokers being worked for is given.

62. A real estate broker is aware that a brutal murder was committed on the property. Is the broker required to tell a prospective buyer?

   a. No, the broker is not required to disclose the murder because it is a not a material fact.

   b. The broker is prohibited from disclosing the murder because it is not a material fact and is confidential.

   c. The broker must disclose the murder if the buyer puts the request in writing.

   d. It would be a violation of the Fair Housing Act not to disclose the murder.

63. The Consent to Dual Agency should be signed by the buyer

   a. when he or she signs the buyer representation agreement.

   b. when he or she first looks at an "in-house" listing.

   c. before he or she fills out an offer to purchase.

   d. when the offer is accepted.

64. When a real estate firm is representing the buyer and the seller in the same transaction, the company could use

   a. dual agency.

   b. designated agency.

   c. either **a** or **b**

   d. both **a** and **b**

65. Betty's hairdresser friend Mary Lou introduced her to some people who wanted to buy a house. Betty eventually sold the people a house and made a nice commission. When can Betty reward Mary Lou for the referral?
- **a.** never, because Mary Lou doesn't have a license
- **b.** once the purchase and sale agreement is signed
- **c.** after the closing
- **d.** once all of the contingencies in the contract are met

66. The term *comp* refers to
- **a.** operating expense ratios.
- **b.** recent nearby sales similar to the subject property.
- **c.** complimentary information.
- **d.** free services offered by a broker.

67. Loan-to-value ratio refers to the relationship between
- **a.** the former mortgage and the new one.
- **b.** the value of the building and the value minus depreciation.
- **c.** the amount of the loan and the value of the property.
- **d.** the amount of the loan and the value of the land.

68. The broker sells a building for $569,888 with a 5.25% commission fee. The amount of commission due to the broker is
- **a.** $19,219.21
- **b.** $108,550.09
- **c.** $229,191.20
- **d.** $29,919.12

69. A buyer contacts a real estate agent to help the buyer find a home. At the first meeting, the agent is required by law to
- **a.** explain how the agent will be paid for his or her services.
- **b.** disclose any material defects in the property that the buyer called on.
- **c.** discuss agency possibilities and determine how the agent and the buyer will work together.
- **d.** qualify the buyer with regard to financing.

70. Two weeks after the closing, Salesperson Earl receives a thank-you note from his buyers and a check in the amount of $500 made out to him. Earl cashes the check and takes the whole family out for a night on the town. Which of the following is true in this situation?
- **a.** Earl's actions were entirely proper.
- **b.** It is permissible for Earl to keep the money if the broker approves it in writing.
- **c.** Earl should have turned the money over to his broker.
- **d.** As long as the check was sent more than 60 days after the closing, Earl can accept it.

71. When an agent represents both the buyer and the seller in the same transaction without his or her knowledge or permission,
- **a.** it is undisclosed dual agency and illegal in Connecticut.
- **b.** it is undisclosed dual agency and permitted in Connecticut.
- **c.** the agent is a designated agent for both parties and can proceed.
- **d.** the agent is required to use a subagent to make his or her actions legal.

72. Some contracts require performance by only one party and are known as
   a. unilateral contracts.
   b. vicelateral contracts.
   c. monolateral contracts.
   d. sololateral contracts.

73. When an agent in Connecticut leaves one firm to join another, he or she must
   a. give the broker the required "Change of Brokerage" form.
   b. do nothing. The burden of notifying the Connecticut Real Estate Commission is the broker's responsibility.
   c. notify the Connecticut Real Estate Commission of the change and pay a $25 fee.
   d. send his or her license and a letter of termination to the Commission. The agent gets his or her license back when the new broker takes responsibility for the agent.

74. Miriam, a real estate salesperson, is driving through a neighborhood when she see a sign that says "FSBO—Call 555-0000." What does FSBO mean?
   a. for sale by offers
   b. real estate brokers not allowed
   c. for sale by owner
   d. for sale by appointment only

75. Joanna has a lease and pays $1,000 per month, which includes all of her utilities. This is known as a
   a. net lease.
   b. gross lease.
   c. ground lease.
   d. percentage lease.

76. A condominium buyer in Connecticut has the right to cancel the contract and get the deposit back within
   a. five days of signing the contract.
   b. five business days of receiving the resale documents from the seller.
   c. ten days of the seller mailing the resale documents.
   d. It's a contract; the buyer can't cancel it.

77. Willow Realty has an in-house sale and the broker appoints Jan to represent the buyers. Jan is a(n)
   a. designated agent.
   b. dual agent.
   c. facilitator.
   d. assigned agent.

78. The owner of a building tells an agent that he wants to get $500,000 and the broker can keep any money over that amount. The building sells for $575,622. How much is the broker's commission?
   a. $75,622
   b. $7,562.20
   c. 6% of $575,622, or $34,537.32
   d. The broker gets no commission.

79. A lease is an example of a(n)
   a. unilateral contract.
   b. bilateral contract.
   c. unbound contract.
   d. desultory contract.

80. FIRREA pertains to
   a. real estate agency.
   b. executing contracts.
   c. the delegation of government powers.
   d. appraisal.

81. To reduce liability, a property manager would buy a(n)
   a. liability insurance policy.
   b. life insurance policy.
   c. automobile insurance policy.
   d. annuity.

82. A broker sold a building for $973,455 and earned a commission of $34,070.93. What percentage of the sale price did the agent earn?
   a. 5.5%
   b. 6.0%
   c. 2.6%
   d. 3.5%

83. One agent in the firm is an agent for the buyer and another agent in the firm is the agent of the sellers. Does the firm have a potential conflict of interest?
   a. No, as long there are two separate agents involved.
   b. Yes, because the agents and the firm represent both parties in the same transaction.
   c. No, the firm does not represent anyone; it is the individual agent's.
   d. none of the above

84. In Connecticut, what is the legal age of competence?
   a. 18
   b. 19
   c. 20
   d. 21

85. Origination fees are also called
   a. loan fees.
   b. application fees.
   c. broker's fees.
   d. finder's fees.

86. Which of the following is NOT a protected class in Connecticut?
   a. sexual orientation
   b. source of income
   c. credit rating
   d. marital status

87. The usury rate establishes the maximum amount of interest that can be charged to borrow money. In Connecticut, the usury rate on real estate loans is
   a. 20%.
   b. 28%.
   c. 37%.
   d. There is no limit to the interest on real estate loans.

88. In Connecticut, a property manager is allowed to lease vacant space only if
   a. he or she has a real estate license.
   b. he or she has an attorney draw up the lease.
   c. the owner is present during negotiations.
   d. it is specifically permitted in his or her property management agreement.

89. A couple lives in an 1872 house with their four-year-old daughter. They know that there is most likely some lead paint in the house, so they have their daughter tested for lead and the tests show no lead in her system. Are the parents required to take any action with regard to the lead?
   a. They must remove all lead paint because there is a child under six years of age in the home.
   b. They are not required to do anything because the tests showed no lead in the child's blood.
   c. They must abate any surfaces that are defective.
   d. They don't need to do anything at the moment, but the child must be tested every four months.

90. FIRREA was enacted to save the S&Ls. What is an S&L?
  a. service and loans
  b. security and loans
  c. savings and loans
  d. standards and loans

91. A property is 200 feet across the front and back and 150 feet along the side. How many acres is the property?
  a. .688 acres
  b. 6.88 acres
  c. 30 acres
  d. .5 acres

92. Ferris is selling his house and there is an unused underground oil tank next to the house. Given these circumstances, which of the following is true?
  a. State law requires the removal of the tank prior to the sale of the property.
  b. It would be illegal for a real estate agent to list the property for sale with the tank in the ground.
  c. Ferris should just keep quiet about the tank.
  d. Most lenders and/or insurance companies will insist that the tank be removed prior to closing.

93. John, a software engineer, has a neighbor who wants to sell his house. John calls his friend Mazzie, who is a Connecticut broker, and refers his neighbor to her, asking Mazzie to pay him a 10% referral fee for sending her business. The house sells and Mazzie refuses to pay John. Is John entitled to collect the referral?
  a. Yes, as long as the referral was discussed before the listing was taken.
  b. Yes, as long as the neighbor who was referred approves of the fee in writing.

  c. Yes, but only if both he and Mazzie have real estate licenses and the referral fee was agreed to up front.
  d. Referral fees are illegal in Connecticut.

94. In Connecticut, the primary type of foreclosure is
  a. judicial foreclosure and sale.
  b. deed in lieu of foreclosure.
  c. quitclaim foreclosure.
  d. strict foreclosure.

95. In the sale of real estate, the seller is obligated to convey
  a. an environmentally clean site.
  b. a good and marketable title.
  c. personal property.
  d. a leased fee title.

96. A house may have a UST, and in Connecticut, that would require a disclosure by the sellers. What is a UST?
  a. UFFI standard trust
  b. unintended security trauma
  c. underground storage tank
  d. undeveloped single tangibility

97. Harry's property has been foreclosed by Liberty Bank. Harry owed the bank $210,000 and the property appraised for $195,000. The bank will make up the difference by
  a. refinancing the property.
  b. seeking a deficiency judgment.
  c. having Harry arrested and held until he can raise the money.
  d. The bank is stuck with the loss and can do nothing.

98. Which of the following is NOT done by the broker in Connecticut to prepare for the closing?
- **a.** the title search
- **b.** maintaining an accurate and complete file on the transaction
- **c.** explaining the closing process to the client
- **d.** coordinating inspections, appraisals, and document processing

99. A buyer is planning to purchase a house for $425,000 with a 20% down payment. The bank will give a loan for the balance at 7% interest only. What is the monthly payment?
- **a.** $2,827.54
- **b.** $23,800
- **c.** $2,262.03
- **d.** $1,983.33

100. Maurice showed his buyer clients, the O'Brians, a number of buildings, but none of them seemed right. In fact, they never even went inside the properties because there always seemed to be something wrong with the location or appearance. Today, Maurice found out that the O'Brians bought one of the properties that he showed them. Is Maurice entitled to any commission?
- **a.** Yes, if the O'Brians signed an exclusive buyer agency agreement with him and agreed to pay his fee.
- **b.** Yes, because he introduced them to the property.
- **c.** No, because all he did was introduce them to the property. He was not the predominant procuring cause of the sale.
- **d.** No, because his buyer representation agreement had expired.

101. A listing agreement will automatically terminate if
- **a.** the seller changes his or her mind.
- **b.** the seller is adjudicated insane.
- **c.** the seller won't agree to having a sign in the yard.
- **d.** nobody responds to the advertising.

102. Edwin and Roberta each own real estate companies and they are good friends. They often have dinner together, and because of their friendship, they decide not to compete with each other. They agree to charge the same commissions. Is this allowed?
- **a.** Yes, because no other brokers were involved in the agreement.
- **b.** No, because it is a violation of Connecticut License Law and the Sherman Anti-Trust Act.
- **c.** Yes, because it is not a permanent arrangement and the parties could change it at any time.
- **d.** Yes; it is protected by the National Privacy Act because only two parties are involved.

103. Yuan met with his real estate broker over dinner to discuss the purchase of an investment property. Yuan and the broker consumed a considerable amount of wine, and at the end of the meal, they completed a purchase and sale agreement for one of the broker's listings. If the seller accepts the agreement, is it valid?
- **a.** Yes, because Yuan is over the age of 18.
- **b.** No, it is voidable by Yuan because he had had too much to drink and would be considered legally incompetent.
- **c.** No, it is void because it is illegal to drink and sign a contract.
- **d.** Yes, because in spite of the drinks, the parties knew what they were doing.

104. In Connecticut, all residential listing agreements must disclose the presence of
  a. UFFI.
  b. EMF.
  c. radon.
  d. USTs.

105. Appraisal reports must be presented
  a. in writing.
  b. verbally.
  c. with full supporting documentation.
  d. It is up to the client how it is presented.

106. In Connecticut, who pays the property expenses for the day of the closing?
  a. seller
  b. buyer
  c. closing attorney
  d. lender

107. Under Connecticut law, confidential information remains confidential
  a. forever.
  b. until the agency relationship terminates or expires.
  c. for 180 days after the termination of the agency relationship.
  d. until it becomes public or common knowledge or the agent is required to disclose it in a court of law.

108. Elijah is taking a listing and wants to be sure that he will be paid a commission even if the sellers sell it on their own. He should use a(n)
  a. exclusive right to sell.
  b. exclusive agency.
  c. open listing.
  d. net listing.

109. In Connecticut, the most common method of describing property is the
  a. government survey method.
  b. lot, block, and plot method.
  c. metes and bounds method.
  d. rectangular survey method.

110. An iron pin located on the corner of a lot is considered
  a. a monument.
  b. a hazard.
  c. the Point of Beginning.
  d. It has no significance.

► Answers

1. **d.** The broker is breaking Connecticut law.
2. **d.** Connecticut has no requirement that a person actually practice real estate prior to getting a broker's license.
3. **c.** Book value is cost less accumulated depreciation.
   $300,000 − (12 × $3,000) $36,000 = $264,000
4. **a.** Real estate lacks liquidity.
5. **b.** Placing the money in the operating account is the crime of commingling; taking it out and spending it is the crime of conversion.
6. **c.** The contract is voidable by the minor.
7. **d.** No license is required to a sell a business where no real estate is involved.
8. **b.** Most appraisals require the use of all three approaches.
9. **a.** The Planning Commission looks at the social and economic needs of the community in order to plan for the future.
10. **c.** Police power allows the government to make rules to protect the public health, safety, and welfare.
11. **a.** The gas station will be "grandfathered in" as a nonconforming use.
12. **d.** The college received 15% of the total.
    63% + 10% + 12% = 85% given to the family.
    100% − 85% = 15% to the college.
    College contribution of $30,000 ÷ 15% = $200,000 total estate.
    The daughter received 12% × 200,000 = $24,000.
13. **a.** All leasehold estates will someday expire.
14. **b.** Taking buyers to or away from neighborhoods because of the type of people who live there is the crime of steering.
15. **b.** Points are based on the amount of the mortgage, $500,000 − $50,000 (10% down payment) gives a mortgage of $450,000 × 2% = $9,000.
16. **c.** The FHA insures loans to low-income and first-time home buyers.
17. **d.** 44 feet + 50 feet + 50 feet = 144 feet.
18. **d.** $935,980 × .0165 = $15,443.67.
19. **c.** An acre contains 43,560 square feet.
20. **d.** In Connecticut, a salesperson must include his or her broker's name in all advertising.
21. **a.** You must have the written permission of the property owner to place a real estate sign.
22. **b.** Agency must be discussed and determined at the first face-to-face meeting where real estate is discussed.
23. **b.** Reconciliation is not a government power.
24. **d.** The loan gets paid off more quickly, resulting in less interest being paid.
25. **b.** Even when acting in a private transaction, a licensee must disclose that fact.
26. **b.** The transfer of real estate is called *alienation*.
27. **b.** Real estate laws are primarily designed to protect the public.
28. **c.** The agent should complete the form and keep it for his or her records. If the consumer enters into a transaction, the form should be attached to the purchase and sale agreement.
29. **a.** *Jones v. Mayer* reaffirmed the Civil Rights Act of 1866 that banned discrimination based on race and color.
30. **d.** Each agency sets its own commissions, and these may be negotiable between the broker and the client.
31. **b.** Eminent domain is an example of involuntary transfer.

32. a. They are entitled to a $500,000 ($250,000 each) tax exemption.

33. c. A legally enforceable agreement is a contract.

34. b. Earnest money must be deposited in the escrow or trust account within three banking days of the last signature going on the contract.

35. b. Commingling is the crime of mixing client money with the broker's own funds. Client money should always go in a separate escrow or trust account.

36. c. Mortgage brokers have no money of their own to lend. They broker loans between lenders and borrowers.

37. c. Client monies should always be placed in the escrow or trust account.

38. a. The money from escrow accounts should go to CHFA unless the client requests to keep the interest. In that instance, the broker can charge a reasonable fee for processing,

39. b. The U.S. government defines an appraisal as a professional opinion. It does not determine the value, it estimates it, and it doesn't have to be in writing, although it usually is. The type of value determined could be market value, but it could also be salvage value, depreciated value, or some other type of value.

40. a. There needs to be a description of the property, but not a "legal" description. That is required for a deed.

41. a. An exclusive seller's agent works only for sellers. They may work with buyers as customers.

42. c. This transaction is an option to purchase.

43. a. All listings must have a fixed expiration date and cannot automatically extend.

44. c. This law banned discrimination based on race, color, religion, and national origin. Later acts and amendments added gender, disability, and familial status.

45. a. The Financial Institutions Reform, Recovery, and Enforcement Act required that appraisers in federally related transactions be licensed.

46. a. The building has a value of $750,000 × 80% = $600,000.
$600,000 ÷ 27.5 = 21,818.18.

47. b. Anything collected over $500,000 goes to the Connecticut General Fund.

48. c. The DVA (Department of Veterans Affairs) guarantees loans to qualified veterans.

49. d. The agent is required to disclose only material facts. He or she would not be allowed to disclose information that is confidential.

50. a. Anyone who signs an agreement is entitled to a copy at the time it is signed.

51. d. False statements are misrepresentation or fraud.

52. b. A listing agreement is a bilateral contract and cannot be terminated by one side without the consent of the other side. The sellers could be liable for damages, and if they list with another broker, they could be liable for two commissions.

53. b. The closing is when all the promises are fulfilled; the buyers get the title and the sellers get their money.

54. d. They could also file a complaint at the federal level with the Department of Housing and Urban Development (HUD).

55. a. The area of a building is measured in square feet.

56. d. Both state and federal law prohibit discrimination based on disability.

57. b. $250,000 ÷ 50,000 = $5.

58. **c.** Because it is owner-occupied and no real estate agent is involved, the owner can legally discriminate on any basis other than race or color.

59. **b.** A buyer's agent represents a buyer.

60. **c.** A salesperson can be paid only by his or her own broker.

61. **d.** A salesperson could work for more than one broker if the brokers agreed in writing.

62. **a.** The broker is not required to disclose the murder, but is not prohibited from disclosing it. If a buyer who is making a *bona fide* offer to purchase requests the information in writing, the agent must pass the request on to the seller, who can decide whether to answer the request or not.

63. **c.** The Consent to Dual Agency is not required until a buyer client is making an offer on one of your firm's listings. It should be completed before the offer is filled in.

64. **c.** In this situation, the firm could use either dual or designated agency depending on company policy and the preferences of the clients.

65. **a.** A licensee cannot share a commission with a person who does not have a license.

66. **b.** *Comp* is short for competitive or comparative sales.

67. **c.** The relationship between the amount of the loan and the value of the real estate is referred to as the loan-to-value ratio.

68. **d.** $569,888 \times 5.25\% = \$29,919.12$.

69. **c.** The agent is required to discuss agency at the first substantive meeting.

70. **c.** Earl can accept money compensation only for real estate–related activities from his broker. He should have turned the check over to the broker immediately.

71. **a.** In Connecticut, an agent is prohibited from acting as a dual agent without the written consent of both parties.

72. **a.** A unilateral contract requires performance from one side only.

73. **c.** It is the agent's responsibility to notify the Real Estate Commission and pay the transfer fee.

74. **c.** FSBO stands for "for sale by owner."

75. **b.** It is a gross lease because the rent is gross income to the landlord, who must pay all of the property expenses.

76. **b.** The buyer has the right to review the resale documents for five days.

77. **a.** Jan is designated to represent the buyers and can give them the full range of fiduciary duties.

78. **d.** The listing is an illegal net listing and the broker is not entitled to a commission.

79. **b.** A lease is a bilateral contract.

80. **d.** The Financial Institutions Reform, Recovery, and Enforcement Act (FIRREA) deals with banking and appraisal.

81. **a.** A property manager would reduce risk through liability insurance.

82. **d.** $\$34,070.93 \div \$973,455 = .035$, or 3.5%.

83. **b.** The firm is a dual agent, which always presents the potential for a conflict of interest.

84. **a.** Eighteen years is the age of competence in Connecticut.

85. **a.** They are called loan fees or discount fees.

86. **c.** Credit rating is not a protected class.

87. **d.** There is no usury rate for real estate loans that are more than $5,000.

88. **a.** In Connecticut, you have to have a real estate license to lease property or collect rent.

89. **c.** If there are defective paint surfaces, they must be abated because there is a child under six in the home. If the child had elevated levels of lead in the blood, further action could be required.

90. c. S&L stands for savings and loan association, sometimes called *savings banks.*

91. a. $200 \times 150 = 30,000$ square feet

$30,000 \div 43,560$ (the number of square feet in an acre) $= .688$

92. d. There is no law requiring the removal of in-ground oil tanks, but lenders and insurance companies want them removed or sealed.

93. c. Referrals can be given only to people who have a real estate license.

94. d. Most foreclosures in Connecticut are strict foreclosure.

95. b. Sellers are expected to deliver good title to the purchasers.

96. c. Sellers must disclose the existence of underground storage tanks if they know about them.

97. b. The bank will go to court and seek a deficiency judgment for the balance that is due.

98. a. In Connecticut, the buyer's attorney usually does or arranges for the title search.

99. d. $425,000 - 20\%$ ($85,000) $= $340,000$ loan amount

$340,000 \times 7\% \div 12 = $1,983.33$ monthly payment

100. a. Maurice could collect only if the buyers had promised to pay him. He was not the predominant procuring cause of the sale and would not be due a commission from the sellers or seller's agent.

101. b. If the seller were adjudicated insane or in some other way was incompetent to continue in the agency relationship, it would automatically terminate.

102. b. It is illegal under state and federal law.

103. b. The fact that they had been heavily drinking would create a voidable offer. Yuan could get out of the contract if he chose to, so it is not valid.

104. a. All residential listing agreements should have a place for the seller to disclose knowledge of urea formaldehyde foam insulation.

105. d. The client decides how it is presented. A court presentation could be verbal.

106. a. It is our practice in Connecticut (but not a legal requirement) that the seller pay the property expenses through the day of the closing.

107. d. It is confidential forever unless it becomes public or common knowledge or the agent is required to reveal it in court.

108. a. With an exclusive right to sell, Elijah will get paid if the listing sells during the period of the agreement regardless of who put the transaction together.

109. c. The most common way of describing property in Connecticut is the metes and bounds method.

110. a. The iron pin is a surveyor's monument showing exactly where the corner is.

▶ Scoring

Again, evaluate how you did on this practice exam by finding the number of questions you got right, disregarding, for the moment, the ones you got wrong or skipped. If you achieve a score of at least 77 questions correct, you will most likely pass the Connecticut Real Estate Sales Exam.

If you did not score as well as you would like, ask yourself the following: Did I run out of time before I could answer all the questions? Did I go back and change my answers from right to wrong? Did I get flustered and sit staring at a difficult question for what seemed like hours? If you had any of these problems, be sure to go over the LearningExpress Test Preparation System in Chapter 2 to review how best to avoid them.

You probably have seen improvement from your first two practice exam scores and this one; but if you didn't improve as much as you would like, following are some options:

If you scored below the passing score on each section, you should seriously consider whether you are ready for the exam at this time. A good idea would be to take some brush-up courses in the areas you feel less sure of. If you don't have time for a course, you might try private tutoring.

If you scored close to the minimum passing score, you need to work as hard as you can to improve your skills. Go back to your real estate license course textbooks to review the knowledge you need to do well or use the LearningExpress book, *Practical Math Success in 20 Minutes a Day*. Also, reread and pay close attention to the information in Chapter 4, Connecticut Real Estate Refresher Course; Chapter 5, Real Estate Math Review; and Chapter 6, Real Estate Glossary. It might be helpful, as well, to ask friends and family to make up mock test questions and quiz you on them.

Now, revise your study schedule according to the time you have left, emphasizing those parts that gave you the most trouble this time. Use the table on the next page to see where you need more work, so that you can concentrate your preparation efforts. After working more on the subject areas that give you problems, take the fourth practice exam in Chapter 9 to see how much you have improved.

EXAM 3 FOR REVIEW

Connecticut Real Estate Sales Exam 3 Subject Areas	Question Numbers (Questions 1–110)
Property Ownership and Land Use Controls and Registrations	9, 10, 11, 13, 23
Valuation and Market Analysis	3, 4, 8, 39, 45, 66, 80, 90, 105
Financing	16, 24, 36, 48, 67, 85, 87, 94, 97
Laws of Agency	41, 49, 59, 64, 71, 77, 83
Mandated Disclosures	22, 28, 63, 69, 96, 104
Contracts	6, 33, 40, 42, 52, 72, 79, 101, 103, 108
Transfer of Property	26, 31, 53, 95, 98, 106
Practice of Real Estate	19, 32, 51, 55, 74, 75, 81, 92, 100, 102, 109, 110
License Law/Rules and Regulations	1, 2, 5, 7, 20, 21, 25, 27, 30, 34, 35, 37, 38, 43, 47, 50, 56, 60, 61, 62, 65, 70, 73, 76, 78, 84, 88, 89, 93, 107
Real Estate Math	12, 15, 17, 18, 46, 57, 68, 82, 91, 99
Fair Housing	14, 29, 44, 54, 58, 86

9 ▶ Connecticut Real Estate Sales Exam 4

CHAPTER SUMMARY

This is the last of the four practice tests in this book based on the Connecticut Real Estate Sales Exam. Using all of the experience and strategies that you gained from the other three exams, take this exam to see how far you have come.

THIS IS THE LAST practice exam in this book, but it is not designed to be any harder than the other three. It is simply another representation of what you might expect on the real test. Just as when you take the real test, there should not be anything here that surprises you. In fact, you probably already know what is in a lot of it! That will be the case with the real test, too.

For this exam, pull together all the tips you have been practicing since the first practice exam. Give yourself the time and the space to work. Because you won't be taking the real test in your living room, you might take this one in an unfamiliar location, such as a library. Make sure you have plenty of time to complete the exam in one sitting. In addition, use what you have learned from reading the answer explanations on previous practice tests. Remember the types of questions that have caused problems for you in the past, and when you are unsure, try to consider how those answers were explained.

After you have taken this written exam, you should try the computer-based test using the CD-ROM found at the back of this book. That way, you will be familiar with taking exams on computer.

Once again, use the answer explanations at the end of the exam to understand questions you may have missed.

▶ Connecticut Real Estate Sales Exam 4 Answer Sheet

1.	ⓐ	ⓑ	ⓒ	ⓓ
2.	ⓐ	ⓑ	ⓒ	ⓓ
3.	ⓐ	ⓑ	ⓒ	ⓓ
4.	ⓐ	ⓑ	ⓒ	ⓓ
5.	ⓐ	ⓑ	ⓒ	ⓓ
6.	ⓐ	ⓑ	ⓒ	ⓓ
7.	ⓐ	ⓑ	ⓒ	ⓓ
8.	ⓐ	ⓑ	ⓒ	ⓓ
9.	ⓐ	ⓑ	ⓒ	ⓓ
10.	ⓐ	ⓑ	ⓒ	ⓓ
11.	ⓐ	ⓑ	ⓒ	ⓓ
12.	ⓐ	ⓑ	ⓒ	ⓓ
13.	ⓐ	ⓑ	ⓒ	ⓓ
14.	ⓐ	ⓑ	ⓒ	ⓓ
15.	ⓐ	ⓑ	ⓒ	ⓓ
16.	ⓐ	ⓑ	ⓒ	ⓓ
17.	ⓐ	ⓑ	ⓒ	ⓓ
18.	ⓐ	ⓑ	ⓒ	ⓓ
19.	ⓐ	ⓑ	ⓒ	ⓓ
20.	ⓐ	ⓑ	ⓒ	ⓓ
21.	ⓐ	ⓑ	ⓒ	ⓓ
22.	ⓐ	ⓑ	ⓒ	ⓓ
23.	ⓐ	ⓑ	ⓒ	ⓓ
24.	ⓐ	ⓑ	ⓒ	ⓓ
25.	ⓐ	ⓑ	ⓒ	ⓓ
26.	ⓐ	ⓑ	ⓒ	ⓓ
27.	ⓐ	ⓑ	ⓒ	ⓓ
28.	ⓐ	ⓑ	ⓒ	ⓓ
29.	ⓐ	ⓑ	ⓒ	ⓓ
30.	ⓐ	ⓑ	ⓒ	ⓓ
31.	ⓐ	ⓑ	ⓒ	ⓓ
32.	ⓐ	ⓑ	ⓒ	ⓓ
33.	ⓐ	ⓑ	ⓒ	ⓓ
34.	ⓐ	ⓑ	ⓒ	ⓓ
35.	ⓐ	ⓑ	ⓒ	ⓓ
36.	ⓐ	ⓑ	ⓒ	ⓓ
37.	ⓐ	ⓑ	ⓒ	ⓓ

38.	ⓐ	ⓑ	ⓒ	ⓓ
39.	ⓐ	ⓑ	ⓒ	ⓓ
40.	ⓐ	ⓑ	ⓒ	ⓓ
41.	ⓐ	ⓑ	ⓒ	ⓓ
42.	ⓐ	ⓑ	ⓒ	ⓓ
43.	ⓐ	ⓑ	ⓒ	ⓓ
44.	ⓐ	ⓑ	ⓒ	ⓓ
45.	ⓐ	ⓑ	ⓒ	ⓓ
46.	ⓐ	ⓑ	ⓒ	ⓓ
47.	ⓐ	ⓑ	ⓒ	ⓓ
48.	ⓐ	ⓑ	ⓒ	ⓓ
49.	ⓐ	ⓑ	ⓒ	ⓓ
50.	ⓐ	ⓑ	ⓒ	ⓓ
51.	ⓐ	ⓑ	ⓒ	ⓓ
52.	ⓐ	ⓑ	ⓒ	ⓓ
53.	ⓐ	ⓑ	ⓒ	ⓓ
54.	ⓐ	ⓑ	ⓒ	ⓓ
55.	ⓐ	ⓑ	ⓒ	ⓓ
56.	ⓐ	ⓑ	ⓒ	ⓓ
57.	ⓐ	ⓑ	ⓒ	ⓓ
58.	ⓐ	ⓑ	ⓒ	ⓓ
59.	ⓐ	ⓑ	ⓒ	ⓓ
60.	ⓐ	ⓑ	ⓒ	ⓓ
61.	ⓐ	ⓑ	ⓒ	ⓓ
62.	ⓐ	ⓑ	ⓒ	ⓓ
63.	ⓐ	ⓑ	ⓒ	ⓓ
64.	ⓐ	ⓑ	ⓒ	ⓓ
65.	ⓐ	ⓑ	ⓒ	ⓓ
66.	ⓐ	ⓑ	ⓒ	ⓓ
67.	ⓐ	ⓑ	ⓒ	ⓓ
68.	ⓐ	ⓑ	ⓒ	ⓓ
69.	ⓐ	ⓑ	ⓒ	ⓓ
70.	ⓐ	ⓑ	ⓒ	ⓓ
71.	ⓐ	ⓑ	ⓒ	ⓓ
72.	ⓐ	ⓑ	ⓒ	ⓓ
73.	ⓐ	ⓑ	ⓒ	ⓓ
74.	ⓐ	ⓑ	ⓒ	ⓓ

75.	ⓐ	ⓑ	ⓒ	ⓓ
76.	ⓐ	ⓑ	ⓒ	ⓓ
77.	ⓐ	ⓑ	ⓒ	ⓓ
78.	ⓐ	ⓑ	ⓒ	ⓓ
79.	ⓐ	ⓑ	ⓒ	ⓓ
80.	ⓐ	ⓑ	ⓒ	ⓓ
81.	ⓐ	ⓑ	ⓒ	ⓓ
82.	ⓐ	ⓑ	ⓒ	ⓓ
83.	ⓐ	ⓑ	ⓒ	ⓓ
84.	ⓐ	ⓑ	ⓒ	ⓓ
85.	ⓐ	ⓑ	ⓒ	ⓓ
86.	ⓐ	ⓑ	ⓒ	ⓓ
87.	ⓐ	ⓑ	ⓒ	ⓓ
88.	ⓐ	ⓑ	ⓒ	ⓓ
89.	ⓐ	ⓑ	ⓒ	ⓓ
90.	ⓐ	ⓑ	ⓒ	ⓓ
91.	ⓐ	ⓑ	ⓒ	ⓓ
92.	ⓐ	ⓑ	ⓒ	ⓓ
93.	ⓐ	ⓑ	ⓒ	ⓓ
94.	ⓐ	ⓑ	ⓒ	ⓓ
95.	ⓐ	ⓑ	ⓒ	ⓓ
96.	ⓐ	ⓑ	ⓒ	ⓓ
97.	ⓐ	ⓑ	ⓒ	ⓓ
98.	ⓐ	ⓑ	ⓒ	ⓓ
99.	ⓐ	ⓑ	ⓒ	ⓓ
100.	ⓐ	ⓑ	ⓒ	ⓓ
101.	ⓐ	ⓑ	ⓒ	ⓓ
102.	ⓐ	ⓑ	ⓒ	ⓓ
103.	ⓐ	ⓑ	ⓒ	ⓓ
104.	ⓐ	ⓑ	ⓒ	ⓓ
105.	ⓐ	ⓑ	ⓒ	ⓓ
106.	ⓐ	ⓑ	ⓒ	ⓓ
107.	ⓐ	ⓑ	ⓒ	ⓓ
108.	ⓐ	ⓑ	ⓒ	ⓓ
109.	ⓐ	ⓑ	ⓒ	ⓓ
110.	ⓐ	ⓑ	ⓒ	ⓓ

► Connecticut Real Estate Sales Exam 4

1. A buyer plans to give a 33% down payment on a house being purchased for $321,788. That amount of the down payment is
   a. $64,357.60
   b. $257,430.40
   c. $106,190.04
   d. $215,597.96

2. A seller gives Beatrice a listing on his property and indicates to her that he has also listed this property with other brokers. The type of listing Beatrice got was
   a. an exclusive right to represent.
   b. an exclusive agency.
   c. an open.
   d. a net.

3. A seller wants to sell his house for $300,000. He states that he doesn't care how much commission the broker gets, as long as he nets his $300,000. This type of compensation is known as
   a. a net commission and is illegal in Connecticut.
   b. a net commission and is often used with the seller's written permission.
   c. a premium commission fee and is common.
   d. a sandwich commission and is rare but completely legal.

4. To be valid, a mechanic's lien in Connecticut must be
   a. filed within 90 days of the start date of the construction.
   b. filed within 60 days of the completion of the work.
   c. filed within 90 days of the completion of the work.
   d. filed within 120 days of the completion of the work.

5. A deposit is given with an offer to purchase because
   a. it is required by contract law.
   b. it is the only means to fully bind the offer.
   c. the deposit effectively takes the property off the market.
   d. it shows that the buyers are serious.

6. A real estate listing is
   a. a list of all the properties for sale in a certain area.
   b. an employment agreement between a broker and a client.
   c. an employment agreement between a broker and a salesperson.
   d. an agreement to put a seller's property on your firm's list.

7. A property is assessed at $824,566. The real estate tax rate in the town is 15.66 mils. What are the annual taxes for this property?
 a. $12,912.70
 b. $824.57
 c. $52,654.28
 d. $129,127.04

8. In Connecticut, the priority of liens is usually established by the date of
 a. execution of the lien.
 b. recording of the lien.
 c. the court filing of the lien.
 d. issuance of the judgment.

9. Angela served in the military and now is buying a home for $185,000 using a veteran's loan. Angela will be able to finance what percent of the purchase price?
 a. 100%
 b. 98%
 c. 95%
 d. 90%

10. All of the following are true about appraisers EXCEPT
 a. they are impartial third parties.
 b. the appraisal may be verbal or in writing.
 c. the appraiser's fee is a percentage of the value of the property being appraised.
 d. they must be licensed to do federally related appraisals.

11. At the first face-to-face meeting at which real estate is discussed, a Connecticut real estates salesperson must discuss one subject before any other. That subject is
 a. the commission.
 b. lead paint.
 c. the buyer's financial qualifications.
 d. Connecticut agency law.

12. A neighbor has been crossing Holly's land several times a week to get to the nearby shopping mall. Holly is concerned that the neighbor might be able to eventually get a prescriptive easement. Holly should
 a. contact an attorney.
 b. write the neighbor a letter telling him or her to cease and desist.
 c. write the neighbor a letter granting permission to cross the property.
 d. put up a physical barrier so the neighbor can't get access to the property.

13. When Conrad bought his home, there was an easement in the deed for the neighbors to drive their car to a nearby pond. Conrad has owned the house for 18 years, and during that time, as far as Conrad knows, the neighbors have never used the easement. What is the status of the easement?
 a. Once an easement, always an easement.
 b. Because they didn't use it for more than 12 years, they have lost all of their rights.
 c. Because it has been abandoned for 15 years, Conrad could go to court and have the easement extinguished.
 d. none of the above

14. In Connecticut, the responsibility for disclosing the presence of UFFI lies with
   a. the seller.
   b. the buyer agent.
   c. the listing broker.
   d. the home inspector.

15. A buyer has made an offer to purchase contingent on a home inspection within 14 days. The offer is accepted and the buyer asks the agent to recommend a home inspector. The agent should
   a. recommend a home inspector.
   b. not recommend a home inspector, because this would be a violation of Connecticut statutes.
   c. give the buyer a list of qualified homes inspectors to choose from.
   d. explain that an inspection is not really needed and recommend that the buyer not waste his or her money.

16. Alfredo, a Connecticut real estate broker, heard at a party about a property that was for sale without a broker. The next day, he brought a buyer to the property, and after some negotiation, a sale was consummated. Alfredo sent a bill to the seller for his commission and the seller refused to pay. Can Alfredo collect a commission from the seller?
   a. Yes, the seller allowed Alfredo to show the property and worked through him to put the sale together. This created an implied agency relationship, so the seller owes a commission.
   b. No, Alfredo had no written contract with the seller, so the seller doesn't have to pay.
   c. Yes, the seller always has to pay a commission when a real estate agent is involved.
   d. No, Alfredo worked for the buyer, so the buyer should pay the commission.

17. In Connecticut, to acquire land by adverse possession, a person must use it for
   a. 12 years.
   b. 15 years.
   c. 20 years.
   d. 25 years.

18. Meredith gets a call from a buyer who wants to see Meredith's new listing. At the first meeting, the buyer refuses to sign a representation agreement or a Disclosure for Unrepresented Persons. What should Meredith do?
   a. She can't work with the buyer unless something is signed.
   b. Show the listing. After all, she tried to get the buyer to sign.
   c. She should refer the buyer to another agent.
   d. She should fill out the Disclosure for Unrepresented Persons indicating that the buyer refused to sign it and then show the property.

19. In Connecticut, the conveyance tax is paid by
   a. the seller.
   b. the buyer.
   c. the lender.
   d. the seller's attorney.

20. While showing her listing to prospective buyers, Leslie refers to the falling down porch as "charming" and describes the weed-choked back yard as "a delightful wildflower garden." What Leslie is doing is called
   a. fraud.
   b. misrepresentation.
   c. illegal.
   d. puffery.

21. To file for a prescriptive easement, all of the following are true EXCEPT
  a. the use was continuous.
  b. the use was without permission of the property owner.
  c. the use was for at least ten years.
  d. the use was out in the open and not hidden.

22. A prospective purchaser in Connecticut has found the right house and wants to buy it. The real estate agent will help the buyer draw up
  a. a purchase and sale agreement.
  b. a binder that will act as a contract if the attorneys don't draw one up within the prescribed time period.
  c. a nonbinding binder.
  d. It could be any of the above depending where in Connecticut you are.

23. Single-family appraisals for lenders are usually done on a form called the
  a. USPAP.
  b. URAR.
  c. RESPA.
  d. CERCLA.

24. The tenant signs a six-month lease. This is known as a(n)
  a. estate for years.
  b. estate from period to period.
  c. estate at sufferance.
  d. tenancy by the entirety.

25. While she is taking the listing, the seller explains to Wanda that there is an old oil tank in the yard that hasn't been used since they converted to gas 17 years ago. The seller instructs Wanda not to tell anyone about the tank. What should Wanda do?
  a. Wanda must follow the instructions of her client.
  b. Wanda should refuse the listing.
  c. Wanda should report the seller to the Real Estate Commission for attempted fraud.
  d. Wanda should explain to the seller that she has to disclose the existence of the tank because it is a material fact.

26. In Connecticut, leases for longer than one year
  a. must be in writing.
  b. must be recorded at the town hall.
  c. are illegal.
  d. both **a** and **b**

27. In Connecticut, all of the following are true about rental security deposits EXCEPT
  a. they must be kept in a separate bank account.
  b. the landlord must pay interest on them.
  c. they can't exceed two months' rent.
  d. they are meant to cover the last two months' rent.

28. A title defect is also known as
  a. malicious fraud.
  b. streamlining.
  c. a cloud.
  d. a gray aberration.

29. Terri is showing property to prospective buyers and they seem very interested. They ask her if anyone who lived in the property ever had HIV or AIDS. Terri should

   a. answer the question as honestly and accurately as she can.

   b. ask them to put the question in writing and she will give it to the seller to answer.

   c. explain that it would be a violation of state and federal Fair Housing Law to discuss this subject.

   d. suggest that the buyers talk to the local Board of Health.

30. A landlord should give the tenant a copy of the rules and regulations

   a. before the tenant signs the lease.

   b. when the tenant first breaks the rules.

   c. when the tenant asks for them.

   d. by posting them in a conspicuous place.

31. Upon the death of a sole proprietor broker, the deceased broker's spouse can continue the brokerage operation

   a. when she completes the requirements for a broker's license.

   b. when she gets a temporary two-year license.

   c. under her spouse's license until she gets one of her own.

   d. when she gets a temporary one-year license.

32. The lease is over and the tenant has gone. What must a Connecticut landlord do with the security deposit?

   a. The landlord keeps the deposit, but must give the interest to the tenant.

   b. The landlord must return the deposit within 30 days or account for why he or she is retaining it.

   c. The landlord can apply the deposit to any damage done by the tenant, but not to any rent that is owed.

   d. The landlord must return the deposit within 15 days and can keep any interest that has accrued.

33. A listing agent has an exclusive right to sell agreement to represent a seller's property consisting of four acres of land and a large commercial building. During the period of the listing, some potential buyers had a serious interest in the property, but during a thunderstorm, the building was struck by lightning and burned to the ground. The agent believes that he could have completed the transaction and is therefore due a fee. Given these facts, which of the following statements is true?

   a. Under Connecticut law, if the agent can prove there was *bona fide* interest on the part of the buyers, a fee is due.

   b. The destruction of the property terminated the listing before any written offer or contract was negotiated, so no fee is due.

   c. The seller owes only a 25% commission under Connecticut law.

   d. If the building was insured, then the seller must keep the property on the market.

34. A Connecticut tenant paid a security deposit equal to one and a half months' rent. How much interest does the landlord have to pay on the security deposit?
   a. 1.8% per annum
   b. 2.4% per annum
   c. 4% per annum
   d. The rate is set by the Connecticut Banking Commissioner and varies from year to year.

35. Margie finds a buyer for her listing. A purchase and sale agreement is negotiated, and the buyers get their financing and are ready to close. The day before closing, the sellers back out of the deal. Margie feels she is due a commission. Is she?
   a. Yes, she produced ready, willing, and able buyers who were acceptable to the sellers.
   b. No, the transaction has to close before a commission is earned.
   c. Yes, the sellers didn't have a valid reason for terminating the sale, so they owe a commission.
   d. You can't tell from the information provided.

36. A tenant has a one-year lease, but leaves after only six months. The landlord
   a. must make a diligent effort to rent the property and can demand that the old tenant continue to pay rent until a new tenant is in place.
   b. can keep the tenant's belongings in lieu of the unpaid rent.
   c. can demand that the tenant fulfill the rental contract and pay the remaining six months' rent.
   d. can do nothing about this situation.

37. All appraisal reports must
   a. be in writing.
   b. be in conformity with USPAP.
   c. be on the URAR.
   d. contain the required RESPA disclosures.

38. A Connecticut real estate license is valid for
   a. one year.
   b. two years.
   c. three years.
   d. five years.

39. Ngyun came to Connecticut four months ago and speaks no English. Because of this,
   a. he cannot own real estate in Connecticut.
   b. he is required to hire a Connecticut licensed broker in order to buy real estate.
   c. if he buys real estate, he must sign the required language disclaimer.
   d. he can buy and sell real estate in Connecticut.

40. A real estate client is someone who
   a. empowers another to act as his or her agent.
   b. wants to buy real estate.
   c. wants to sell real estate.
   d. signs the mandatory agency disclosure.

41. If a tenant in Connecticut is more than ten days late in paying the rent, the landlord may
   a. terminate the lease.
   b. lock the tenant out of the unit until the rent is paid.
   c. forfeit one month's interest on the tenant's security deposit.
   d. confiscate the tenant's belongings.

42. John Smith owns an apartment building with a gross annual income of $56,700. The annual operating expenses are $15,600. Rob Doe, a buyer, is willing to purchase the building if he can get it at a price that yields him a capitalization rate of 8.5% or better. What is the most that Rob will pay?
- **a.** $481,950
- **b.** $349,350
- **c.** $483,529
- **d.** $132,600

43. A listing agent receives two offers on her listing. One of the offers states "time is of the essence," while the other offer does not include this phrase. Is there a difference between the offers?
- **a.** There is no difference because all offers are "time is of the essence."
- **b.** Yes, "time is of the essence" means all parties must meet the dates and deadlines set forth in the contract.
- **c.** "Time is of the essence" just means that you should move quickly.
- **d.** The offer without "time is of the essence" is the stronger offer.

44. A Connecticut landlord has an apartment that she rents out for $11,400 per year. What is the maximum security deposit she can collect on this unit?
- **a.** $900
- **b.** $1,800
- **c.** $2,700
- **d.** whatever the market will allow

45. In Connecticut, a real estate agency must keep its records for at least
- **a.** five years.
- **b.** seven years.
- **c.** ten years.
- **d.** 12 years.

46. All of the following describe the possible legal status of a contract EXCEPT
- **a.** void.
- **b.** voidable.
- **c.** unenforceable.
- **d.** arm's length.

47. According to Connecticut statutes, a deed must be recorded how soon after closing?
- **a.** within 24 hours
- **b.** within 48 hours
- **c.** within three business days
- **d.** within a reasonable time

48. An agent in Connecticut lists a house for sale that was built in 1965. What potential environmental issues should the agent be concerned about?
- **a.** lead paint
- **b.** asbestos
- **c.** urea formaldehyde insulation
- **d.** all of the above

49. In Connecticut, a real estate salesperson may hold the escrow deposits
- **a.** if he or she is a certified escrow holder.
- **b.** as long as he or she has written permission of the broker.
- **c.** never.
- **d.** as long as the amount of the deposit is less than $1,000.

50. Elvira wants to give extra exposure to her listings, so she sends information to brokers who are not members of her MLS. Does Elvira have to share her commission with one of these outside brokers?
   a. She can offer to share her commission through a co-broker agreement to induce these brokers to show the property, but she is not obligated to share her commission with them.
   b. Yes, because sending them the information created a "vicarious compensation liability."
   c. Yes, because if she didn't share, it would be misleading and fraudulent.
   d. No, because she is prohibited by Connecticut statute from compensating agents who don't belong to an MLS.

51. A person who dies without a will is said to have died
   a. intestate.
   b. testate.
   c. codicil.
   d. devise.

52. In Connecticut, a salesperson can become self-employed and work without a broker
   a. after working five years under a licensed broker.
   b. after working five years under a licensed broker and can document participation in 50 successful transactions.
   c. if he or she passes the unaffiliated salesperson exam.
   d. never.

53. Russell's home in Connecticut is being foreclosed because he did not keep up with the mortgage payments. Russell may redeem the property
   a. any time prior to the sale under the statutory right of redemption.
   b. any time prior to the sale under the equitable right of redemption.
   c. within six months after the sale under the equitable right of redemption.
   d. never. Connecticut has no right of redemption.

54. In Connecticut, the person who records the deeds is called the
   a. assessor.
   b. town clerk.
   c. first selectperson.
   d. recorder of deeds.

55. Connecticut towns are required to physically revalue real properties at least every
   a. eight years.
   b. ten years.
   c. 12 years.
   d. 15 years.

56. Which of the following phrases in an advertisement could trigger further disclosures?
   a. VA and FHA financing available
   b. fixed- and adjustable-rate financing
   c. as low as $550 per month
   d. 95% financing is possible

57. Olga has just gotten her new tax assessment and feels it is much too high. Olga needs to talk to
   a. the local board of tax review.
   b. the Connecticut board of tax review.
   c. the state tax assessor's office.
   d. the local tax assessor's office.

58. The Connecticut conveyance taxes are based on
   a. the amount of the mortgage.
   b. assessed value of the property conveyed.
   c. the sale price.
   d. the date of the closing.

59. Thomas has just won a judgment against a Connecticut real estate broker. If he wants to use the Real Estate Guaranty Fund, Thomas has a right to
   a. recover the amount of the judgment and all court costs and lawyer's fees from the fund.
   b. recover up to $10,000 from the fund, including court costs and legal fees.
   c. recover up to $25,000 from the fund, including court costs and legal fees.
   d. nothing, because the fund was not meant for this situation.

60. In order to become a real estate agent in Connecticut, a person must be at least
   a. 16 years old.
   b. 18 years old.
   c. 21 years old.
   d. Age is not a factor in obtaining a real estate license in Connecticut.

61. Constance is negotiating a lease for an apartment that will allow her to operate her plant-sitting business on the premises and she asks her broker if she ought to consult an attorney. The broker should
   a. tell her that the attorney would cost more than the rent, so she shouldn't bother.
   b. tell her that with a very simple transaction like this, with very little money involved, an attorney is unnecessary.
   c. tell her that she is always free to consult an attorney, but it is a waste of money in this situation.
   d. never advise against the use of an attorney.

62. Net operating income divided by the capitalization rate equals
   a. the debt service.
   b. the property value.
   c. the annual percentage rate.
   d. the annual interest rate.

63. In Connecticut, dower and curtesy are
   a. an integral part of our laws.
   b. recognized on a case-by-case basis.
   c. always enforced between married couples.
   d. not recognized or enforced.

64. A listing agreement is an example of a(n)
   a. bilateral contract.
   b. unilateral contract.
   c. unenforceable contract.
   d. descriptive contract.

65. The person who receives title to real property is known as the

- **a.** grantor.
- **b.** grantee.
- **c.** recipient.
- **d.** receptee.

66. A buyer broker works for the buyer. In Connecticut, who pays the buyer broker's fee?

- **a.** The buyer has to compensate the buyer agent.
- **b.** The seller compensates all of the agents in the transaction.
- **c.** Compensation is based on the terms negotiated in the buyer agency agreement.
- **d.** The buyer and seller split the cost of the buyer agent.

67. Most married couples in Connecticut take title as joint tenants with a right of survivorship. What happens to the ownership when they divorce?

- **a.** It is automatically extinguished and becomes a tenancy in common.
- **b.** It reverts to a tenancy by the entirety.
- **c.** It becomes a tenancy at sufferance.
- **d.** Nothing "automatically" happens, but usually, the divorce decree changes it to a tenancy in common.

68. In Connecticut, a deed shows title in the name of a husband and wife. Unless stated to the contrary, ownership is assumed to be

- **a.** joint tenancy with a right of survivorship.
- **b.** tenancy in common.
- **c.** in severalty.
- **d.** tenancy by the entirety.

69. Connecticut statutes say that all brokers shall cooperate with other brokers in marketing a property

- **a.** if they can't sell it themselves.
- **b.** when it is in the seller's best interest to do so.
- **c.** if the other brokers ask them to.
- **d.** if the broker is a member of the MLS.

70. When a lender allows a borrower to continue to control and use assets pledged as collateral for the loan, this is known as

- **a.** retention.
- **b.** titling.
- **c.** hypothecation.
- **d.** a collateral usage situation.

71. Eva has been notified that she passed the Connecticut salesperson's exam. In order to activate her license, she must

- **a.** pay the first year's license fee.
- **b.** affiliate with a broker and pay the first year's license fee.
- **c.** do nothing. She passed the test and that is all she needs to do.
- **d.** affiliate with a broker. She paid the fee when she registered to take the test.

72. Marianna has been parking her car on her neighbor's land for years. One day, the neighbor tells her not to park there anymore. Marianna decides to file for a prescriptive easement. How long would she have to have been continuously using her neighbor's land in Connecticut to establish the right to a prescriptive easement?

- **a.** ten years
- **b.** 12 years
- **c.** 15 years
- **d.** 20 years

73. In Connecticut, property is usually transferred using a
   a. grant deed.
   b. bargain and sale deed.
   c. quitclaim deed.
   d. warranty deed.

74. For a real estate salesperson to become a broker in Connecticut, he or she must
   a. be a salesperson for two years and take an additional 60 hours of education, including 30 hours of appraisal, and pass the broker's exam.
   b. pass the broker's exam.
   c. get the sponsorship of three persons who are brokers.
   d. Salespeople can't become brokers. The requirements are completely different.

75. According to Connecticut statutes, agency disclosures and buyer agency agreements must be kept by the broker for
   a. one year.
   b. three years.
   c. five years.
   d. seven years.

76. When doing a title search in Connecticut, the documents affecting title will be found in the
   a. county courthouse.
   b. district land records office.
   c. town clerk's office.
   d. tax assessor's office.

77. How many acres are contained in a parcel of land that is 121 feet wide and 240 yards deep?
   a. 1
   b. $1\frac{1}{2}$
   c. 2
   d. $2\frac{1}{2}$

78. Eugene owns a rental property occupied by a tenant. Eugene's wife has no ownership in the rental property. Eugene has decided to sell the property. In Connecticut, who is required to sign the listing agreement?
   a. Eugene and his wife must sign because they are married.
   b. Eugene and the tenant must sign because the tenant's interests would be affected by the sale.
   c. Only Eugene has to sign.
   d. Eugene, his wife, and the tenant all have interests, so they must all sign.

79. Arthur owns a house in Hartford and decides to retire to his cottage down on the shore in Old Saybrook. His son, Arthur Jr., wants to buy the house but has limited financial resources, so Arthur gives him a very favorable price. This is an example of
   a. ratification.
   b. an arm's-length transaction.
   c. a non-arm's-length transaction.
   d. undue influence.

80. Rita has $86,576 remaining on her 8.5% mortgage. Her monthly payment is set at $852.56 for principal and interest. How much of her next payment will go to repay principal?
   a. $116.76
   b. $239.31
   c. $613.25
   d. $735.80

81. Graciella has decided to sell the house in Connecticut that she has owned for the past 11 years, but she finds that she has lost her copy of the deed and has no proof of ownership. What does Graciella need to do?
   a. She will need to contact her attorney and pay to have a new deed drawn up.
   b. Nothing. The deed is recorded on the land records and that is all the proof she needs.
   c. Her attorney will need to file a suit for quiet title to clear up this mess.
   d. Graciella can't sell the house until the deed is found.

82. In order for a purchase and sale agreement to be valid, it must contain
   a. a deposit.
   b. the name of the listing broker.
   c. consideration.
   d. the full name of the lender.

83. In Connecticut, a property owner may exempt how much of the value of his or her home from debt collection for involuntary liens?
   a. $25,000
   b. $50,000
   c. $75,000
   d. $100,000

84. In Connecticut, the Grand List is
   a. a list of all the taxable property in a town, both real and personal.
   b. a list of all the properties for sale at any given time.
   c. a list of all the licensed brokerage firms in a county.
   d. a list of all the real estate transactions that have taken place during the calendar year.

85. In Connecticut, a recorded deed
   a. proves that the deed is valid.
   b. is required, and if the deed is not recorded, title does not pass.
   c. is evidence of title.
   d. is not necessary.

86. When a tenant pays the rent in cash, a Connecticut landlord
   a. must give the tenant a receipt even if the tenant doesn't ask for it.
   b. can't accept it. Only checks or credit cards are allowed.
   c. must report it along with all cash receipts to the Connecticut Rental Commission on a quarterly basis.
   d. doesn't need to do anything special.

87. A landlord is allowed to make reasonable rules for the property. Which of the following rules would NOT be allowed in Connecticut?
   a. The tenants must keep personal belongings out of the common areas.
   b. Trash must be placed in the receptacle provided by the landlord.
   c. The landlord is not responsible for personal injuries that occur on the premises.
   d. No tampering with fire or smoke detectors.

88. Which of the following is NOT a protected class under Connecticut's Public Accommodation Act?
   a. gender
   b. sexual orientation
   c. creed
   d. credit record

89. New home contractors
   a. must have a state license from the Contractor's Commission.
   b. must register with the Department of Consumer Protection.
   c. must serve under a licensed contractor for five years and complete 150 hours of required education in order to get a license.
   d. have no special requirements in Connecticut.

90. Zoning ordinances typically regulate the
   a. number of occupants allowed in a building.
   b. permitted uses for a parcel of land.
   c. maximum rent that can be charged in a zone.
   d. adherence to state and federal Fair Housing Laws.

91. The Connecticut Real Estate Commission has
   a. seven members.
   b. eight members.
   c. nine members.
   d. ten members.

92. Holly has made an offer to purchase Dan's property. Dan really likes the offer and accepts it with one minor change; he moves the closing date from June 4 to June 6 because he will be away on vacation on June 4. Dan has
   a. accepted Holly's offer and created a contract.
   b. created a novation.
   c. made a counteroffer that Holly could refuse.
   d. rescinded Holly's offer.

93. Special assessments are levied
   a. when the town runs short of funds during the fiscal year.
   b. as a way of generating extra income for the town without raising taxes.
   c. to pay for improvements or services that benefit only a few properties.
   d. by the state to bring a town into compliance with state tax standards.

94. A listing or buyer agency agreement is
   a. a unilateral contract.
   b. an employment agreement.
   c. an executed contract.
   d. able to be terminated by either party at any time.

95. The Bundle of Rights includes all of the following EXCEPT
   a. the right to possess.
   b. the right to control.
   c. the right to exclude.
   d. the right to appurtenance.

96. To prepare a will in Connecticut, a person must be at least
   a. 16 years of age.
   b. 18 years of age.
   c. 21 years of age.
   d. There is no age restriction.

97. A person dies in Connecticut and has no legal heirs. After how many years will the property escheat to the state?
   a. seven years
   b. 15 years
   c. 20 years
   d. 25 years

98. Which of the following types of properties are NOT covered by the Connecticut Common Interest Ownership Act?
   a. apartment buildings
   b. condominiums
   c. cooperatives
   d. planned unit developments

99. If the Connecticut Real Estate Commission asks an agent to cooperate in an investigation, the agent should
   a. get permission from his or her broker.
   b. not get involved.
   c. cooperate fully.
   d. not answer any questions until receiving legal counsel.

100. Before refusing, suspending, or revoking a real estate license or imposing a fine, the Real Estate Commission must
   a. notify the licensee of the charges.
   b. get permission from the attorney general.
   c. obtain a judgment from the judicial system.
   d. file a notice suspendis on the land records.

101. A Connecticut real estate agent can receive a fee or commission for assisting a buyer in obtaining a mortgage loan if the agent
   a. has a license as a mortgage originator.
   b. discloses in writing that he or she is getting a fee for placing the mortgage.
   c. gets a written consent to dual agency.
   d. A Connecticut real estate licensee cannot get paid for originating a mortgage.

102. A buyer could get out of the purchase and sale agreement for any of the following reasons EXCEPT
   a. he or she did not have an attorney present when it was signed.
   b. he or she had been drinking when it was signed.
   c. he or she cannot read or write.
   d. he or she was under the age of 18 when it was signed.

103. An excellent source of mortgage funding for Connecticut residents is the
   a. Federal National Mortgage Association (Fannie Mae).
   b. Connecticut Housing Finance Authority (CHFA).
   c. Federal Home Loan Mortgage Corporation (Freddie Mac).
   d. New England Financial Services Administration (NEFSA).

104. A Connecticut real estate licensee can be paid for giving an opinion of value if
    a. the client agrees in writing to the fee.
    b. the subject property is within the licensee's area of expertise.
    c. the fee is less than $250.
    d. the opinion of value is related to a real estate transaction and the fee is debited from any commission received.

105. Mary Alice, a licensed Connecticut salesperson, is renting a room in her own home and she is not doing it through an agency but by word of mouth. Alex asks to rent the room and Mary Alice refuses, saying she only wants to rent to women. Which of the following is true?
    a. Mary Alice can do this because it is not listed with the MLS.
    b. Mary Alice can do this because it is a safety issue.
    c. Mary Alice can't do this because she has a real estate license.
    d. Mary Alice can't do this because she should have advertised "Women Only."

106. The most common proof of ownership used in Connecticut is
    a. the attorney's certificate of title.
    b. the Torrens system.
    c. title search warranty.
    d. a seller certification with acknowledgement.

107. From a real estate agent's perspective, net listings are
    a. ideal for situations in which the probable sale price is uncertain.
    b. a good type of listing to use when the seller wants to net a certain figure.
    c. something to be avoided.
    d. to be used only if the seller won't agree to any of the other types of listings.

108. The obligation for completing the Connecticut property condition disclosure report falls on the
    a. seller.
    b. listing agent.
    c. buyer agent.
    d. home inspector.

109. Dissolving a co-ownership could involve
    a. a suit for dissolution.
    b. a suit for partition.
    c. a suit for cancellation.
    d. a suit for separation.

110. Connecticut Public Act 490 establishes that Connecticut farm, forest, and open space lands
    a. can be developed for residential purposes.
    b. must be preserved from development to protect the quality of life.
    c. can qualify for reduced property taxes under certain circumstances.
    d. are exempt from all property taxes.

► Answers

1. **c.** .33 × $321,788 = $106,190.04
2. **c.** An open listing can be given to many different agencies and only the agency that sells the property gets a commission.
3. **a.** This is a net listing or net commission, which is strictly prohibited in Connecticut.
4. **c.** Mechanics' liens must be filed within 90 days of the completion of the work or the day work stopped.
5. **d.** Earnest money deposits are not required. They are given to demonstrate the seriousness of the buyers.
6. **b.** Listings are employment agreements between a client and a real estate firm.
7. **a.** $824,566 × .01566 = $12,912.70
8. **b.** The date the lien was recorded at the town hall is the usual standard for establishing priority.
9. **a.** Veteran's loans can be 100% of the purchase price up to certain limits.
10. **c.** The fees cannot be contingent upon the value arrived at.
11. **d.** The first thing an agent must do is inform a prospective client about agency and decide how they will work together.
12. **a.** Preventing a prescriptive easement is not as simple as putting up a barrier or writing a letter. It is best to use an attorney so that it will be done properly.
13. **c.** Abandoning an easement for 15 years gives the serviant tenement the right to have it extinguished.
14. **a.** The seller should disclose the presence of UFFI if the seller knows it is there.
15. **c.** It is always best to give a list of experts whenever possible to avoid charges of collusion.

16. **b.** No. Alfredo had no written contract with the seller, so the seller doesn't have to pay. In fact, participating in the transaction without a written employment agreement from either the buyer or the seller is a violation of Connecticut license law and could cost Alfredo his real estate license.
17. **b.** You must use someone else's land for 15 years in order to claim adverse possession.
18. **d.** Meredith can't force the buyers to sign something and she has a duty to the seller to show the property.
19. **a.** The seller pays the conveyance tax.
20. **d.** Puffery or sales talk is legal exaggeration on the part of a salesperson.
21. **c.** The period of use is 15 years.
22. **d.** Practices vary widely across the state when it comes to the real estate agent's role in drawing up paperwork.
23. **b.** The uniform residential appraisal report is usually used for single-family homes.
24. **a.** A lease for a specific period of time is known as an estate for years.
25. **d.** If the seller refuses to cooperate, then Wanda should not take the listing.
26. **d.** Leases for longer than a year should be in writing and recorded.
27. **d.** The security deposit can be used to cover rent with the landlord's permission, but that is not the purpose.
28. **c.** A defect is a cloud on the title.
29. **d.** Discussing the disability of previous owners would be illegal under federal and Connecticut law.
30. **a.** The tenant should know about the rules before he or she signs the lease.
31. **a.** To operate the business, she would have to have a Connecticut broker's license.

32. b. The security deposit and any interest it has earned belong to the tenant. The landlord can retain it only to cover damage by the tenant or unpaid rent.

33. b. Destruction of the property terminates the listing.

34. d. The Connecticut Banking Commissioner announces the rate on the first of each year, and it can never go lower than 1.5% per annum.

35. d. Whether or not a commission was earned will depend on the language in the listing agreement. Usually, producing a ready, willing, and able buyer is sufficient to earn a commission, but the agreement could have had language that said no commission is earned until passing of title.

36. a. The landlord is owed the rent for the balance of the lease, but must make a diligent effort to relieve the tenant of this burden by finding a new tenant.

37. b. Appraisals must conform to the Uniform Standards of Professional Appraisal Practice.

38. a. Real estate licenses must be renewed annually.

39. d. A person who does not speak English would not be prohibited from buying or selling real estate in Connecticut. An agent would need to take steps to assure that this person fully understood the transaction.

40. a. A client is someone who hires an agent to act on his or her behalf.

41. c. A tenant who is more than ten days late in paying the rent forfeits that month's interest on the security deposit.

42. c. $56,700 − $15,600 = $41,100 net operating income
$41,100 ÷ .085 = $483,529.41 maximum sale price

43. b. "Time is of the essence" has a powerful legal impact because it means the parties must get everything done on or before the deadline or face liability for being late.

44. b. The maximum security deposit is two months' rent.
$11,400 ÷ 12 = $900 per month rent
$900 × 2 = $1,800 maximum security deposit

45. b. Records must be retained for a minimum of seven years. This includes all contracts, agency agreement, escrow fund records, etc. It is acceptable to keep them in an electronic format as long as they can be printed.

46. d. Arm's length is not a recognized legal status.

47. d. Deeds must be recorded within a reasonable time.

48. d. All of these substances were banned for use in residential after this house was built, and the presence of any of them must be disclosed.

49. c. Salespersons are never allowed to hold escrow deposits. Only brokers can do that.

50. a. In order for a non–MLS agent to demand that Elvira pay compensation, there would need to be a written agreement co-brokering the listing.

51. a. A person who had no will died intestate.

52. d. In Connecticut, a salesperson must always be affiliated with a licensed broker.

53. b. Connecticut has only an equitable right of redemption in mortgage foreclosures.

54. b. In Connecticut, the town clerk is responsible for maintaining the land records.

55. c. Connecticut requires physical revaluation every 12 years and statistical revaluation every four years.

56. c. The monthly payment is a "trigger term" under Regulation Z and it means that an advertiser would need to disclose the other terms such as purchase price, mortgage amount, interest rate, and number of payments.

57. a. The local board of tax review has the authority to make an adjustment in Olga's assessment if a mistake was made.

58. c. The conveyance taxes (state and local) are based on the sale price of the property.

59. c. Thomas can collect up to $25,000 and must sign over his rights in the judgment to the Real Estate Commission.

60. b. A person cannot get a license until he or she is 18 years old.

61. d. A real estate agent should never advise a client not to use an attorney.

62. b. Dividing net operating income by the capitalization rate gives the property value that would yield that rate of return.

63. d. Dower and curtesy are not part of Connecticut law and are not recognized.

64. a. A listing agreement is a promise in exchange for a promise; a bilateral contract.

65. b. The grantee is the person receiving title to real property.

66. c. There is no required or standard way that a buyer agent gets paid. It is the subject of negotiation between the buyer and the buyer agent.

67. d. The divorce decree usually extinguishes the joint tenancy and replaces it with a tenancy in common.

68. b. Whenever a deed in Connecticut does not indicate how title is to be taken between two or more people, it is always assumed to be a tenancy in common.

69. b. A Connecticut broker is required to share the listing with other brokers when it is in the seller's best interest.

70. c. Hypothecation is using an asset that has been pledged as security for a loan.

71. b. To activate a salesperson's license, a person must affiliate with a broker and pay the license fee.

72. c. You must use another person's land continuously for 15 years to establish the right to a prescriptive easement.

73. d. Warranty deeds are the usual way of transferring title in Connecticut.

74. a. To become a broker, you must be a salesperson for two years, pass 60 hours of classes, and pass the broker's exam.

75. d. Connecticut law requires brokers to keep all records for seven years.

76. c. Land records are kept in the town where the land is located in the town or city clerk's office.

77. c. 240 yards × 3 feet = 720 feet
720 feet × 121 feet = 87,120 square feet
87,120 square feet ÷ 43,560 square feet = 2 acres

78. c. The wife has no interest in the property because she is not on the deed, and the tenant's rights are protected by the lease. Only Eugene needs to sign the listing.

79. c. This is a non-arm's-length transaction and would not be good to use in an appraisal.

80. b. A year's interest on the present debt would be $86,576 × .085 = $7,358.96.
$7,358.96 ÷ 12 = $613.65.
The monthly payment of $852.56 less the interest of $613.25 leaves $239.31 to go toward principal.

81. b. Graciella does not need a copy of the deed to convey the property. The fact that it is recorded on the land records is sufficient.

82. c. In order for a contract to be valid, there must be consideration, but that doesn't have to be money such as a deposit. A binding promise in exchange for a binding promise is sufficient consideration.

83. c. A homeowner may claim an exemption for $75,000. This is based on fair market value less any consensual liens, so it is the first $75,000 of equity in the home.

84. a. The Grand List is maintained by the town and shows all of the taxable property in the town.

85. c. A recorded deed is evidence of title, but not proof. A person could record a false deed and this would not be enough to transfer title.

86. a. When the tenant pays in cash, he or she must get a receipt even if he or she doesn't specifically request one.

87. c. This type of "hold harmless" clause is not enforceable in Connecticut. The landlord cannot require the tenants to waive their rights.

88. d. You could discriminate against a person because of his or her credit record in Connecticut.

89. b. New home contractors must register with the Department of Consumer Protection and the town building officials must check the registration certificate before issuing any building permits.

90. b. The zoning commission is concerned with how land will be used in the different zones within a town.

91. b. The Connecticut Real Estate Commission is made up of eight members, five of whom are in the real estate business (three brokers and two salespeople) and three persons who are members of the public.

92. c. By making a change in the original offer, Dan has created a counteroffer. Holly could refuse to accept the change and walk away with no penalty.

93. c. Special assessments apply only to those properties that benefit from a town improvement, such as sewer or water lines.

94. b. Buyer agency and listing agreements are employment agreements and as such are considered personal contracts that can be terminated by the death of either party.

95. d. The Bundle of Rights includes the rights to possession, control, enjoyment, exclusion, and disposition.

96. b. In preparing wills, the age of consent is 18, as it is in most other situations in Connecticut.

97. c. The time period for escheat in Connecticut is 20 years.

98. a. The Common Interest Ownership Act covers situations in which there are 12 or more properties whose ownership requires a financial contribution for the maintenance of common areas.

99. c. A licensee has a duty to cooperate truthfully and fully with the Real Estate Commission.

100. a. The Commission must notify a licensee of any pending action that would affect his or her license or result in a fine.

101. b. A licensee can get paid for originating a mortgage if he or she discloses to the buyer using the statutory form.

102. a. A person does not have to have an attorney present when he or she signs a purchase and sale agreement; however, the agreement should provide an opportunity for an attorney to review the contract within a reasonable amount of time.

103. b. The Connecticut Housing Finance Authority is a source of mortgage financing for low-income or first-time home buyers.

104. d. An agent can get paid a reasonable fee to do a CMA related to a real estate transaction. If the transaction results in a commission, the fee must be deducted from the commission.

105. c. Mary Alice is not allowed to discriminate based on gender by Connecticut and federal law because a licensee (herself) is involved in the transaction.

106. a. The attorney's certificate of title is the most common proof of ownership used in Connecticut; however, it is not a guarantee.

107. c. Net listings are illegal in Connecticut and should never be used.

108. a. It is the seller's responsibility to complete the property condition disclosure report.

109. b. A suit for partition would be used when the co-owners cannot agree on how to dissolve the ownership.

110. c. This law allows owners of farm, forest, or open space of a certain size to apply for a property tax reduction in return for agreeing to keep the property off the market for a period of ten years.

▶ Scoring

Once again, in order to evaluate how you did on this last exam, find the number of questions you answered correctly. The passing score for this practice exam is 77 correct answers (70%), but just as on the real test, you should be aiming for something higher than that on these practice exams. If you haven't reached a passing score on both sections, look at the suggestions for improvement at the end of Chapter 8. Take a look at the table following to see what problem areas remain.

The key to success in almost any pursuit is complete preparation. By taking the practice exams in this book, you have prepared more than many other people who may be taking the exam with you. You have diagnosed where your strengths and weaknesses lie and learned how to deal with the various kinds of questions that will appear on the test. So, go into the exam with confidence, knowing that you are ready and equipped to do your best.

EXAM 4 FOR REVIEW

Connecticut Real Estate Sales Exam 4 Subject Areas	Question Numbers (Questions 1–110)
Property Ownership and Land Use Controls and Registrations	17, 21, 54, 55, 57, 58, 67, 68, 72, 76, 83, 84, 85, 90, 93, 95
Valuation and Market Analysis	10, 23, 37, 62, 79, 104
Financing	8, 9, 53, 70, 103
Laws of Agency	2, 40, 107
Mandated Disclosures	11, 14, 18, 25, 48, 56, 108
Contracts	5, 6, 22, 24, 43, 46, 64, 78, 82, 92, 94, 102, 109
Transfer of Property	19, 28, 47, 51, 65, 73, 81, 97, 106
Practice of Real Estate	12, 13, 15, 16, 20, 33, 35, 36, 39, 50, 61, 66
License Law/Rules and Regulations	3, 4, 26, 27, 30, 31, 32, 34, 38, 41, 44, 45, 49, 52, 59, 60, 63, 69, 71, 74, 75, 86, 87, 89, 91, 96, 98, 99, 100, 101, 110
Real Estate Math	1, 7, 42, 77, 80
Fair Housing	29, 88, 105

How to Use
the CD-ROM ▶

SO YOU THINK you are ready for your exam? Here's a great way to build confidence and *know* you are ready: Use LearningExpress's Real Estate Licensing Tester AutoExam CD-ROM software developed by PEARSoft Corporation of Wellesley, Massachusetts. The disk, included inside the back cover of this book, can be used with any PC running Windows 95/98/ME/NT/2000/XP. (Sorry, it doesn't work with Macintosh.) The following description represents a typical "walk through" of the software.

To install the program:

1. Insert the CD-ROM into your CD-ROM drive. The CD should run automatically. If it does not, proceed to Step 2.
2. From Windows, select **Start**, then choose **Run**.
3. Type D:\Setup
4. Click **OK**.

The screens that follow will walk you through the installation procedure.

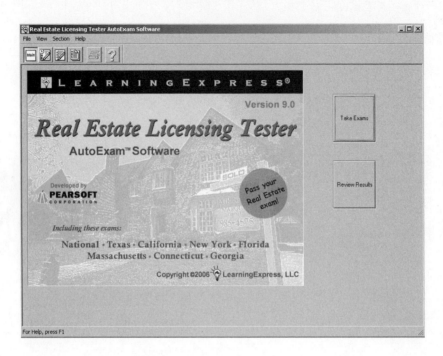

From the Main Menu, select **Take Exams**. (After you have taken at least one exam, use **Review Exam Results** to see your scores.)

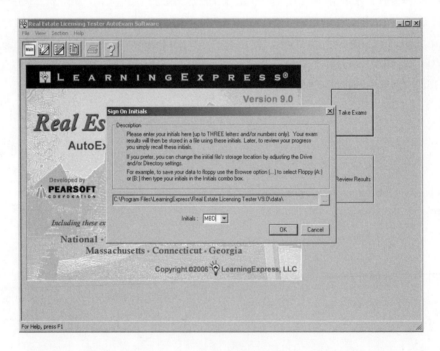

Now enter your initials. This allows you to record your progress and review your performance for as many simulated exams as you would like. Notice that you can also change the drive and/or folder where your exam results are stored. If you want to save to a floppy drive, for instance, click on the **Browse** button and then choose the letter of your floppy drive.

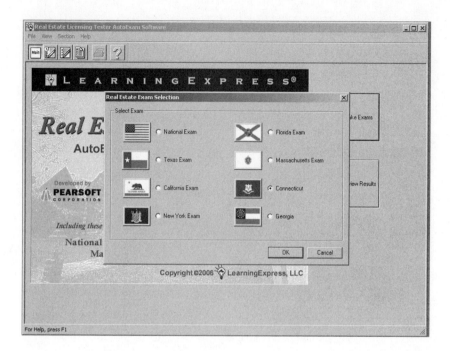

Now, because this CD-ROM supports eight different real estate exams, you need to select your exam of interest. Let's try Connecticut, as shown above.

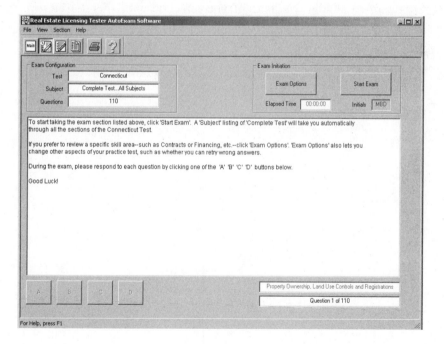

Now you are into the **Take Exams** section, as shown above. You can choose **Start Exam** to start taking your test, or **Exam Options**. The next screenshot shows you what your **Exam Options** are.

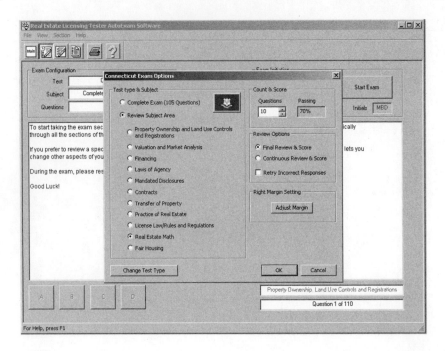

Choosing **Exam Options** gives you plenty of options to help you fine-tune your rough spots. How about a little math to warm up? Click **Review Subject Area**, and then the **Real Estate Math** option. Choose the number of questions you want to review right now. On the right, you can choose whether to wait until you have finished to see how you did (**Final Review & Score**) or have the computer tell you after each question whether your answer is right (**Continuous Review & Score**). Choose **Retry Incorrect Responses** to get a second chance at questions you answer wrong. (This option works best with **Review Subject Area** rather than **Complete Exam**.) If you have chosen the wrong exam, you can click **Change Test Type** to go back and choose your exam. When you finish choosing your options, click **OK**. Then click the **Start Exam** button on the main exam screen. Your screen will look like the one shown next.

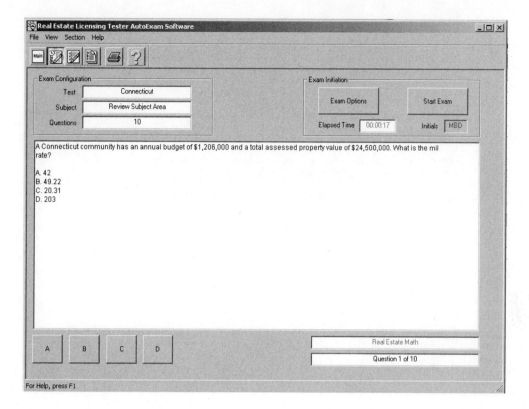

Questions come up one at a time, just as they will on the real exam, and you click on A, B, C, or D to answer.

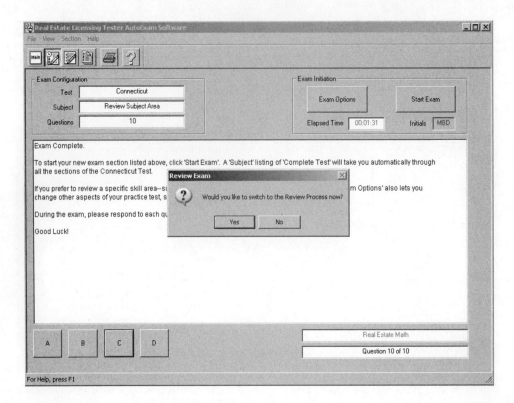

When you have finished your exam or subject area, you will have the option of switching to **Review Results.** (If you don't want to review your results now, you can always do it later by clicking on the **Review Exams Section** button on the toolbar.) When you use **Review Results**, you will see your score and whether you passed. The questions come up one at a time. Under **Review Options**, you can choose whether to look at all the questions or just the ones you missed. You can also choose whether you want an explanation of the correct answer displayed automatically under the question.

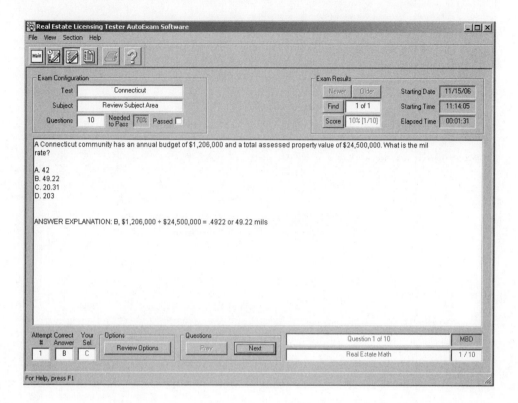

When you are in the **Review Results** section, click on the **Find** button to look at all the exams you have taken.

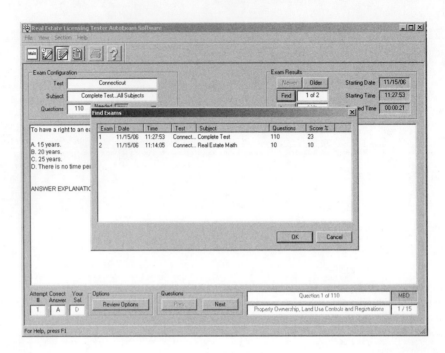

By default, your exam results are listed from newest to oldest, but you can sort them by any of the headings. For instance, if you want to see your results arranged by score, you can click on the **Score %** heading. To go to a particular exam you have taken, double-click on it.

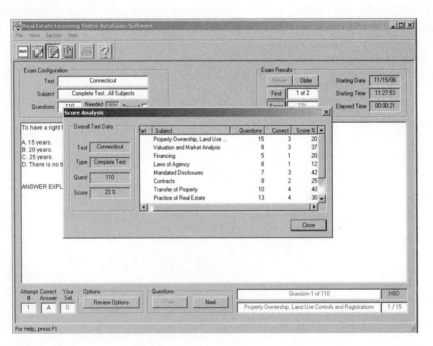

In the **Review Results** section, if you click on the **Score %** button, you will get a breakdown of your score on the exam you're currently reviewing. This section shows you how you did on each of the subject areas on the exam. Once again, you can sort the subject areas by any of the column headings. For instance, if you click on the

Score % heading, the program will order the subject areas from your highest percentage score to your lowest. You can see which areas are your strong and weak points, so you will know what to review.

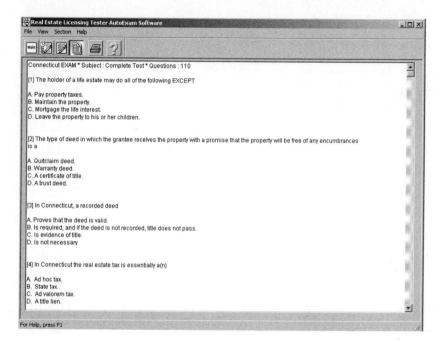

What's that? No time to work at the computer? Click the **Print Exams** menu bar button and you will have a full-screen review of an exam that you can print out, as shown above. Then take it with you.

For technical support, call 800-295-9556.